The First Book of

PC Tools™ 7

The First Book of

PC Tools™ 7

Gordon McComb

iii

Revised by Joe Kraynak

A Division of Macmillan Computer Publishing
11711 North College, Carmel, Indiana 46032 USA

For Amy

© 1992 by SAMS

THIRD EDITION
FIRST PRINTING

International Standard Book Number: 0-672-27371-3
Library of Congress Catalog Card Number: 91-62356

Screen reproductions in this book were created by means of the program Collage Plus from Inner Media, Inc., Hollis, NH.

Special thanks to C. Herbert Feltner for assuring the technical accuracy of this book.

Printed in the United States of America

Publisher
Richard Swadley

Publishing Manager
Marie Butler-Knight

Managing Editor
Marjorie Hopper

Development Editors
Lisa Bucki and Greg Bushyeager

Manuscript Editor
Judy Brunetti

Technical Reviewer
C. Herbert Feltner

Cover Artist
Held & Diedrich Design

Indexer
Jill D. Bomaster

Production Team
*Beth J. Baker, Jeff Baker, Scott Boucher, Betty Kish,
Bob LaRoche, Howard Peirce, Mary Beth Wakefield*

Contents

viii

6   *Managing Disks with Shell, 151*

7   *Running Programs with Shell, 179*

8   *Backing Up Your Hard Disk, 197*

X

xi

Introduction

You purchased Central Point Software's PC Tools because you have work to do, so let's get right to the point.

This is a book on learning how to use PC Tools version 7.0. With the information contained in this book, you'll be able to use PC Tools to supervise your computer, manage your hard disk drive, run other programs, recover files that have been damaged or erased, inspect your disks for hidden damage, and lots more. *The First Book of PC Tools 7* is a beginner's guide to get you started using PC Tools in your everyday computing.

PC Tools is a complex program, but this book pares it all down to a manageable size. You'll learn everything you need to know to use PC Tools for routine computing chores, including copying files, copying disks, verifying disks, "unerasing" lost files, starting programs, backing up your hard drive, even writing and editing with the PC Tools word processor.

How to Use This Book

The Chapters in this book are organized in the same manner that you are likely to use to PC Tools program.

▶ Chapter 1 introduces you to PC Tools and explains its component parts, the concept of its user interface, and the minimum hardware you need to use the program.

▶ PC Tools is composed of several stand-alone programs, yet all follow the same user interface standards. Chapter 2 explains how to use PC Tools interface, including keyboard and mouse control.

▶ Chapter 3 explains how to use PC Tools with the Windows program.

▶ Chapter 4 introduces Shell, the main component of PC Tools, and explains how to run individual tools from the DOS prompt.

▶ Chapter 5 illustrates how to use Shell to manage files on your floppy and hard disks.

▶ Chapter 6 tells you how you can manage your computer disks, including copying floppy disks, verifying and comparing disks, formatting data disks, and managing subdirectories on your hard drive.

▶ Chapter 7 shows you how to run other programs directly from PC Tools Shell.

▶ Chapter 8 explains how to use PC Tools for creating backups for the data on your hard drive. You'll learn how to perform quick and easy backups weekly and even daily.

▶ If you've ever accidentally erased a file or even an entire hard disk (or think you might someday), you'll want to read Chapter 9 on using PC Tools to recover lost files and disks.

▶ Chapter 10 details the procedures for maintaining your computer's hard disk drive, including periodically testing the drive for errors (even "hidden" ones), and ways to increase hard drive efficiency.

▶ Chapter 11 explains how to use the System Information program to answer questions you have about your computer, such as how much memory it has and what kind of floppy disk drives it has. You'll also learn about VDefend, an anitvirus program that will warn you of incoming viruses.

▶ PC Tools comes with an assortment of handy desk accessory programs, including a word processor and data manager. Chapter 12 introduces these desk accessories, providing quick start help for the word processor, data manager, and communications terminal.

▶ Chapter 13 provides the basics of using PC Tools on a network and using the new PC Tools Commute program, which allows you to control another computer from a different location.

Although you don't have to read this book from cover to cover and in order, at the very least you should start by reading Chapters 1 and 2 (and 3, if you're using PC Tools with Windows). These provide an overview of PC Tools and detail how to access its features and capabilities.

Conventions Used in This Book

You need to know about the conventions used in this book before you can dive head first into it. The following is a list of the conventions used to make learning PC Tools 7 more enjoyable and effective.

► This is a beginner's quickstart guide to PC Tools, but it assumes you have worked with the IBM PC and its disk operating system (DOS). If you are unfamiliar with DOS or how to use your computer, read the instruction manual that came with the computer, or consult one of the many fine books on using the PC and DOS. A good place to start is *The First Book of MS-DOS*, published by SAMS.

Many chapters include step-by-step Quick Steps that help you promptly master a command or function of PC Tools. The Quick Steps outline *the commonly used* PC Tools commands. Refer to the inside front cover of this book for an alphabetical list of Quick Steps.

► PC Tools can be controlled via the keyboard or a mouse. You'll learn how to use both in Chapter 2. For clarity and convenience, instructions for commanding PC Tools do not provide specific steps for using either the keyboard or the mouse. Rather, you'll read "Select the XYZ command..." and have the choice of using the mouse, the keyboard or both.

► PC Tools uses an interface similar to the one found on Microsoft Windows 3.0. If you're familiar with the Windows interface, you'll be up and running on PC Tools in no time. But if the use of windows, pull-down menus, and dialog boxes is new to you, be sure to read Chapter 2 for a thorough introduction to the PC Tools interface.

► Each chapter includes a summary to help you review what you learned and check your progress.

► Screen messages or prompts appear in computer type.

► Text you type appears in colored computer type.

▶ This icon notes PC Tools 7 features or procedures that may require particular care.

 This icon indicates special situations to watch out for.

Acknowledgments

The people deserving the most credit for this book are the software developers at Central Point Software. With PC Tools 7, they not only improved an already excellent product, but they added several exciting features to make a computer do what it's supposed to be able to do. Special thanks go to Debbie Hess, graphics/project specialist at Central Point, for providing us with the PC Tools software and for her continued support of our work, and to Ken Dietz for technical support.

Thanks to Marie Butler-Knight, publishing manager, for providing us the opportunity to work on this project. Thanks to Lisa Bucki and Greg Bushyeager, development editors, who helped structure the book and guide it through its initial stages. Thanks also to Judy Brunetti, manuscript editor, who forced us to face our assumptions and clarify our prose.

Thanks to Herb Feltner, technical support person at SAMS, who offered his usual patience and expertise in answering our questions and making sure we had the equipment we needed, and providing us with a thorough technical edit of the manuscript. Thanks also to Richard Leach of Macmillan Computer Publishing for his help on the networking chapter.

Without these folks, this book would not be.

xvi

Trademarks

All terms mentioned in this book that are known to be trademarks or service marks are listed below. In addition, terms suspected of being trademarks or service marks have been appropriately capitalized. SAMS cannot attest to the accuracy of this information. Use of a term in this book should not be regarded as affecting the validity of any trademark or service mark.

dBASE III and dBASE IV are trademarks of Ashton-Tate Corporation.

IBM, IBM PC, and IBM PC AT are registered trademarks of International Business Machines Corporation. IBM PC XT and PS/2 are trademarks of International Business Machines Corporation.

Lotus 1-2-3 is a registered trademark of Lotus Development Corporation.

Macintosh is a trademark licensed to Apple Computer Corporation.

Microsoft Word and Microsoft Windows are trademarks of Microsoft Corporation.

WordPerfect is a registered trademark of WordPerfect Corporation.

WordStar is a registered trademark of MicroPro International.

MCI Mail is a service mark of MCI Communications Corporation.

EasyLink is a service mark of The Western Union Telegraph Company.

CompuServe is a registered trademark of CompuServe Information Service, an H & R Block Company.

xvii

An Introduction to PC Tools

In This Chapter

- ▶ *Component parts of PC Tools*
- ▶ *Basics of the PC Tools user interface*
- ▶ *PC Tools with Windows*
- ▶ *Network support and remote computing*
- ▶ *Operating modes of PC Tools*
- ▶ *Minimum hardware needed*

Some computer programs can be described in a sentence or two. Explaining PC Tools takes paragraphs of descriptive prose, because it does so many things. It's a DOS shell, a hard disk backup utility, a data recovery system, a word processor, a data manager, an electronic appointment keeper, a telecommunications program, a data encrypter, and lots more.

PC Tools wears many hats and performs the duty of perhaps a half-dozen software packages.

What PC Tools Provides

PC Tools offers the following functions:

DOS Shell—controls your computer with easy-to-use menus rather than cryptic DOS commands.

Data Protection and Recovery—protects loss of data and retrieves data from erased or damaged files and disks.

Hard Disk Backup—stores an archival copy of your hard disk data.

Desktop Accessories—provides "pop-up" tools you can use with almost any PC program.

System Information and Optimization—increases your knowledge of your computer and increases your computer's performance.

Network Support and Remote Computing—transfers files directly from one computer to another and runs a computer from a remote location.

This chapter begins by taking a closer look at each of these important functions. It also discusses the PC Tools user interface, operating modes, and hardware requirements.

DOS Shell

The core of PC Tools is a DOS shell, a menu-driven program that not only provides near-instant access to PC Tools commands but also to many common DOS functions. In addition, you can use the PC Tools Shell to start other programs, such as Lotus 1-2-3 or WordPerfect. Instead of starting and ending your programs at the DOS prompt (c>), Shell provides a neat and easy-to-use menu interface. With Shell you can:

▶ View files and directories on a floppy or hard disk.

▶ Run a stand-alone PC Tools program (one that can be run from the DOS prompt), such as PC-Cache or PC Secure (more about these later in the chapter).

2

▶ Run any other DOS-compatible program.

▶ Perform routine DOS chores like copying, moving, and comparing files, but with the benefit of menu-driven commands and easy-to-understand prompts.

▶ Print, view, and edit document files.

▶ Maintain hard disk directories, including creating, deleting, renaming, and moving subdirectories.

▶ Restructure the organization of data on a hard disk to make it more efficient.

▶ Undelete files that have been deleted previously.

Shell contains seven pull-down menus: File (shown in Figure 1.1), Disk, Options, View, Special, Tree, and Help. In addition, context-sensitive help is available by pressing the F1 function key or by selecting F1 Help with the mouse. (*Context-sensitive help* is one-step help that the program determines you need on a given command. You can also select a help topic from a master index.)

3

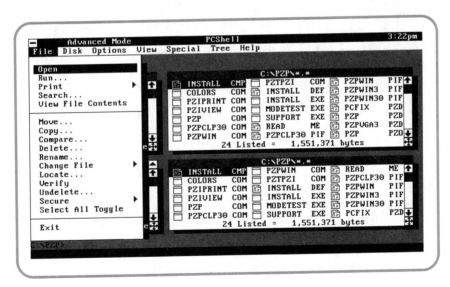

Fig 1.1   *The File pull-down menu.*

Shell is the main component of PC Tools and is the utility you'll use most often. Because it's so versatile and useful, several chapters of this book are devoted to helping you learn its commands and features.

Data Protection and Recovery

One of the most important features of PC Tools is its capability to restore information accidentally erased from files and disks. The PC Tools data protection and recovery system is composed of several units:

▶ Delete Tracker and Delete Sentry.

▶ Undelete command.

▶ VDefend (antivirus program).

▶ Mirror program.

▶ Unformat program.

▶ PC Format program.

▶ DiskFix program.

▶ PC Secure command.

4

The Undelete command and file restoration programs work separately or together to help you recover from accidental erasure of files, hard disk crashes, and even from reformatting hard and floppy disks. The four recovery programs can run from Shell, directly from the DOS prompt, or from the Windows program.

Delete Tracker and Delete Sentry

When you delete a file, only the first letter of the file's name is deleted in the *file allocation table* (*FAT*)—the index of the files on a diskette or hard disk. This tells DOS that it's okay to write another file onto the disk where the deleted file resides. The actual contents of the file remain on the disk until replaced with new data. As long as you don't record any new information on the disk, you can retrieve any files that you've accidentally deleted.

Delete Tracker keeps a record of all files on disk and their complete names. If you delete a file by mistake, you can usually recover it simply by selecting its name from a list. Delete Sentry provides additional protection for your file by keeping a copy of each file in a hidden directory (\SENTRY) on your hard disk. If anything happens to the file in its original location on disk, you can retrieve the copy that Delete Sentry made from the \SENTRY directory.

Undelete Command

The Undelete command, found in the Shell program on the File menu, works together with the Delete Tracker or Delete Sentry. It also works with DOS to help you retrieve accidentally erased files by using the DOS ERASE or DEL command, or another delete command within a program.

The undelete operation is automatic: Just select the Undelete command. If you installed Delete Tracker or Delete Sentry, Undelete will display a list of the deleted files that can be recovered. You simply select the file(s) from the list. If you did not install Delete Tracker or Delete Sentry, you'll have to supply the first letter of the deleted file's name. In special situations, you may need to control the undelete process directly, and PC Tools provides a means to retrieve lost files manually.

Undelete is also included as a Windows program, offering the same simple graphics interface used by all Windows programs.

5

VDefend

VDefend (VDEFEND.COM or VDEFEND.SYS) protects your system from viruses. If you get files or programs from colleagues or from outside computer information services, your computer may get infected by a computer virus. When these bugs get into your system, they can wipe out the data on your hard disk. VDefend works in the background to notify you of incoming viruses and prevent these viruses from infecting your system and wiping out files.

Mirror Program

The Mirror program (MIRROR.COM) is designed to provide protection against accidental ERASE (like ERASE *.*), RECOVER, or FORMAT of a hard disk. Mirror keeps a clone of the all-important file allocation table (or FAT) of a hard disk, along with a mirror image of the root directory recorded on the drive. The FAT tells the computer where to locate the files stored on a disk. If the FAT is damaged or accidentally erased, all of the files on the disk can be lost; because even though they are still contained on the disk, there's no way to retrieve them.

The root directory of a hard disk contains many important files, including CONFIG.SYS and AUTOEXEC.BAT, as well as the first level of subdirectories. Its loss—although not as critical as the FAT—can make reconstruction of your hard disk time-consuming and difficult.

Each time Mirror is run (preferably one or more times a day), it resamples the FAT and root directory and stores that information in a backup file. In the event of an accidental ERASE, RECOVER, FORMAT, or damaging hard disk crash, the Mirror backup file can reconstruct the missing data.

Unformat Program

The reconstruction of the mirrored FAT is performed by an adjunct program, Unformat. Unlike Mirror, which is a preventive maintenance program and should be run often, Unformat (UNFORMAT.EXE) is used only when needed. In fact, running Unformat when you don't need to can cause you to lose files you recently created. You can also use Unformat if you haven't been using Mirror to take regular snapshots of the FAT and root directory, but you may lose some files because Mirror will not have its backup file to work with.

PC Format Program

PC Format provides an additional preventive measure against loss of data. It prevents you from accidentally formatting a disk that contains data, and it makes it more difficult to accidently format your hard disk.

The PC Format program (PCFORMAT.EXE) is a replacement for the DOS FORMAT.COM program. In fact, during the installation process, PC Tools automatically replaces the DOS FORMAT.COM program file with PC Format. Your original FORMAT.COM is renamed FORMAT!.COM so that you can still use it, but you must explicitly enter FORMAT! at the DOS prompt.

DiskFix Program

The DiskFix program seeks out, reports, and optionally repairs disks automatically. While you have control over the repair process, it is completely automatic, so you don't need to know a thing about how your DOS disks work (although it can help). When DiskFix first starts, it checks the critical portions of the drive you specify (such as floppy disk drive A: or hard disk drive C:). If DiskFix finds errors, it report them and then asks if you want to repair the damage.

The DOS CHKDSK command also offers some of the reconditioning DiskFix provides, but DiskFix is easier to use and offers greater flexibility. Note that not all disk damage can be successfully repaired. Some data may be irretrievably lost, especially if the damage occurred some time ago, but DiskFix greatly increases your chances of recovering, especially if you run the program often.

Hard Disk Backup

A movie director often orders a second take as protection or as a backup, even if the first is perfectly good. The information on a hard disk is often treated the same way. Because weeks, months, and even years' worth of data can be stored on a hard disk, making an archival copy of it in the event of catastrophe is not only common sense, but it is essential to good computing practice.

If you use a hard disk (and you probably are if you're running PC Tools), making backups should be a part of your regular routine. In the event of a mishap (the hard disk crashes, you totally corrupt the hard disk using a DOS command like FDISK, or the computer is stolen), the data from the hard disk is safely stored on floppy disks and can be readily retrieved.

PC Tools provides an efficient hard disk backup utility called CP Backup. You can run this backup utility (CPBACKUP.EXE) either from within PC Shell or directly from the DOS prompt. It handles both backup *and* restoration (reclaiming previously stored data from the floppy disks back onto the hard disk).

CP Backup, whose opening screen is shown in Figure 1.2, gives you full control over the backup process. This includes selecting subdirectories and files to include in the backup, determining the type of backup media to use, verifying backed up data against the original on disk, and selecting the backup method.

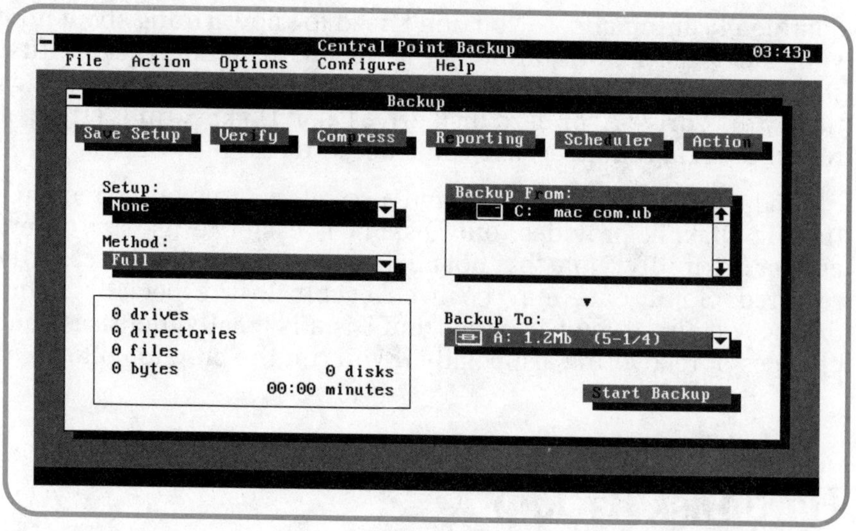

Figure 1.2   Central Point Backup (CP Backup) lets you make archival backups of your hard disk.

8

CP Backup automatically compresses files so that you need fewer disks to hold the archive data. For example, depending on the actual data on your hard disk, you can cram about 20M of data into just 10 or 12 1.44M, 3-1/2" disks. Data compression also reduces time, so you're more likely to perform regular backups of your hard disk. It takes about 10 to 15 minutes to back up 20M worth of hard disk data.

The first time you use CP Backup, the program asks a number of set-up questions about your computer system and the type of media you'll be using (tapes or floppy disks) for the backups. The questions aren't repeated on subsequent uses of CP Backup, and you can change and resave your set-up selections at any time.

If you have Windows, you can run CP Backup for Windows. In addition to the speed and reliability that the regular CP Backup offers, CP Backup for Windows lets you run the backup operation in the background, allowing you to continue working while you're backing up your disk. You can even schedule automatic backups to back up your system when you're not there.

PC Secure

If you work for the government or for a company manufacturing goods under contract from the government, your computer data may be considered confidential or classified. To prevent the data from falling into the wrong hands, you may be required to encrypt it so that only you or other authorized persons are able to read it and use it. Or, you may need to create or edit sensitive information like personnel records that you don't want others to look at. The PC Secure utility scrambles program and data files to an extent that even the largest supercomputers in the world can't crack their code.

PC Secure uses the *Digital Encryption Standard (DES)* encoding system, which shuffles the data in a seemingly random order. A *software key* locks and unlocks the data. Without the key, it is highly unlikely (but theoretically not impossible) that anyone else will be able to retrieve the file and look at it.

A little-known feature of the PC Secure utility (named PCSECURE.EXE) is a file-compression command used to shrink program and data files into smaller packets. You don't need to encrypt the file to compress it. However, you might want to compress a data file before sending it over the phone lines with a modem. With a size savings of 20 to 60 percent when compressed, your time on the modem will be less and your phone bills lower. The receiver needs a copy of PC Tools (or at least PC Secure, which can be run from the DOS prompt or from Shell) to uncompress the data and turn it into a readable form.

9

Desktop Accessories

How many times have you looked for your desktop calculator, only to find someone walked off with it? PC Tools contains its own calculator—four different types, in fact—plus a number of other useful desktop accessories, including a word processor, a data manager, an appointment book, a telecommunications program, and a macro editor.

As with PC Shell, The PC Tools Desktop Manager (or just plain Desktop) can be loaded into your computer directly at the DOS prompt as a *stand-alone program*, or it can be loaded into memory and used as a *terminate-and-stay-resident (TSR) program* (also known as a *memory-resident program*). A memory-resident program (or TSR) is one that remains in your computer's memory (that is, it stays resident) when you quit (terminate) the program. Whenever you need the Desktop tools, just press the Desktop hot keys, Ctrl-Spacebar. *Hot keys* consist of two or more keys pressed together to start and exit a TSR program. You can change Desktop to use a different set of hot keys (for example, Ctrl-Shift).

PC Desktop contains the following miniprograms:

Notepads. A fairly full-featured word processor (but no match for WordPerfect or Microsoft Word). Features: opens both ASCII and WordStar files.

Outlines. A special-purpose word processor designed to create outlines; it is also called "a thought organizer." Features: expands and collapses headings; indents for multiple levels.

Databases. An information storage and retrieval system for keeping tabs on moderate amounts of data. Features: data file-compatibility with dBASE III and IV; an automatic phone dialer.

Appointment Scheduler. An electronic calendar that keeps track of your appointments and other things you must do. It even sounds an alarm to remind you of lunch breaks or important meetings. Features: links with macros (see Macro Editor) for automated control of your computer so you can run programs when you're not there.

Modem Telecommunications. A "smart" terminal utility that lets you make calls from a modem, communicate with other computer users (or automated computer systems), and send or receive files electronically. Features: Hayes AT-command compatible with full autodial and autoanswer capability.

FAX Communications. Lets you send and receive FAX transmissions while you use your computer for something else. It requires an Intel (or compatible) FAX board in your computer or in a network. Features: selectable resolution (high, standard), delay FAX broadcast, and auto dialing.

Macro Editor. Another specialized word processor designed for writing scripts (which contain a series of keystrokes). You can play back the scripts later, by pressing a single keystroke to perform a task requiring several keystrokes. Features: wide program compatibility; the macros can be used within Desktop, other PC Tools or non-PC Tools programs, and DOS.

10

Clipboard. Stores bits of cut or copied text from the Desktop applications or from other programs. Features: adds cut-and-paste capabilities to programs that otherwise can't share data.

Calculators. A set of algebraic, financial, scientific, and programmer's calculators for use at a moment's notice. Features: algebraic calculator includes memory; all calculators can be programmed with macros to perform complex routines; the algebraic, scientific, and financial calculators include a scrolling tape.

Utilities. A collection of miscellaneous tools that lets you configure PC Shell and Desktop.

Autodialer. (For use with a modem.) Lets you dial the phone using a phone number appearing on your computer screen.

PC Tools Desktop is best used as a TSR program, where you can access it from within any program. For example, pop up Desktop while working with Lotus 1-2-3 and access the Appointment Scheduler to check the day's events. Or jot down a particularly brilliant thought with Notepads while you're busy putting your company's books in order.

The opening screen for Desktop is simple and clutter-free, as shown in Figure 1.3. Only the main Desktop menu is present, providing access to the miniprograms available under PC Tools Desktop. Desktop employs the same keyboard and mouse conventions as Shell and the other PC Tools programs.

11

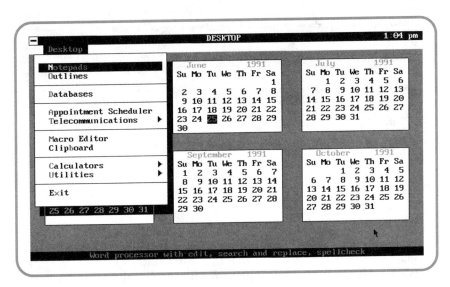

Figure 1.3   The opening screen of Desktop.

System Information and Optimization

In addition to providing help with your daily work, PC Tools offers features that provide information about your system and ways of improving its performance.

System Information

Many times a user will purchase a system that is set up and ready to go. That's great until you need to know something about your system. With the System Information program, you can get information about the size of your hard disk, the type of floppy disk drives you have, the amount of memory installed on your system and what programs are currently using it, and lots more. (See Figure 1.4.)

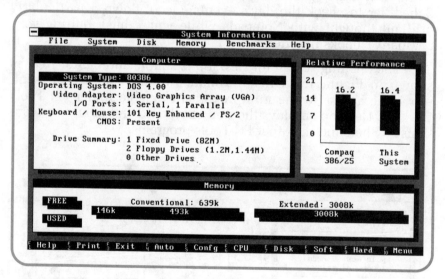

Figure 1.4   The System Information program tells you all you need to know about your computer.

Compress

Imagine the data tracks on a disk uncoiled into a straight line, like a piece of string. As you store information on the disk, the string fills up, starting on one end and proceeding to the other. As you fill the disk, each program and document file is stored as a self-contained unit.

If you remove a file or two, you'll create a gap in the string. The next program or document you place on the disk will jam into the empty slot and the remaining data will be distributed to other portions of the disk. The more small gaps that are on the disk, the more a particular program or document file might be fragmented throughout the disk.

Over the course of several weeks or months of use, the typical hard disk will consist of hundreds of files, with many of them fragmented in at least one place, as illustrated in Figure 1.5. The separation of individual pieces of the file can impair disk drive performance: The heads in the drive must shuttle back and forth over the surface of the disk to pick up all the bits and pieces of the scattered file. Perhaps worse, a fragmented file is harder to retrieve when accidentally erased and is more likely to be corrupted permanently in the event of a DOS or disk error.

13

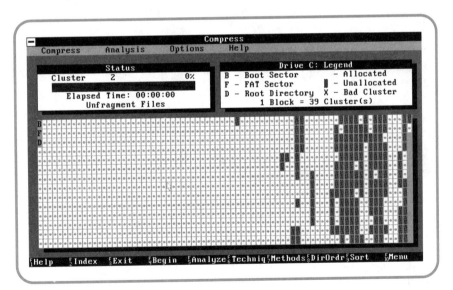

Figure 1.5   File fragmentation causes files to be scattered over the surface of the disk.

The PC Tools Compress utility (called COMPRESS.EXE) examines the files on a hard or floppy disk and rearranges them to eliminate fragmentation. Compress can be started directly at the

DOS prompt or from Shell. Although compressing (or defragmentizing) a large hard disk can take up to several hours depending on the capacity of the hard disk and the speed of your computer, the effort is worth the wait in the long run.

PC-Cache

PC-Cache (PC-CACHE.COM) allows you to partition some of the memory in your computer (either the base 512K or 640K of RAM, or expanded) and use it to speed up hard and floppy disk access. *RAM (Random-Access Memory)* is the electronic memory where your system temporarily stores the information it's using.

A *memory cache* works by storing the most frequently used information in the computer's RAM, so that the computer doesn't have to access the hard disk every time it needs a particular scrap of data. Although the savings in time are but brief flashes, tiny fractions of a second will add up over a long period to greatly enhance efficiency. In addition, wear and tear on the drive decreases because the mechanism isn't being used as often.

PC-Cache is fully programmable: You can tell it how much memory to use as a cache, where to find the memory (base or expanded), and even to display the savings it has achieved since first turned on.

Network Support and Remote Computing

More and more computers are being connected to one another every day. Businesses are networking their computers in order to save time transferring files and communicating important information throughout the company. More users are connecting their computers to other computers via modem to harness the information and power of other computers. PC Tools has kept up with this trend by offering increased network support and a new communications program called Commute.

Network Support

PC Tools can be installed in a write-protected directory on a *network server* (the network's central computer). PC Tools can then be accessed by anyone hooked into the network. Features such as Undelete, FileFind, and VDefend are then accessible companywide. Any user on the network can access system information about the network. Network users can even access the Workgroup Scheduler to schedule appointments among themselves.

CP Commute

CP Commute is a communications program that lets you connect your computer to another computer and take control of it. If you work at home, you can connect your home computer to your office computer, via modem, and transfer files between the two computers. If your office is networked, you can access the network from a remote location. You can even run another program that's on your office computer.

15

Commute is also useful if you work on team projects. You can connect two computers and then collaborate on a project with one of your colleagues. If you're often called upon to help your fellow workers with their computer woes, you can use Commute to take control of a computer and figure out what's going wrong. You and your colleague can then discuss the problem, through your computers, until you come to some resolution.

The PC Tools Concept

PC Tools is not one huge program but many small ones. In fact, PC Tools consists of over 150 individual files, many of them contributing a small function, application, or subprogram to the PC Tools repertoire. Although you don't need all these files to take advantage of the basic features of PC Tools, Appendix A details each major PC Tools file: what it does, how it's used, and when it's needed.

User Interface

Despite its hodge-podge foundation, the individual files of PC Tools create a near seamless integration of DOS power tools. The various utilities share a common interface. This interface employs pull-down menus and *point-and-shoot commands* (commands that you select rather than type), similar to the interface used on a Macintosh. Because the various components of PC Tools are based on similar operating techniques, once you master one PC Tools program, you can graduate to the others quickly.

Like the Macintosh, IBM OS/2 Presentation Manager, and Microsoft Windows, the new PC Tools uses a more graphical interface. In addition, PC Tools provides pull-down menus, pop-up dialog boxes, and movable windows, as shown in Figure 1.6. PC Tools appears in color on a color display (EGA or VGA recommended) or monochrome on a black-and-white display. You don't need a graphics display adapter to use PC Tools.

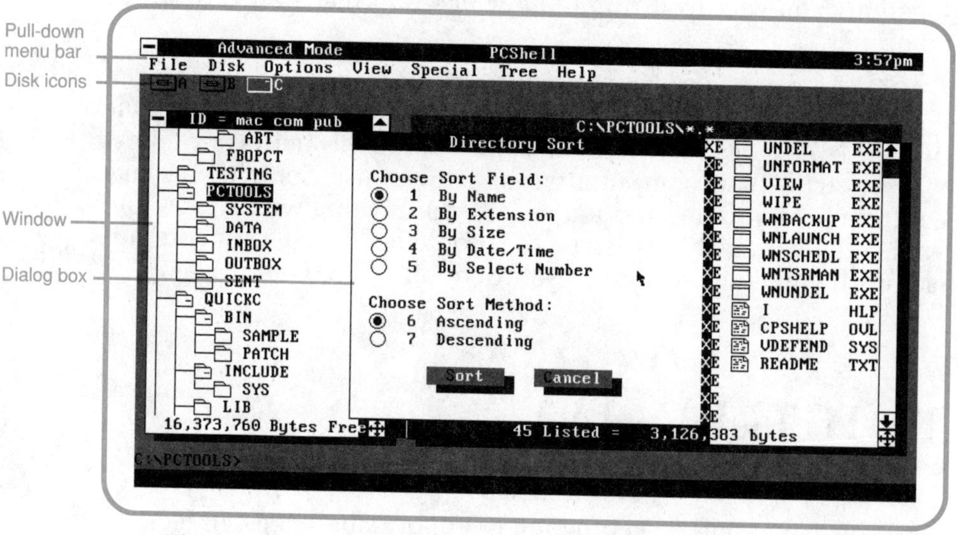

16

Figure 1.6   Icons, prompts, moveable windows, and dialog boxes make PC Tools commands easy to use.

PC Tools with Windows

If you use PC Tools with Windows, you'll see PC Tools take on a different look, as shown in Figure 1.7. By taking advantage of the graphical interface that Windows offers, PC Tools provides an even more intuitive way to use the tools. You simply select the icon that represents the tool you want to use.

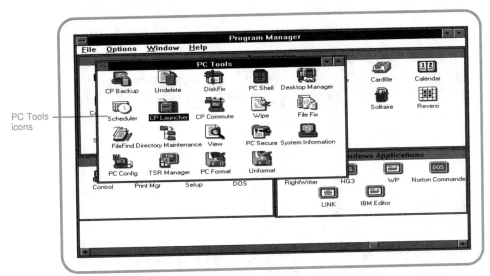

PC Tools icons

Figure 1.7 *You can run PC Tools in the Windows environment.*

17

Mouse Support

PC Tools fully supports mice: the Microsoft Mouse (version 6.14 or higher), the Logitech/Dexxa Mouse (version 3.4 or higher), and any of the many other models compatible with these. Although a mouse is not mandatory, you'll find PC Tools is best used with a rodentia desktopus (that's Latin for desktop rodents).

If you don't already own a mouse, you may want to consider purchasing one, even if PC Tools is the only program you use that supports a mouse. You can buy a Microsoft or Microsoft-compatible mouse for under $75 these days (I bought mine for $35 at a computer swap meet), and they connect to your computer through a standard serial port or special mouse expansion board.

Accessing Commands with the Keyboard

Although a mouse is most convenient, PC Tools also offers direct keyboard control; Function keys F1 through F10 are assigned to the most common commands. A message bar, which appears at the bottom of the screen shown in Figure 1.8, reminds you which keys to press to invoke various commands. You can get on-line, context-sensitive help at any point in PC Tools by pressing F1 or clicking on F1 Help with the mouse.

18

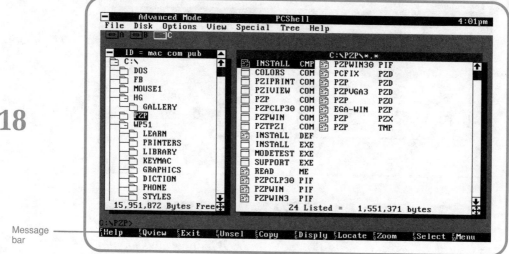

Message bar

Figure 1.8 The message bar is located at the bottom of the screen.

Hard Disk or Floppy?

PC Tools is aimed at hard disk users. The program comes shipped on several disks and requires a great deal of disk space for proper operation. Most of the PC Tools programs are aimed at hard disk management and administration. To run PC Tools, your computer must have a hard disk and at least one floppy disk drive.

Operating Mode

The PC Tools programs consist of two main programs: PC Shell and Desktop. As detailed later in this chapter, Shell provides a means of accessing the PC Tools programs and DOS commands under a familiar pull-down menu system. Desktop provides a number of handy miniprograms or desktop accessories, including a word processor and telecommunications terminal program.

You can load both Shell and Desktop into your computer in one of two ways:

▶ As a *stand-alone program*, Shell and Desktop are run like any other ordinary PC software. Enter the name at the DOS prompt, and the program runs. Quit the program, and you return
to DOS.

▶ A *memory-resident program* or *terminate-and-stay-resident program (TSR)* loads into a portion of the computer's RAM and makes room for other programs. You can then access the program by pressing a certain combination of keys, called *hot-keys*. Running the program in this way allows you to use your computer for regular tasks and call up Shell or Desktop from within DOS or one of your regular programs, such as Lotus
1-2-3 or WordPerfect.

19

Hardware Compatibility

PC Tools operates with almost any IBM PC or clone. Directly supported are the IBM PS/2 (all models), PC, PCjr, XT, and AT. The program also works with most "IBM compatibles," which include Compaq, Epson, and Dell. Most generic clones, such as the no-name brand models available at some computer swap meets and mail order, should work as well.

PC Tools needs MS-DOS or PC DOS version 3.0 or higher. However, you are advised to use the latest version of DOS that works with your computer. Once you have started PC Tools under a recent version of DOS, you can use the program to work with disks formatted under any version of DOS.

In addition to an IBM PC or a reasonable clone, you need at least 512K of memory in your computer. While PC Tools will work with just 512K of RAM, you're better off with the full complement of 640K. If your computer is equipped with expanded (LIM 4.0 standard) memory, PC Tools will use it when possible. Expanded memory is particularly handy when using Shell in memory-resident mode, rather than as a stand-alone program run directly from DOS.

You need just one floppy disk drive when using PC Tools with the recommended hard disk. However, if you plan on doing disk-to-disk copying, a pair of similar media drives (two 5-1/4", for example) is helpful.

Automated Installation

20

PC Tools comes with an installation program, INSTALL. You must use this program to transfer the contents of the PC Tools disks to your hard disk. The files are compressed (to save space); simply copying the files from floppy to hard disk does not install the programs properly.

INSTALL is menu driven, as shown in Figure 1.9, and needs little explanation to use it. To start INSTALL, insert the PC Tools installation diskette into the floppy drive. Change to the drive that contains the installation diskette, type `install`, and press Enter. Follow the on-screen prompts until installation is complete. If you need help at any time, press F1.

What You Have Learned

This chapter began with an explanation of PC Tools and the menu-driven interface it shares with all its programs and miniprograms. The chapter also discussed the following:

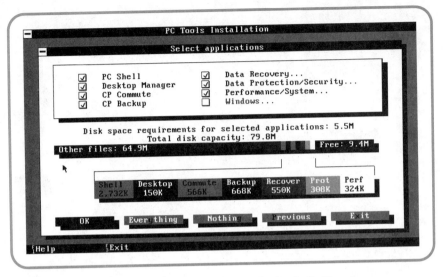

Figure 1.9   A sample screen from the installation program.

21

▶ Four core functions of PC Tools are the DOS shell, data recovery, hard disk backup, and desktop accessories.

▶ Shell provides a means of accessing the PC Tools programs and DOS commands under an intuitive pull-down menu system.

▶ Desktop provides a number of miniprograms you can use both independently or with other DOS programs.

▶ Both Shell and Desktop can be loaded into the computer directly from the DOS prompt as stand-alone programs, or as terminate-and-stay-resident (TSR) or memory-resident programs.

▶ You can access on-line, context-sensitive help anywhere within PC Tools by pressing the F1 function key or clicking on F1 Help in the message bar.

▶ PC Tools requires MS-DOS or PC DOS version 3.0 or higher, but the latest version of DOS is recommended.

▶ The computer must have a hard disk and at least 512K of RAM (640K is recommended); PC Tools can access LIM 4.0 expanded memory.

Getting Started with PC Tools

In This Chapter

- ▶ *Starting PC Shell and Desktop*
- ▶ *Using either program in memory-resident mode*
- ▶ *Navigating through PC Tools*
- ▶ *Using the keyboard and mouse*

It takes but a moment to get started with PC Tools. Installing it is nearly automatic, starting it up is quick and easy, and navigating your way around the program is as simple as pressing keys (or moving a mouse) and watching menus and windows scroll by.

Yet for all its plainness, you'll want to give certain consideration to how you install PC Tools and how best to load the program into your computer's memory. And, if you've never used a pull-down menu system with windows, you may not know how to enter commands in PC Tools.

This chapter details everything you need to know to get started using the PC Tools *utilities* (the programs that make up PC Tools). It describes:

- ▶ The contents of the PC Tools package.
- ▶ How to run the Shell program.

▶ How to run the Desktop program.

▶ How to navigate through the PC Tools programs, using either the keyboard or mouse.

▶ How to use pull-down menus, windows, and dialog boxes.

▶ Tips on mastering mouse and keyboard control of PC Tools.

▶ How to access the on-line help facility.

Package Contents

PC Tools comes on a series of disks and is accompanied by several manuals. The exact composition of the package depends on the specific version of PC Tools and its release date. As of this writing, PC Tools 7 comes with both 5-1/4" and 3-1/2" disks.

24

The following manuals detail different aspects of PC Tools:

▶ *Upgrader's Handbook* explains the version 7.0 enhancements, including its new features.

▶ *Getting Started/Tips for Windows* explains the installation and configuration of PC Tools and the basics of working with PC Tools. It also includes tips for using PC Tools in the Microsoft Windows 3.0 environment.

▶ *DOS Shell/File Manager* covers PC Shell.

▶ *Data Recovery and System Utilities* covers Undelete, DiskFix, Mirror, Unformat, the data monitors (Delete Sentry and Delete Tracker), PC-Cache, Compress, PC Format, PC Secure, VDefend, and System Information.

▶ *Desktop Manager* covers Desktop.

▶ *Hard Disk Backup* covers CP Backup and Restore.

▶ *Windows Utilities* explains CP Backup for Windows, the Windows Undelete program, and the CP Launcher.

▶ *Commute* covers the Commute program.

Throughout this book, you will be referred to one of these manuals for additional information on certain advanced topics. Keep this book and the PC Tools manuals handy at all times when using the PC Tools program.

> ▶ **Tip:** Last-minute updates to the program or corrections to the manual can be found in the README.TXT file located on one of the PC Tools disks. Be sure to view or print this file as soon as possible after installing PC Tools. PC Tools includes its own file viewing and printing features, so you don't need a word processor to examine the README.TXT file. (Refer to Chapter 5.)

Let's assume the PC Tools programs have already been installed on your computer. The INSTALL program, provided with PC Tools, makes installation quick and simple. Let's also assume you're using PC Tools with a hard disk.

Running PC Shell

25

You can run PC Shell in a number of ways, depending on how you configured the program during installation. The Program Configuration screen for Shell offered two options:

1. *Run PC Shell*. This option adds a command to your AUTOEXEC.BAT file that runs the Shell as a stand-alone program automatically when you start your computer.
2. *Load PC Shell*. This option loads PC Shell into memory whenever you start your computer. You can then run the program in memory-resident mode by pressing Ctrl-Esc.

> ▶ **Note:** With *memory-resident* programs, you can run two programs at once and switch from one program to the other by using hot keys, such as Ctrl-Esc. *Stand-alone* means that a program is not memory-resident. The program remains in memory only while you're using it.

If you chose not to configure PC Shell in either of these ways, you can run or load the program from the DOS prompt. If you want to run PC Shell from Windows, read Chapter 3. Then, skip ahead to the section "Working Your Way Through PC Tools" for information on using PC Tools once it's up and running.

Running PC Shell from the DOS Prompt

You can run Shell as a stand-alone program from the DOS prompt, as the following Quick Steps describe. The INSTALL program adds a PATH statement to your AUTOEXEC.BAT file so you can start Shell at any DOS prompt, regardless of the subdirectory you're currently in. You don't need to change the current directory of your hard disk to use PC Tools.

Q Running Shell from the DOS Prompt

1. Type **c:** and press Enter.   Logs onto the C hard disk
   (If your copy of PC Tools   drive.
   is on another drive,
   substitute another letter for C.)

2. Type **pcshell** and press Enter.   Starts Shell   □

In a few moments, the PC Shell opening screen appears, like the one in Figure 2.1. (The names of directories and files will be different, reflecting the contents of your hard disk.)

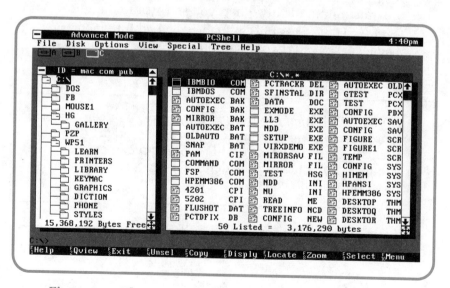

Figure 2.1   The PC Shell opening screen.

Loading PC Shell as a Memory-Resident Program

If you chose not to have PC Shell loaded automatically on startup, you can load it as a memory-resident program from the DOS prompt. (See the following Quick Steps.) You can then run Shell while working in another program. (Note: Memory constraints may prohibit you from running Shell within all PC programs.)

Q Loading Shell as a Memory-Resident Program

1. Type **c:** and press Enter. (If your copy of PC Tools is on another drive, substitute another letter for C.)

   Logs on to the C hard disk drive.

2. Type **pcshell** **/r** and press Enter.

   Loads Shell in memory-resident mode. The screen in Figure 2.2 appears, showing available memory. □

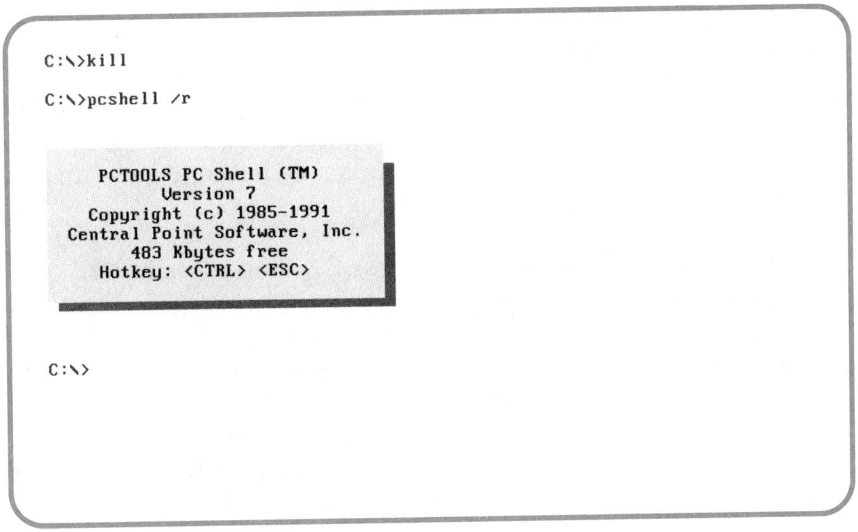

27

```
C:\>kill

C:\>pcshell /r


        PCTOOLS PC Shell (TM)
              Version 7
        Copyright (c) 1985-1991
    Central Point Software, Inc.
            483 Kbytes free
        Hotkey: <CTRL> <ESC>



C:\>
```

Figure 2.2   Shell information window when loaded in memory-resident mode.

The Shell is now in your computer's memory and is ready to run whenever you need it. (Note: You should avoid using Shell if available memory dips below about 25K.) You can run another program (for example, a word processing program). If you want to use Shell, you don't have to exit the program you're working in. Just press Ctrl-Esc (hold down the Ctrl key and press Esc), and the PC Shell opening screen appears, as in Figure 2.1.

Running PC Shell as a Memory-Resident Program

If you installed Shell to run in memory-resident mode on startup or if you loaded it as a memory-resident program from the DOS prompt, you can now start and exit the Shell using the hot keys: Control (Ctrl) and Escape (Esc). Holding down the Ctrl key and pressing Esc galvanizes Shell from its idle state in memory and activates it so you see it on the screen. To leave the Shell, press Ctrl-Esc again, and you return to the program you were working in.

28

Leaving PC Shell

The procedure for leaving Shell depends on whether it was run as a memory-resident or stand-alone program:

> *For a stand-alone program*, press F3, then press Enter.
>
> *For a memory-resident program*, press Ctrl-Esc.

If you've loaded Shell as a memory-resident program and want to unload it completely from the computer's memory, exit the Shell, type `kill` at the DOS prompt, and press Enter. This removes Shell (and any other PC Tools memory-resident programs) from the computer's RAM, freeing the space for other programs.

Running Desktop

You can run Desktop in the same manner as Shell, depending on how you configured the program during the installation. The Program Configuration screen for Desktop, however, offered only one option: Load Desktop. If you selected this option, Desktop is automatically loaded as a memory-resident program whenever you start your computer. If you did not select this option, you can run Desktop as a stand-alone program or load it as a memory-resident program from the DOS prompt, as the following Quick Steps describe:

> ▶ **Tip:** If you plan on using the Desktop's Calendar to notify you of appointments in advance, you should load Desktop as a memory-resident program. If Desktop is not in memory, it cannot interrupt your work to notify you.

29

Running Desktop from the DOS Prompt

If you run Desktop as a stand-alone program at the DOS prompt, Desktop stays in memory only until you exit Desktop. The INSTALL program adds a PATH statement to your AUTOEXEC.BAT file so that you can start Desktop at any DOS prompt.

 Running Desktop from the DOS Prompt

1. Type **c:** and press Enter. (If your copy of PC Tools is on another drive, substitute another letter for C.)	Logs onto the C hard disk drive.
2. Type **desktop** and press Enter.	Starts Desktop. □

In a few moments, the Desktop program loads and presents you with the screen shown in Figure 2.3.

Loading Desktop as a Memory-Resident Program

If you chose not to have Desktop loaded automatically on startup, you can load it as a memory-resident program from the DOS prompt:

Pull-down menu bar

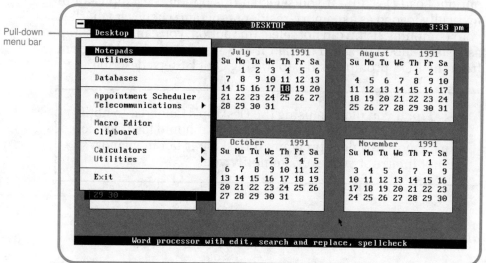

Figure 2.3   The Desktop opening screen.

Q **Loading Desktop as a Memory-Resident Program**

1. Type **c:** and press Enter. (If your copy of PC Tools is on another drive, substitute another letter for C.)

   Logs onto the C hard disk drive.

2. Type **desktop** /r and press Enter.

   Loads Desktop in memory-resident mode. ☐

Desktop is now in your computer's memory and ready to run whenever you need it. (Note: You should avoid using Desktop if available memory dips below about 25K.) If you want to run another program (for example, a word processing program), and then use Desktop, you don't have to exit the program you're working in. Just press Ctrl-Spacebar, and the Desktop pull-down menu bar appears, as in Figure 2.3; however, you won't see the calendar.

> ▶ **Tip:** If you want the calendar to appear in memory-resident mode, add the /cs switch when you load Desktop at the DOS prompt. That is, enter `desktop /r /cs` at the prompt. If Desktop is already loaded in memory, enter `kill` at the DOS prompt first.

Running Desktop as a Memory-Resident Program

If you installed Desktop to load on startup or if you loaded it as a memory-resident program from the DOS prompt, you can now start and exit the Desktop using the hot keys: Control (Ctrl) and Spacebar. Holding down the Ctrl key and pressing the Spacebar activates the Desktop so you see it on the screen. To leave the Desktop, press Ctrl-Spacebar again, and you return to the program you were working in. You can change the hot keys used to activate Desktop, as described in Chapter 12.

31

Leaving Desktop

The procedure for leaving Desktop depends on how it was loaded:

> ***For a stand-alone program***, press F3.
> ***For a memory-resident program***, press Ctrl-Spacebar.

If you loaded Desktop as a memory-resident program and want to completely unload it from the computer's memory, exit the Desktop, type `kill` at the DOS prompt, and press Enter. Note that if Shell is also currently loaded into memory, using the KILL command will remove it also.

Working Your Way Through PC Tools

Each of the programs in the PC Tools repertoire follows the same user interface. All embrace pull-down menus, scrollable windows, and dialog boxes in a similar fashion to the Microsoft Windows screens.

A typical PC Tools screen is shown with its component parts identified in Figure 2.4. These are:

Menu bar. The menu bar contains the pull-down menus. Select one of the items in the menu bar and the menu drops into view.

Menu. Menus contain commands which you can select with the mouse or keyboard.

Message bar. The message bar contains messages to guide you through the use of PC Tools, without the need to consult the manual or on-line help. When no menu or command is selected, the message bar contains a list of function keys (F1, F2, and so on) you can press (or select with your mouse) to invoke common commands. When a menu command is highlighted, a short, single-line description of the command is provided as a reference.

Application window. The application window contains the text or data for the PC Tools application, whether it be Shell, Desktop, Compress, or any other application. Some applications, such as Shell, can display more than one window at a time. Each window provides a different view of the data presented by the application.

Pull-Down Menus

Pull-down menus offer a convenient and uncluttered method of selecting commands, because you can quickly and easily see the available choices. Each menu contains a specific set of commands. The commands are generally grouped by function within the menus so you can find them more easily.

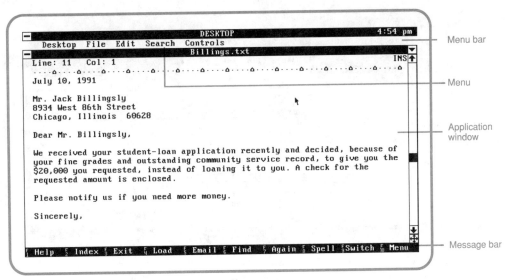

Figure 2.4   Parts of a PC Tools screen interface.

PC Tool's pull-down menus are the locking type. Once you open the menu, it stays there until you select a command, select another menu, or cancel the menu.

You can control the menus in PC Tools using either a keyboard or mouse (or a combination of the two). Both have their advantages and disadvantages. You'll find, however, that while some commands can be invoked quickly by pressing one or two keys, operating PC Tools goes much faster when you have a mouse by your side.

The way items are written and grouped in menus tells you much about the nature of the commands, as shown in Figure 2.5.

Lines separating commands act as group boundaries: The commands in one group are generally related to one another to locate them more easily.

An *ellipsis (...)* following a command means that PC Tools provides additional options and selections, presented with a dialog box, as detailed later.

A *right arrow* following a menu item means that selecting the command pops up a submenu.

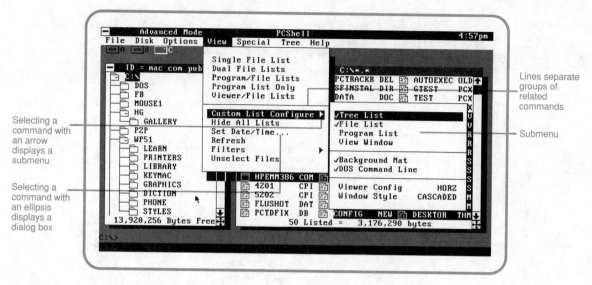

Selecting a command with an arrow displays a submenu

Selecting a command with an ellipsis displays a dialog box

Lines separate groups of related commands

Submenu

Figure 2.5 *A pull-down menu with ellipses (additional information needed after choosing the command) and arrows (additional submenu).*

34

PC Tools Windows

The windows in PC Tools are like stacks of paper on a desk. They divide the screen into many parts, so you can peer into several computing "portholes" at once. While PC Tools is designed to display windows from just one program, the windows provide a convenient and intuitive method for working with files, disks, and subdirectories.

PC Tools windows contain many components. Get to know them, and you'll be able to use PC Tools more efficiently. Most of the window features are used exclusively with the mouse, although alternative commands for accomplishing the same tasks are provided for keyboard control. The component parts of PC Tools windows are shown graphically in Figure 2.6.

Window border. The border displays the boundaries of the window. Even if the screen displays several windows at once, only one window at a time can be *active* (meaning keystrokes and commands affect that window and not the others). The title bar of the active window is highlighted, as illustrated in Figure 2.7. On a color monitor, the active window appears in color. On a monochrome monitor, the active window is bold. Many windows can be moved, by sliding them around the screen using the title bar, as you'll see later.

Close box. The close box closes the window. In some cases, closing the window exits the application; this is especially true when using PC Tools utilities from within Shell.

Size box. The size box changes the size of the window, from a small postage size square to full screen.

Maximize/Minimize box. If this box contains a triangle pointing up, you can click on it to enlarge the window so it takes up the whole screen. If the triangle is pointing down, you can shrink the window by clicking in the box with your mouse.

Scroll bars. When the window contains more data than PC Tools can show in one screen, you must scroll information to view the rest of it. Windows can have horizontal scroll bars to scan the text back and forth, vertical scroll bars to move the text up and down, or both.

35

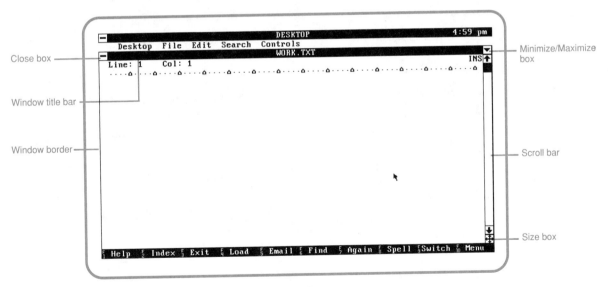

Figure 2.6   The parts of a window.

While all windows have borders, only some windows provide a close box, size box, and scroll bars. The full complement of window controls is generally available only on those windows where you can write and edit text or select from among a set of directories or files. Information windows, such as the one shown in

Figure 2.8, have nothing to select or edit, so the window controls (except the close box) are omitted. Table 2.1 summarizes the features of PC Tools windows and when they are present.

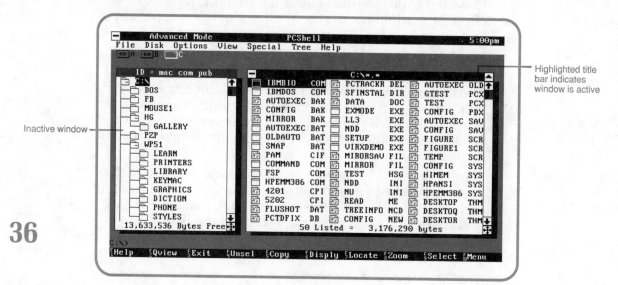

Figure 2.7   *Highlighted window is currently active.*

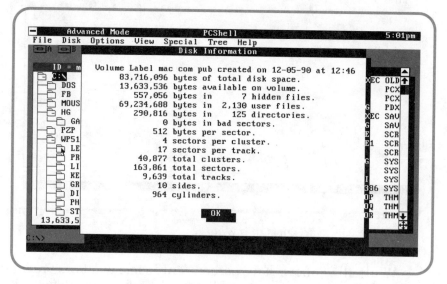

Figure 2.8   *An informational window lacks scroll bars, resize boxes, and many other controls.*

Table 2.1   *Window Features Comparison*

Feature	Present in All Windows
Border	Yes
Close Box	Yes
Size Box	No
Scroll Bars	No

Dialog Boxes

Working with PC Tools is like carrying on a conversation: You issue commands (via menus) to PC Tools and it responds with warnings, comments, questions, and messages. These exchanges from PC Tools are displayed in dialog boxes. The boxes are much like windows, except you can't generally move, size, or scroll a dialog box.

The types of dialog boxes vary, but all contain "buttons" you press to indicate your answer or preference. Almost all dialog boxes contain at least two such buttons: **O**K (or **Y**es or some other go-ahead command) and **C**ancel or E**x**it. You "press" these buttons, as if they were real-life objects, by selecting them with the keyboard or by pointing to them with the mouse.

There are five main types of dialog boxes: Prompt, Message and Warning, Option, List, and Text. Two or more of these types may be combined in one composite box.

Prompt boxes. A prompt asks you to complete a certain task before the remainder of the command is executed. As illustrated in Figure 2.9, for example, a Prompt dialog box may ask you to insert a disk into drive A: so that data can be recorded on it. PC Tools may sense automatically that you have completed the task. If not, you may need to answer by pressing a button in the dialog box.

Message and Warning boxes. PC Tools is about to do something it thinks you should know about. You read the message and respond (see Figure 2.10).

Option boxes. PC Tools wants you to select one or more options, as illustrated in Figure 2.11, before it carries out the command. For example, if you've selected the Sort command, you must indicate the type of sort you want (ascending or descending, for instance) before the actual sorting can begin. The options are check boxes or radio buttons; you select these in a similar fashion to the **O**K/**Ex**it buttons.

List boxes. PC Tools wants you to select from a list of files or subdirectories, or enter text such as a file name before it completes the command. The list within the dialog box is like a narrow scroll of paper, as shown in FIgure 2.12. If the file or subdirectory you want isn't shown in the list, you can scroll it up or down until the item appears. List boxes are a fancy way of displaying a directory of files.

Text boxes. PC Tools requires a specific entry in order to perform a task. For example, you may need to type a file name in a text box in order to load the file.

38

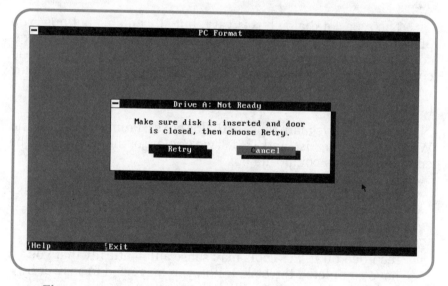

Figure 2.9   A sample Prompt dialog box.

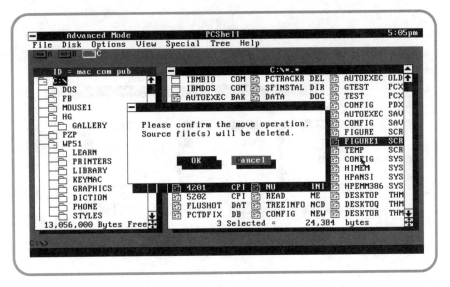

Figure 2.10   A sample Message/Warning dialog box.

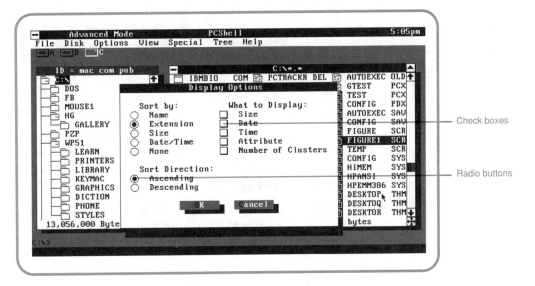

Figure 2.11   A sample Options dialog box.

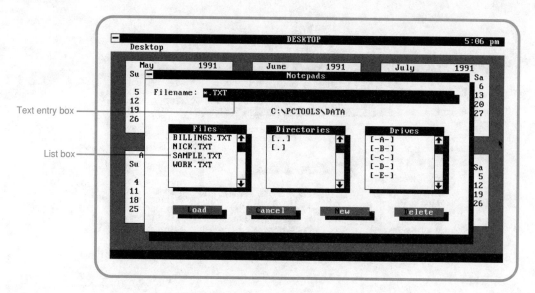

Text entry box ⎯

List box ⎯

Figure 2.12   *A sample dialog box containing list and text boxes.*

Using the Keyboard

The keyboard offers full control over the PC Tools utilities, although you may need to press several keys in succession to perform a single function. However, the most common PC Tools commands have single-key shortcuts. For example, while in Shell, selecting a file and pressing the F5 function key activates the Copy command.

The procedures that follow pertain to all PC Tools utilities. Specific information on using the various commands within the utilities is provided in the chapter that covers each program.

Opening a Pull-Down Menu

To pull down a menu when there isn't one visible, hold down the Alt key and press the first letter (the *quick-key*) of the menu's name (Alt-F for File, Alt-D for Disk, etc.).

> ▶ **Tip:** Pressing the Alt key highlights the menus and their associated quick-key letters in the menu bar. Once any menu in the menu bar is open, you can change menus by pressing the Left or Right Arrow key. Cancel the selection by pressing the Escape key.

Selecting a Command

You can select a command from a menu using either of two methods:

1. Press the highlighted quick-key associated with the command.
2. Highlight the command with the Up and Down Arrow keys.

For instance, to select the Copy command from the File menu (when in Shell), pull down the menu and press the C key (the quick-key for Copy). Or, press the Up and Down Arrow keys until the Copy command is highlighted, then press Enter to select the command.

41

> ▶ **Tip:** Menus are like endless loops. Pressing the Down Arrow key selects each command, in turn, down the length of the menu. Continue pressing the Down Arrow key and the highlighting continues back at the top again. To highlight a command at the bottom of a menu quickly, when starting at the top, merely press the Up Arrow key once.

Canceling a Menu

Press the Escape key to close a menu without selecting a command.

Selecting Items in a Dialog Box

Dialog boxes require that you provide PC Tools with additional information or confirm an action. Many dialog boxes contain more than one item to select, so you must use the keyboard to highlight the item you want to choose, then press the **OK** button (or press the Enter key on the keyboard) to make the final selection. The following actions are commonly performed in dialog boxes using select keys:

Selecting item groups. Use the Tab key to move from one set of items to the next. The selected group is shown highlighted or in a different color.

Selecting action buttons. Use the Tab key to highlight the action button you want (like **OK** or **Ex**it), and then press Enter, or type the highlighted letter in the action button of your choice (the C in **C**ancel, for instance).

Selecting options. After the option group is highlighted (with the Tab key), press the number (or letter) next to the option you want to turn on or off. A dot beside the option means on; no dot means off. You can also select different options by pressing the Up or Down Arrow key to highlight each option in turn and pressing Enter to choose the one you want.

Selecting option check boxes. After you select the option check box, place or remove an X or checkmark in the box by pressing Enter.

Selecting items in a list. After highlighting a list (with the Tab key), press the Up and Down Arrow keys to choose the list item you want.

When the desired options in a dialog box are set, continue by pressing Enter. If you want to cancel the dialog box (and therefore cancel the command that brought the box to the screen in the first place), press the Escape key. You can always use the Escape key to investigate a dialog box without the worry of actually making changes.

Selecting the Active Window

If more than one window is displayed at one time, press the Tab key until the window you want to use is highlighted. Many of the PC Tools programs have other techniques for selecting the active window. These are detailed throughout this book where appropriate.

Scrolling Through a Window

Windows that provide more information than you can see at once usually have scroll bars along the right and bottom edges. (Windows

42

that don't have scroll bars include buttons that allow you to flip through successive windows like pages in a book.) Even though the scroll bars are intended solely for use with the mouse, you can accomplish the same ends with the keyboard by pressing the cursor movement keys. Table 2.2 summarizes the action of the cursor keys when scrolling through a window.

Table 2.2   Cursor Key Scrolling

Key	Action
Page Down	Scrolls the contents of the window down one column or window-full
Page Up	Scrolls the contents of the window up one column or window-full
Down	Scrolls the contents down one line
Up	Scrolls the contents up one line
Home	Scrolls the contents of the window all the way to the top
End	Scrolls the contents of the window all the way to the bottom

43

Closing a Window

For most PC Tools programs, closing the main applications window means quitting the program. To close the window, select the Exit command, usually found in the File menu.

> ▶ **Tip:** The F3 function key serves as a universal exit key. It works whether you are closing a window, dialog box, menu, or application. The Escape key also functions as an exit key.

Moving a Window

Movable windows can be shuttled around the screen with the Move command on the Control menu opened from the upper left corner of the screen (see Figure 2.13). To open the Control menu, hold down the Alt key and press the Spacebar. Select the **M**ove command to display the small Cursor Pad window shown in Figure 2.14. Press the cursor keys (Up, Down, Left, and Right) until the window moves where you want it.

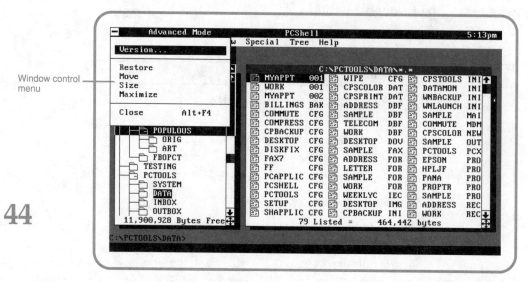

Window control menu

Figure 2.13 *The Control menu lets you control the position and size of the active window.*

44

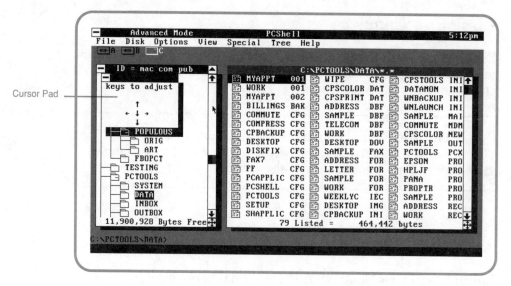

Cursor Pad

Figure 2.14 *The window cursor pad shows you how to change the position of a window.*

Resizing a Window

You can resize a window in much the same way as you can move one. Open the Control menu and choose the **S**ize command. Press the arrow keys to move the right side or the bottom of the window in the selected direction, resizing the window.

Maximizing a Window

Many PC Tools windows can be zoomed between full size (generally the entire screen, minus the menu and message bars) and one preset size. To zoom a window, press F8 or select Ma**x**imize from the Control menu (this works with most PC Tools applications, but not all).

Specific Keyboard Control

45

Specific information on using the keyboard with individual PC Tools programs is provided throughout this book.

Using the Mouse

Using the mouse to select commands, manipulate windows, and choose options from a dialog box is easy to learn. In addition, you don't have to remember which keys do what. PC Tools uses both the left and right mouse buttons (the center button on a three-button mouse is not used).

Although the left and right buttons do different things under some circumstances, you can normally select commands, control windows, and manipulate dialog boxes using either button. In some instances, especially when selecting files from a list or text from within a window, the two buttons behave differently:

▶   The right button scrolls through the list or text.
▶   The left button scrolls through the list of text and highlights (selects) it along the way.

Unlike many other aspects of the PC Tools user interface, the exact nature of the operation of the two mouse buttons differs somewhat between the utilities, so exceptions to this rule are noted in the appropriate chapters throughout this book.

If you are left-handed, you can exchange the operation of the right and left mouse buttons by starting the desired PC Tools program with the /LE parameter. For example, to start Shell and reverse the mouse buttons, enter `pcshell/le` at the DOS prompt.

One of the most important concepts to remember when using the mouse is the difference between the cursor and the mouse pointer, as illustrated in Figure 2.15. The cursor indicates the spot where text will be entered when you type from the keyboard. Or it appears as a rectangular highlight to show a file you have selected. The mouse pointer appears as an arrow or as a rectangular blip of light that moves when you move the mouse. The cursor and mouse pointer may be in separate parts of the screen, so even if the mouse pointer is located over a blank part of the window, it doesn't mean that the text you write will appear there. Rather, it will appear at the cursor.

46

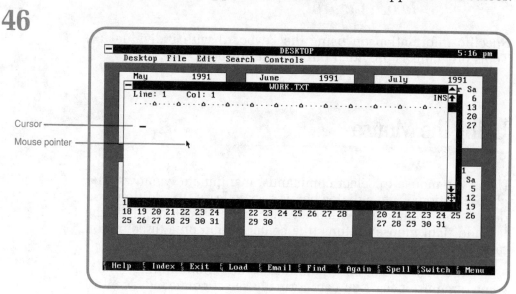

Figure 2.15   *The mouse pointer (visible only when using a mouse) differs from the cursor.*

Using the mouse entails its own vocabulary and set of procedures. There are four basic mouse functions used in PC Tools: moving the mouse pointer, clicking, double-clicking, and dragging.

Moving the mouse pointer means pushing the mouse around the table. The mouse pointer will mimic your hand movements.

Clicking selects things that are directly under the mouse pointer—things like menu commands and dialog box options. When using a word processor, clicking over a character sets the cursor position. To click, hold the mouse still, and press and release the right or left button.

Double-clicking is the same as regular clicking, except that you press and release the right or left mouse button twice in quick succession, without moving the mouse. Generally, double-clicking is used to select an item in a list and to activate the default command (such as open the file or copy the file).

Dragging involves holding down the right or left mouse button while moving the mouse. In most cases, this selects text or files between the point where you started and finished dragging. Release the mouse button when the selection is complete.

47

The procedures that follow pertain to all PC Tools programs. Information on using specific mouse movements within the utilities is provided in the applicable chapters for each program.

Opening a Pull-Down Menu

To pull down a menu with the mouse, move the mouse pointer onto one of the menu names in the menu bar and click once (either button). The menu will drop open. To select another menu, click over another name in the menu bar. Or, drag the mouse pointer over to the menu you want.

Selecting a Command

With the menu you want dropped into view on the screen, select the desired command by clicking on it with the mouse. You can combine menu and command selection in one smooth action, as the Quick Steps describe:

Q **Choosing a PC Tools Command with a Mouse**

1. Click on the menu name in   Selects the menu.
   the menu bar; keep the
   button held down.

2. Drag the mouse pointer to the   Highlights the command.
   desired command.

3. Release the mouse button.   Invokes the command.   □

Canceling a Menu

To cancel a menu after you've opened it, click anywhere outside the menu. You may wish instead to press the Escape key or the F3 function key, as clicking may select a portion of the screen you hadn't intended to select.

Selecting Items in a Dialog Box

If you have a mouse, you don't need to touch the keyboard to select items in a dialog box. Merely point and click at those options you want to engage. To select a dialog box button, for example, position the mouse pointer over it and click once with the right or left mouse button.

Some dialog boxes contain lists of files, disk drives, or directories. These are like miniature windows and have their own scroll bars.

Activating a Window

Only one window can be active at a time. When you want to work in a window, you must activate it. To activate a window using the mouse, click anywhere within the window or on one of its borders. The currently active window is highlighted.

Scrolling Through a Window

The scroll bars along the bottom and right edges of some windows are for the express purpose of scrolling the contents of windows vertically or horizontally. They're made especially for the mouse.

Scroll arrows move the display incrementally, usually one line up or down, or one character left or right. Click in the scroll arrow to actuate them, or hold down the left mouse button to scroll continuously.

The *scroll box* shows the approximate location of the cursor within the contents of the window. To view another part, drag the thumb box along the length of the scroll bar.

> ▶ **Tip:** You can also move to an approximate location within the contents of the window by clicking in the gray area of the scroll bar. For example, to move to approximately two-thirds through a document, click at an area about two-thirds the way down in the vertical scroll bar.

49

Closing a Window

To close a window with the mouse, click once in the close box, located in the upper left corner of the window. To close the program's main window (and exit the program) double-click on the box. On the program's main window, the close box is the same box you select to open the Control menu.

Moving a Window

Not all windows can be moved (for example, informational windows). Those that can are moved by dragging with the mouse. Position the mouse pointer in the title bar of the window, press and hold the right or left mouse button, and drag the window in the direction you want to move it. Release the mouse button when the window is in the proper position.

Resizing a Window

A window with a size box (lower right corner) can be readily resized with the mouse. Drag the size box with the mouse until the window is the shape you want. A window that's been moved and resized is shown in Figure 2.16.

Zooming a Window

In the upper right corner of most windows, you'll see a zoom box containing a triangle. If the triangle is pointing up, you can zoom the window to full size by clicking in the box. If the triangle is pointing down, you can shrink the window by clicking in the box. You can also zoom and unzoom an active window by selecting Maximize or Restore from the Control menu, shown in Figure 2.13.

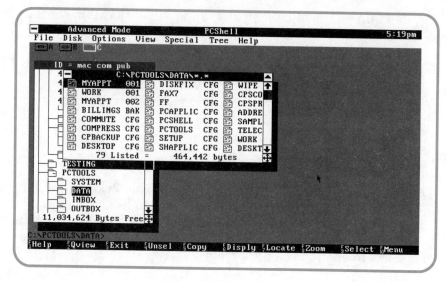

Figure 2.16   A window that's been moved on top of another.

Specific Mouse Control

Specific information on using the mouse with individual PC Tools programs is provided throughout this book.

Becoming Proficient with the Mouse and Keyboard

If you're like most PC Tools users, you'll find a combination of mouse and keyboard control works best and offers the greatest efficiency.

While most functions are more easily and quickly performed by the mouse, some are better suited to direct keyboard control.

Once you get accustomed to PC Tools and are comfortable with its interface, take a moment to think about the best course of action for each function. Do you find it easier to use the mouse or the keyboard for selecting commands from menus? The most common commands are provided function key equivalents (F3 to exit, for example), so instead of using the mouse or keyboard to pull down the File menu and select the Exit command, use the F3 function key. PC Tools presents two, three, and sometimes four different approaches for accomplishing the same goals. It's up to you find the method that works best for you.

This was mentioned in the introduction of this book, but it bears repeating here: Because of the diverse techniques of accessing PC Tools commands, you'll be instructed to perform a certain task by *selecting* a command or *choosing* an option, but without specific mouse or key-by-key instructions for doing so. That way, you are free to pick your favorite method of accessing PC Tools commands.

Occasionally, however, the text gives specific instructions for keyboard or mouse shortcuts, as you've seen in this chapter. The shortcuts can differ between PC Tools programs so, unfortunately, it's not possible to group them all here and get them over with.

51

Getting Help

When you get stuck or forget the meaning of a command or how it works, PC Tools provides a handy on-line help system. The help is context-sensitive, meaning the program identifies the command or function you are about to perform and provides help on it. You can also call up a help index and locate the specific information you desire. You can get help in either of two ways: Press F1 or pull down the Help menu from the pull-down menu bar, as shown in Figure 2.17. The Help menu offers the following options:

Topics—displays general topics about which you can get help.

Index—displays an extensive alphabetical list of items about which you can get help.

Keyboard—displays help for keyboard users.

Basic Skills—offers information about the skills you need to get started.

Commands—displays information about PC Tools commands.

Using Help—teaches you how to use the on-line help system.

About—provides help about specific tasks you may want to perform.

DOS Advice—helps you decide what to do when you're getting DOS error messages.

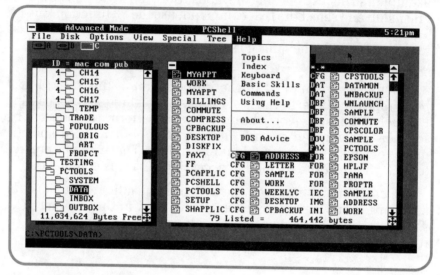

Figure 2.17   The pull-down Help menu offers various help options.

Checking the Bottom Line

Whenever you have a question about a task you're trying to perform, check the message bar at the bottom of the screen. This bar often contains just the information you need.

Using Context-Sensitive Help

PC Tools monitors everything you do with the keyboard or mouse. If you'd like help on a particular command, select it with the keyboard or mouse, then press the F1 function key or select F1 Help from the message bar. Help for that specific command is shown in the Help window, as illustrated in Figure 2.18.

52

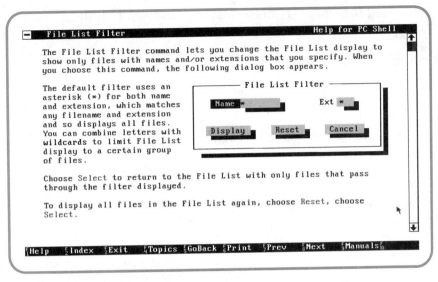

Figure 2.18   Help for the File List Filter command.

53

The Help window works like any other PC Tools window: If you have a mouse, scroll through the contents with the window's scroll bar. If you're using the keyboard, press the Page Up or Page Down key (or the Up and Down Arrow keys to move one line at a time), and press Enter to select the topic. When you're done with help, press the Escape key, the F3 function key, or the X key (for E**x**it) or click with the mouse in the close box.

The Help screen also contains Hypertext links that let you get information about related topics mentioned in the current Help screen. To select a topic, press the Tab key to highlight it and press Enter, or click on it with your mouse.

Using the Help Index

If you want help with a feature you're not currently using or with a topic, you can display an index of help topics. Pull down the Help menu and select **I**ndex. You can then select a topic from the list:

For keyboard users, scroll through the available help topics by pressing the Up and Down Arrow keys.

For mouse users, click on the help topic you want (if it's not visible, use the scroll bars to scroll through the list). Then, press Enter to view the help topic.

Read the Help screen (scroll the text down if it fills more than one window). Close the Help window if you're finished, or select the Index button (use the mouse or press the I key for Index) to view more help topics.

What You Have Learned

This chapter explained how to get started with PC Tools and discussed the basic operating procedures for starting the program and using the interface. You also learned:

▶ PC Shell and Desktop can be run as stand-alone programs at the DOS prompt, as a memory-resident program loaded manually, or as a memory-resident program loaded automatically.

▶ The typical PC Tools screen contains a menu bar, one or more menus, a message bar, and one or more windows.

▶ The most common PC Tools commands have single-key shortcuts.

▶ There are four basic mouse functions used in PC Tools: moving the mouse pointer, clicking, double-clicking, and dragging.

▶ Context-sensitive help provides a help screen of the currently highlighted command.

▶ The Help index offers a list of available help topics.

Using PC Tools with Microsoft Windows 3.0

In This Chapter

▶ *Working in the Windows environment*
▶ *Changing the size and location of windows*
▶ *Running PC Tools from Windows*
▶ *Installing and using CP Launcher*

If Windows is installed on your computer, you can run most of the PC Tools programs directly from Windows. PC Tools also offers three programs designed especially for Windows:

▶ CP Launcher, described later in this chapter.
▶ CP Backup for Windows, described in Chapter 8.
▶ Undelete for Windows, described in Chapter 9.

This chapter provides basic instructions for working with Windows and for running the PC Tools programs from Windows. Specific information on each program is discussed in the chapter that pertains to it.

The Windows Environment

Windows is an operating environment that works with DOS. It sits *on top* of DOS and provides a user-friendly interface to some of DOS' more complicated procedures. When you run Windows, you'll see a screen similar to the one in Figure 3.1. With this graphical interface, you don't type commands; you *select* icons that represent the commands, or you *select* the command from a menu.

To select icons and commands, you can use the keyboard or mouse. When using the mouse, you should be familiar with the following terms:

Move—consists of pushing the mouse on the table. The mouse pointer moves to mimic your hand movements.

Click—means press and release the mouse button. This selects whatever the mouse pointer is resting on.

Double-click—means press and release the mouse button twice in quick succession. This usually activates a command or runs a program.

Drag—consists of moving the mouse pointer over the item you want to select, holding down the mouse button and moving the mouse.

Throughout the text, when you see the term "click" or "double-click," use your left mouse button. If you need to press the right mouse button, it will specifically say so.

Although your screen may look a little different from the one in Figure 3.1, you'll see the Program Manager; this is the Windows program coordinator. The Program Manager allows your computer to run more than one program at a time and transfer information from one windows-compatible program to another.

In addition to the Program Manager, your screen will contain several of the following elements:

Control Menu box. Click on this box or press Alt-hyphen to see the Control menu. This menu lets you move, size, or shrink a window. It will also let you restore a window to its original size. To close a window, double-click on this box.

Title bar. Contains the title of the window. If you have a mouse, you can use the title bar to move the window, as you'll see later.

56

Menu bar. Contains a series of menus you can pull down. To pull down a menu, click on its name or hold down the Alt key and press the underlined character in the menu's name. The menu drops down, showing a list of its options.

Maximize and Minimize buttons. These buttons let you shrink the active window to the size of an icon or maximize the window so it takes up the entire screen.

Border. The window border sets the window off from other windows. If you have a mouse, you can use the borders to change the size of the window.

Program icons. Each program icon represents a program that you can run from Windows. To run a program, you select its icon.

Application icons. If you start a program and then minimize it without leaving the program, the program's icon appears at the bottom of the screen. You can reenter the program by selecting its application icon.

Document icons. If you close a program window, it appears as an icon at the bottom of the screen. The icon looks like a miniature program window. You can restore the window to its original form by selecting its document icon.

Scroll bars. If a window extends beyond the screen borders, you can use the scroll bars to view the undisplayed portion of the window.

57

Displaying the PC Tools Program Window

When you start Windows (by entering `win` at the DOS prompt), you'll see the Windows Program Manager, which you saw in Figure 3.1. The Program Manager contains one or more smaller program windows. Your screen will probably show a Windows Applications window and a Non-Windows Applications window. To display the PC Tools program window, shown in Figure 3.2, pull down the Windows menu and select PC Tools. This window contains a program icon for each PC Tools program you installed.

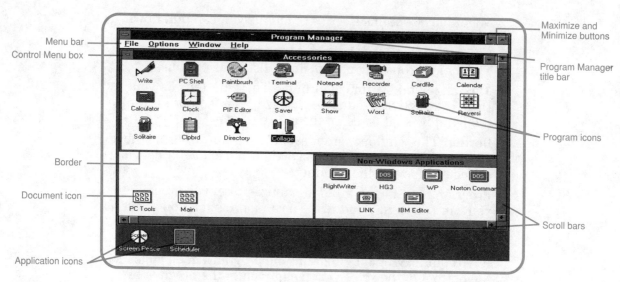

Menu bar

Control Menu box

Border

Document icon

Application icons

Maximize and
Minimize buttons

Program Manager
title bar

Program icons

Scroll bars

Figure 3.1   Windows provides a graphical user interface.

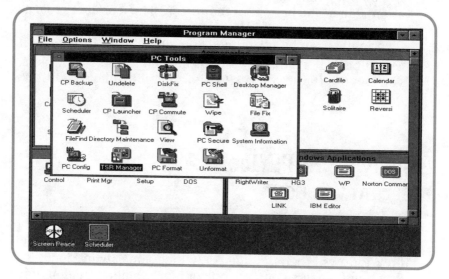

Figure 3.2   The PC Tools program window.

Activating the PC Tools Program Window

Before you can run one of the PC Tools programs, you must activate the PC Tools program window. Because you just displayed the window, it is already active. But if you switch to another window (say, Windows Applications) and then decide to run one of the PC Tools programs, you'll have to switch back to the PC Tools window. (The title bar of the active window is highlighted.) As long as the PC Tools program window is displayed, you can activate the window using your keyboard or mouse.

> ***With the keyboard***, press Ctrl-F6 or Ctrl-Tab repeatedly until the window appears highlighted.
>
> ***With the mouse***, move the mouse pointer anywhere inside the PC Tools program window and click the left mouse button.

59

> ▶ **Tip:** If you can't see the PC Tools Program window or document icon, it's probably hidden behind one of the other windows. A quick way to bring the window into view is to pull down the Windows menu from the Program Manager's pull-down menu bar and select PC Tools. The PC Tools window is restored, moved to the front of the screen, and activated.

Controlling the PC Tools Program Window

As you can see, the program window takes up much of the screen. If you want to use other program windows, this one may be in the way. You have a few options for controlling the window, as you'll see in the following sections. Figure 3.3 shows a sample setup that displays the PC Tools program window without it overlapping the other windows.

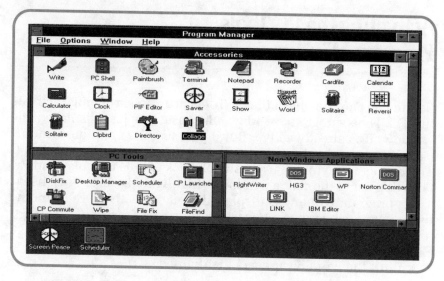

Figure 3.3   *Change the position and size of the PC Tools*
program window to prevent overlap.

Using the Windows Control Menu

One way to manipulate windows is to use the Control menu, shown
in Figure 3.4. To open this menu, activate the PC Tools program
window and press Alt-hyphen, or click on the Control Menu box
with your mouse. The Control menu offers the following options:

Restore. Restores a window to its original size after it was
minimized.

Move. Lets you move the window. After selecting this command, use the arrow keys to move the window.

Size. Lets you change the size of the active window. Select
this command and then use the arrow keys to change the
size of the window.

Minimize. Shrinks the active window to the size of an icon.

Maximize. Enlarges the window so it takes up the entire
screen.

Close. Closes the active window or exits the current
application.

Switch To. If you have more than one Windows-compatible
program running, you can switch from one program to the
other using this command.

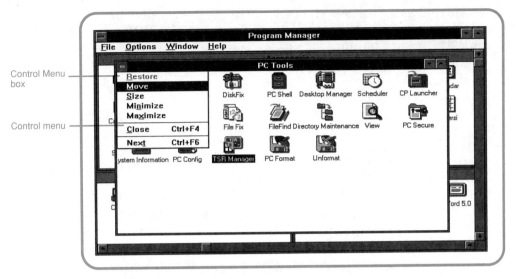

Control Menu box

Control menu

Figure 3.4   The Control menu lets you modify the program window.

> ▶ **Tip:** If you minimize a window and the window disappears without leaving a document icon on screen, the icon is probably hidden behind another window. Move and resize the windows to bring the document icons into view. You can't work with something you cannot see.

Using Your Mouse to Control Windows

If you have a mouse, you can use it to control the size and location of the program window more directly, as shown in Figure 3.5:

Move. To move a window, position the mouse pointer in the window's title bar, hold down the left mouse button, and drag the window where you want it.

Size. To size a window, position the mouse pointer on one of the window's borders (the pointer changes to a double-headed arrow). Hold down the left mouse button and drag the border in the direction you want to move it.

Maximize/Minimize. You can maximize the window by clicking on the Maximize button, or shrink it by clicking on the Minimize button.

Restore. To restore a minimized window, click on its document icon.

In addition to using your mouse to control the various windows, you can use it to move individual icons from one window to another. For example, if you use only a few of the PC Tools programs on a regular basis, you can move their representative icons into a window that contains some free space, as shown in Figure 3.6. To move an icon, move the mouse pointer over the icon, hold down the left mouse button, and drag the icon where you want it to appear.

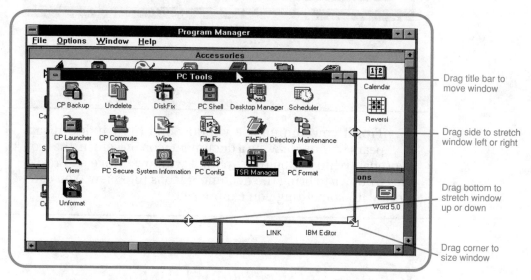

Figure 3.5   Use the mouse to control windows more directly.

▶ **Tip:** If the icons are not aligned neatly in the window, you can have Windows rearrange them. Pull down the Windows menu and select **A**rrange Icons.

Working with Dialog Boxes

When you run a PC Tools Windows program, you may encounter a dialog box, such as the one shown in Figure 3.7. Dialog boxes pop up to request additional information or to prompt you to make a selection. Each dialog box contains one or more of the following elements. You can move among elements by clicking on the element, tabbing to it, or holding down the Alt key and typing the underlined character in the element's name.

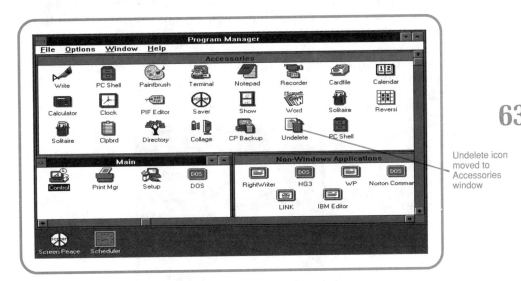

Undelete icon moved to Accessories window

Figure 3.6   You can use your mouse to drag an icon.

Text box. Prompts you to type an entry, such as a path name or file name. Press the Tab key or click inside the text box to activate it. To replace the contents of the box, type your entry. To edit the contents, use the arrow keys to move the cursor, use Del and Backspace to delete existing characters, and then type your corrections.

List box. Provides a list of entries or options from which you can select. To activate the list, press the Tab key or click inside the box. If you have a mouse, use the scroll bar to scroll through the list, or use the Up and Down Arrow keys on the keyboard. To select an item, click on it or highlight it using the arrow keys and press Enter.

63

Pull-down list box. This list box appears with a down arrow to the right of the box. To pull down the list, click on the down arrow or press Alt-Down Arrow. You can then select an item from the list as described above.

Option buttons. Let you select from one or more available options. To turn on an option, highlight it and press Enter or click on it with your mouse. A check mark or dot will appear in the check box or circle next to the option, indicating it is on. You can unselect an option in the same way.

Command buttons. Buttons such as **O**K and **C**ancel let you execute or cancel the options or selections you made. To select a command button, click on it or press Tab until the button is highlighted and then press Enter.

To close a dialog box and save your changes, press Alt-O or click on the **O**K box. To exit without saving your changes, double-click on the Control Menu button or press Ctrl-F4.

64

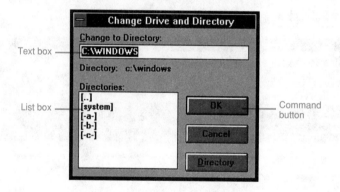

Figure 3.7   Dialog boxes request additional information to carry out a command.

Running PC Tools from Windows

Most of the PC Tools programs don't run much differently in Windows than they do in DOS. However, there is quite a difference in how you run them. If you run the tools from the DOS prompt, you have to enter a command at the prompt, such as `cpbackup`. If you run the tools from the Shell, you select the tool from a menu. In Windows, you simply select the icon for the tool you want to use.

> **With the keyboard**, use the arrow keys to highlight the icon for the tool you want to use. Press Enter.
>
> **With the mouse**, double-click on the icon.

Using CP Launcher

Normally, when you want to run a program in Windows, you have to return to the Program Manager or to one of the program windows. With CP Launcher, however, you can "launch" a program directly from whatever Windows program you're in.

If you installed CP Launcher during the PC Tools installation process, it added an option to the Control menu of every window, as shown in Figure 3.8. The Control menu button appears red, indicating CP Launcher is active. If you did not install CP Launcher, you can install it now by double-clicking on its icon or highlighting the icon (with the arrow keys) and pressing Enter. When CP Launcher is installed, you can use it to run another program:

1. Open the Control menu and select CP **L**auncher.
2. Select the program you want to run from the CP Launcher submenu.

When you install CP Launcher, several programs are added to its menu, but some of your programs will not be listed. You can add programs to the menu at any time. To add a program to the CP Launcher submenu, perform the following Quick Steps:

Adding a Program to CP Launcher

1. Press Alt-hyphen or click on the Control Menu box.

   The Control menu for the active window appears.

2. Select CP Launcher.

   The CP Launcher submenu appears.

3. Select Configure.

The Configure Central Point Launcher dialog box appears as in Figure 3.9.

4. Press Alt-B or click on Browse.

A list of files with the .EXE extension appears in the Files box. These are usually the files that run your programs.

5. To view a list of files on another drive or directory, press Alt-D or click inside the Directories box, and then select a drive or directory from the list. Press Enter or select **O**K.

The [..] entry returns you to the directory above the current subdirectory.

66

6. To view a list of files with a different extension, press Alt-N or click in the Filename box. Type *`.ext`, where *ext* stands for the extension you want to use, and press F4. Then type **0** and select **O**K.

Some programs use the extension .BAT or .COM for the files that execute the program. For example, type *`.com`.

7. Select the file that runs the program from the Files list.

You are returned to the Configure Central Point Launcher dialog box.

8. Press Alt-M or click in the Menu item box.

This is the box that contains the entry that will appear on the CP Launcher submenu.

9. Type the program's name as you want it to appear on the menu.

If you want to run the program by typing a single character, type an ampersand (**&**) before the letter you want to use to run the program. This letter will appear underlined on the menu.

10. Press Alt-S or click on the Save button.

The configuration is saved.

11. Repeat Steps 4-10 for any programs you want to add to the CP Launcher submenu.

This returns you to the Program Manager submenu.

12. Select **O**K.

□

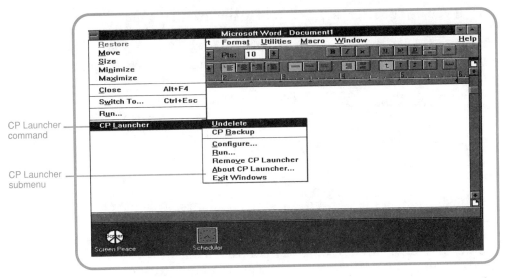

CP Launcher command

CP Launcher submenu

Figure 3.8   CP Launcher adds an option to the Control menu for every window.

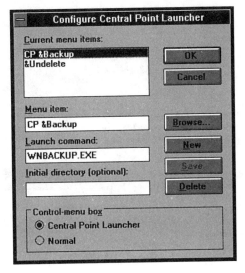

Figure 3.9   You can add or delete program names from the CP Launcher submenu.

If you decide later that you want to remove CP Launcher from the Control menus, open the Control menu and select CP Launcher. From the CP Launcher submenu, select Remove CP Launcher and select OK in the dialog box. The Control Menu box appears in its normal color, and CP Launcher is removed. To reinstall CP Launcher, simply select the CP Launcher icon.

What You'll See with CP Backup and Undelete for Windows

Although Chapters 8 and 9 discuss CP Backup and Undelete for Windows in detail, let's take a look at their opening screens, as shown in Figures 3.10 and 3.11. As you can see, the screens offer a graphical interface that resembles a control panel. To back up your hard disk or undelete files, you simply press the control buttons and select items from a list. (To press a control button, you click on it with your mouse or highlight it and press Enter.)

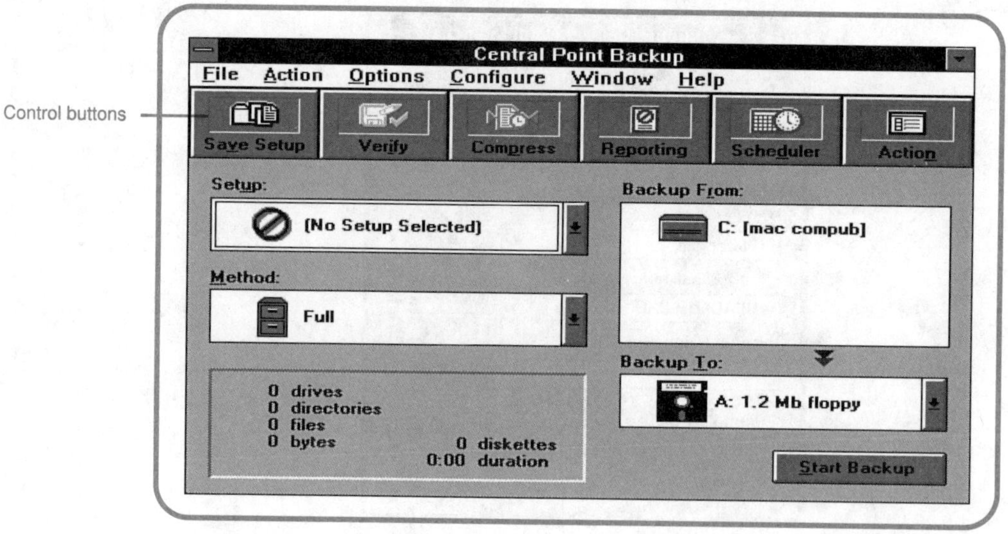

Figure 3.10   With CP Backup for Windows, you can select your options by "pressing" buttons.

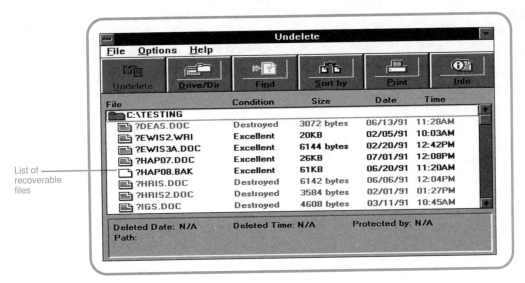

List of recoverable files

Figure 3.11   With Undelete for Windows, you select the directories and files you want to undelete from a list.

What You Have Learned

This chapter explained how to work in the Windows environment and how to run the PC Tools programs from Windows. You also learned:

▶ You can activate a window that's displayed by pressing Ctrl-F6 or clicking inside the window with your mouse.

▶ You can close the active window by double-clicking on the Control Menu box or pressing Ctrl-F4.

▶ You can use the Control menu to move, size, minimize, maximize, restore, or close the active window.

▶ You can run a program from Windows by double-clicking on its icon or by highlighting the icon with the arrow keys and pressing Enter.

▶ The CP Launcher lets you run programs directly from the program in which you're working, without returning to the Program Manager.

Understanding PC Shell

In This Chapter

- ▶ *Loading Shell using special parameters*
- ▶ *Viewing directories and files*
- ▶ *Using the commands in Shell's menus*
- ▶ *Saving your configuration settings*

Shell is the cornerstone of the PC Tools package. It provides the gateway to the PC Tools programs and functions and offers an easy-to-use alternative to DOS. This chapter provides an overview of the features and capabilities of Shell. You'll learn how to run Shell, how to view files and directories, how to move around the directory tree, and more.

In addition, you'll be introduced to Shell's menus and commands, so you'll know what the program offers.

In Review: Running Shell

In Chapter 2 you learned how to start Shell as either a stand-alone or memory-resident program (also known as a TSR program). For your convenience, this section will review the methods of starting Shell. As you may recall, there are five ways to run Shell:

▶ As a stand-alone program it runs automatically when you start your computer.

▶ As a memory-resident program it loads automatically when you start your computer.

▶ As a stand-alone program you load it manually at the DOS prompt.

▶ As a memory-resident program you load it manually at the DOS prompt.

▶ As a stand-alone program you can run it from Windows.

Note: Throughout this and the remaining chapters, we'll use the terms "memory-resident" and "TSR" (for terminate-and-stay resident) interchangeably.

The following steps explain how to run Shell. The steps assume you are using a hard disk drive and are currently logged onto the drive that contains the PC Tools programs, usually drive C. You do not need to change directories if you had the INSTALL program add the PCTOOLS directory to the the PATH statement in your AUTOEXEC.BAT file.

As a stand-alone program at the DOS prompt, type `pcshell` and press Enter.

As memory-resident program at the DOS prompt, type `pcshell/r`, press Enter, then press Ctrl-Esc to activate Shell.

As a memory-resident program loaded on startup, press Ctrl-Esc to activate Shell.

From Windows, double-click on the PC Shell icon or highlight the PC Shell icon and press Enter. See Figure 4.1.

In memory-resident mode, the Control and Escape keys are hot-keys that activate Shell from memory. Under most circumstances, you can activate Shell from within DOS or any application. Some PC programs may require all the memory in your computer, however, and Shell may not run.

You press these same keys to deactivate Shell and return to the DOS prompt or to your application. Remember that even though Shell is deactivated, it still resides in your computer's memory, so you can call it back up any time. It also continues to consume a portion of your computer's RAM, so if you need to reclaim that memory for use by another application, enter `kill` at the DOS prompt. This removes Shell (as well as Desktop, if it has also been loaded as memory-resident) from the computer's RAM. It is important to note that KILL.EXE is a PC Tools program and must be on the currently selected drive, or DOS won't be able to find it.

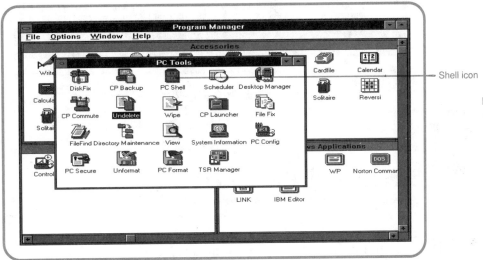

Figure 4.1   To run Shell from Windows, select the icon that looks like a filing cabinet.

> ▶ **Note:** If you're running Shell from Windows, you must exit Shell in order to return to Windows. You cannot run PC Shell in memory-resident mode and hot-key into and out of Shell.

After Shell is loaded (and activated if you're using it in memory-resident mode), your computer screen should look like the screen shown in Figure 4.2. The illustration points out the various components of the Shell display.

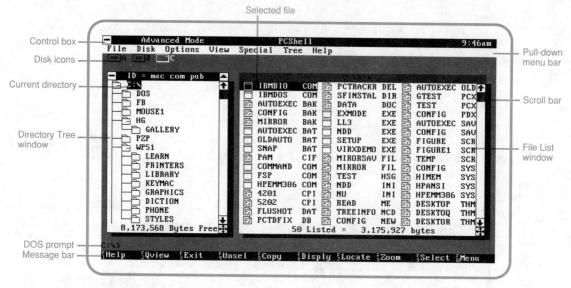

Figure 4.2   *The component parts of the Shell screen.*

74

Special Shell Parameters

Parameters are switches or options you select when you load a program into your computer. Shell supports about a dozen parameters that control the way the program works and interacts with your computer. To use a parameter, enter it after typing `pcshell` at the DOS prompt. You've already learned about one of Shell's parameters: the /R switch that loads Shell as a memory-resident program instead of a stand-alone program. In most cases, you can combine the following switches to activate many options:

/BW

Starts PC Shell in black-and-white mode.

/DQ

Disables the *Quick-Load feature* when activating Shell from the DOS prompt. (Quick-load helps load Shell faster when you activate it; it's used only when Shell is loaded as a memory-resident program.) Use the /DQ switch if you are experiencing problems running Shell as memory resident when activating the program from the DOS prompt.

/FF

Disables screen snow suppression on CGA monitors. Without the /FF switch, screen snow is suppressed when using a CGA monitor, but scrolling takes longer. With the /FF switch, screen snow appears whenever you scroll the contents of a window, but the scrolling goes faster.

/Fn

Changes the default hot-key from Ctrl-Esc to Ctrl-*n*, where *n* is one of the function keys (F1 through F10).

/LCD

Allows you to set the colors to better show on the monochrome screen of the *liquid crystal display (LCD)* panel. It is used on laptop computers with LCDs.

/LE

Exchanges right and left mouse buttons to accommodate left-handed persons.

/IM

Disables the mouse. It is helpful if you are using an older mouse driver that is not supported by PC Tools.

/IN

Used to run Shell in color with a Hercules InColor graphics card (memory-resident mode only).

/Od

Selects a different drive to contain the Shell overlay files (these include PCSHELL.OVL, PCSHELL.IMG, and PCSHELL.THM). Ordinarily, Shell places these overlay files in the drive and directory containing the PC Tools files; you can change it if your drive (or RAM disk) gets too full. Replace the *d* with a drive letter, such as /Oa.

/PS2

Resets the mouse on IBM PS/2 computers upon entering Shell. Use this switch if the mouse cursor does not appear properly.

/R

Loads Shell memory resident. You can control the amount of memory consumed by Shell when it is loaded (but not actually activated) as a memory-resident program. The more RAM consumed, the faster Shell operates, but the less room you have for other applications.

- ▶ /R or /RT or /RTINY consumes about 9K of RAM.
- ▶ /RS or /RSMALL consumes about 70K of RAM.
- ▶ /RM or /RMEDIUM consumes about 90K of RAM.
- ▶ /RL or /RLARGE consumes about 170K of RAM.

/Annn

Allocates a certain amount of RAM when Shell is activated (called up from memory) when loaded as a memory-resident program. The minimum setting for the /A switch is 180K; the maximum is approximately the total amount of RAM in your computer, minus 200K (for example, if your computer has 640K , the maximum /A setting is about 440K). Enter a memory amount after the /A switch, such as /A360, for 360K. The default setting of /A is 200K.

/TRn

Whenever you add, move, or delete a directory, the change may not appear immediately in the directory tree that Shell displays. This command tells Shell to rebuild the tree (directory hierarchy) every *n* number of days. Normally, this is set to 1, but you can increase it if you like to force Shell to examine and rebuild the tree every 2 days, every 3 days, whatever. With a setting of 0 (/TR0), Shell rebuilds the tree every time it is run. Tree rebuilding takes time—about 5 to 10 seconds for the average hard disk.

Table 4.1 offers a quick reference guide to using the parameter switches with Shell running as a stand-alone program from the DOS prompt, or as a memory-resident program.

Table 4.1   Parameter Switches for Shell Operating Modes

	Shell Loaded from DOS Prompt	Shell Loaded as a Memory-Resident Program
/BW	X	X
/DQ		X
/FF	X	X
/Fn		X
/LCD	X	X
/LE	X	X
/IM	X	X
/IN		X
/Od	X	X
/PS2	X	X
/R		X
/Annn	X	X
/TRn	X	X

Using Parameters with Windows

When you select an icon to run a program, Windows looks for the icon's corresponding *program information file (PIF)*. This file contains information about the directory in which the program's executable file is located and the command used to run the program. To use the PC Shell startup parameters with Windows, you must edit PC Shell's PIF to include the parameters, as the following Quick Steps describe:

Q Editing PC Shell's PIF

1. Change to the window that contains the PIF Editor icon.

   This is usually the Accessories window, unless you changed it.

2. Double-click on the PIF Editor icon, or highlight it and press Enter.

   The PIF Editor appears.

3. Pull down the File menu, and select Open.

   The File Open dialog box appears as in Figure 4.3, prompting you to specify which file you want to edit.

4. Activate the Files list box and double-click on `pcshell.pif` or highlight `pcshell.pif` and press Enter.

   The PIF Editor screen for PCSHELL.PIF appears as in Figure 4.4.

5. Press Alt-O or click in the Optional Parameters box.

   The cursor appears in the box.

6. Type the startup parameter(s) you want to use.

   For example, type `/le`.

7. Pull down the File menu and select Save.

   This saves the edited PIF.

8. Press Alt-F4 or double-click on the Control Menu box.

   This closes the PIF Editor. □

Viewing Directories and Files

When Shell is first started, it displays the screen shown in Figure 4.2. (Your directory and file listing will be different, reflecting the contents of your hard disk.) Unless you've used Shell before and changed its configuration (using the Save Configuration File command, introduced later in this chapter), the display will be divided into two windows.

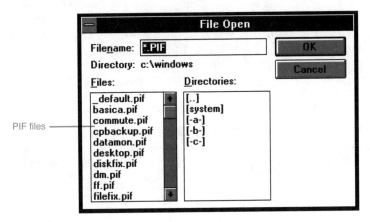

Figure 4.3 *The File Open dialog box asks you to specify which PIF you want to edit.*

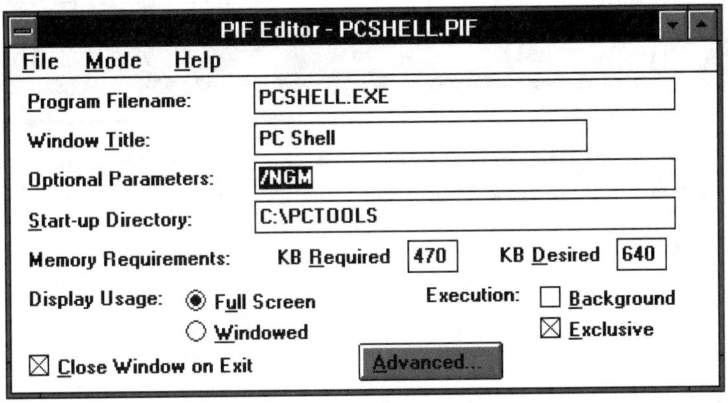

Figure 4.4 *The PIF Editor lets you specify optional parameters.*

The window on the left contains the directory tree of the hard disk drive. The tree represents the organization and layout of the subdirectories. The tree begins at the root directory, listed at the top. Subdirectories are listed alphabetically under the root.

You might consider the first hierarchy of subdirectories as the main trunk of the tree. Subdirectories under the main directories are shown as limbs branching off the trunk. Shell displays the complete hierarchy of subdirectories, even if you have created many subdirectory levels. You may have to use the scroll bars in the Tree window to view the entire hierarchy. The root or subdirectory is always selected (shown highlighted) in the Tree window. This represents the currently active directory.

The window on the right contains the files within the currently active directory. For example, if the root directory is selected in the Tree window, as shown in Figure 4.5, the File List window displays the files contained within the root directory. As you make other subdirectories active, the files in the File List window change.

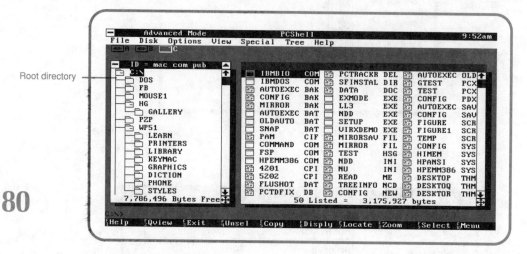

Root directory

Figure 4.5   *The root directory (shown as C:\\) is currently selected in the Tree window.*

80

Moving Around the Tree and File List Windows

The Tree and File List windows behave like any other PC Tools window. You can control the windows using either the keyboard or mouse, as detailed in Chapter 2. Remember that only one window can be active at any time. The active window is highlighted. Press the Tab key to activate a different window or click inside a window to activate it.

Selecting Subdirectories

You select a subdirectory simply by scrolling through the contents of the Tree window.

▶ When using the keyboard, press the Up or Down Arrow key to move through the directory list. Table 4.2 lists some shortcut keys you can use to move through the Tree window quickly.

▶ When using the mouse, select a subdirectory by clicking on it with the left mouse button. Or, hold down the right mouse button and drag up or down to scroll through the tree.

Table 4.2   Shortcut Keys Used in Tree Window

Key	Action
Page Up	Moves selection up one window
Page Down	Moves selection down one window
End	Moves selection to end of tree
Home	Moves selection to beginning of tree

Selecting Files

You will often select a file within the File List window for such tasks as deleting, renaming, or copying the file. To select a single file, highlight it with the cursor keys or click on it once with the left mouse button.

81

Shell allows you to select multiple files for group operations (deleting an entire set of files, for instance). Follow these Quick Steps to select a series of files.

 Selecting a Series of Files with the Keyboard

1. With the cursor keys, highlight the first file you want to select.

2. Press Enter.   Highlights the file in a different color or intensity.

3. Repeat selecting and entering for each file in the series.   □

To deselect a file, highlight it again with the cursor keys and press Enter. The file will no longer appear highlighted.

 Selecting a Series of Files with the Mouse

1. Click on one of the files with the left mouse button.   The selected file is highlighted in a different color or intensity.

2. Repeat the procedure for other
   files in the list.   □

To deselect a file, click on it again with the mouse.

> ► **Tip:** You can select two or more contiguous (adjacent) files
> quickly by using the *drag-select* technique. To drag-select,
> position the mouse pointer over the first file you want to select,
> hold down the right mouse button, and then press and hold
> down the left mouse button. Drag the mouse to move the
> highlight over the other files you want to select. Release the
> mouse buttons when all the desired files are selected. You can
> deselect the files in the same manner.

As with the Tree window, you can use the Page Up, Page Down,
Home, and End keys to move through the file list quickly, as detailed
in Table 4.3.

Table 4.3   Shortcut Keys Used in File List Window

Key	Action
Page Up	Moves selection up one column or window
Page Down	Moves selection down one column or window
End	Moves selection to end of files
Home	Moves selection to beginning of files

If you're using a mouse, you can scroll through the files quickly:
Hold down the right mouse button, and drag up or down to scroll
through the file list.

Automatic Quick File Display and Selection

Shell offers other means for displaying and selecting groups of files
quickly.

► You can display a list of only those files that match the name
or extension you've provided (with and without wild cards)
using the File List Filter command in the Modify Display
submenu.

▶ You can retain the entire list, with the files you chose high-lighted and numbered, using the File Select command.

▶ You can select only those files that match the name or extension you've provided (with and without wild cards) using the File Select Filter command on the Options menu.

> ▶ **Tip:** Press the F9 function key then press Enter three times to select all files quickly. Conversely, press the F4 function key to deselect all files quickly.

The following Quick Steps give the basic procedure for filtering the file list:

Filtering the File List

83

1. Select the subdirectory that contains the files you wish to view.

2. Pull down the View menu and select Filters.

The Filters submenu appears.

3. Select File List.

The File List Filter dialog box appears, as in Figure 4.6, asking you to specify the files you want included in the list.

4. Define the name and/or extension of the files you want to view.

For example, to view only .EXE files, enter EXE in the Ext field. You may use the * and ? DOS wild cards: Enter SHOW?.EXE to find SHOW1.EXE, SHOW2.EXE, SHOWA.EXE, etc.

5. Choose Display.

The file list is updated to show a list of files that match your entry. ☐

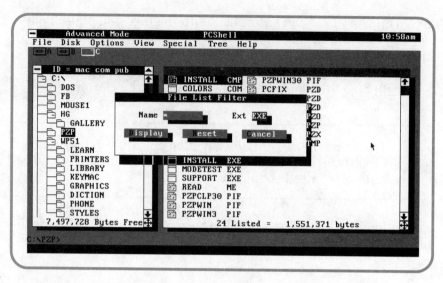

Figure 4.6   The File List Filter dialog box.

84

To return the file list to its original form (unfiltered), repeat Steps 1 to 3, and then select **R**eset. This puts the asterisks back in the Name and Ext text boxes. When you select **D**isplay, the list will return to its original form. You can also select certain groups of files, as the following Quick Steps explain:

 Activating the Select File Filter

1. Choose the subdirectory that contains the files you wish to select.

2. Pull down the View menu and select Filters.

   The Filters submenu appears.

3. Select File **S**elect.

   The File Select Filter dialog box appears, asking you to specify the files you want selected from the list.

4. Define the name and/or extension of the files you want to view.

   For example, to view and select only files with the .DOC extension, enter DOC in the Ext field.

5. Choose **S**elect.

   The file list is updated with the specified group of files highlighted.   □

To return the file list to its original form (unfiltered), pull down the View menu and choose **U**nselect Files. A sample of selected files (all with the .DOC extension) is shown in Figure 4.7.

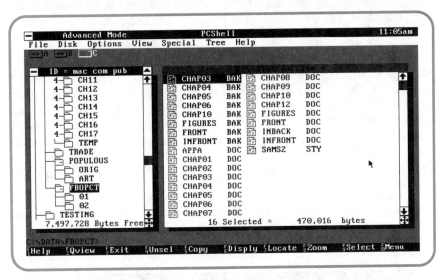

Figure 4.7   File List display showing all .DOC files selected.

Changing the Current Drive

The current drive (with directory and files shown in the Tree and File List windows) is indicated immediately under Shell's pulldown menu bar. The available drives as detected by Shell or indicated with the LASTDRIVE command in your CONFIG.SYS file are listed as A, B, C, etc.; the current active drive is highlighted.

To change the current drive with the keyboard, hold down the control key and type the letter of the drive you want to activate (such as Ctrl-A or Ctrl-B).

To change the current drive with the mouse, click on one of the drive icons under the menu bar. For example, to activate drive C, click on the C icon.

Viewing Two Lists

Shell normally presents a single set of Tree and File List windows, but you can readily add another set of windows to view two trees and file lists at a time. This comes in handy, for example, when copying or moving files between two directories or drives.

To add another set of windows, pull down the View menu and choose **D**ual File Lists. Now four windows are displayed on the screen, as shown in Figure 4.8. To go back to the one-list display, choose **S**ingle File List from the View menu. You can toggle between the Dual and Single File List display by using the Ins and Del keys. Press Ins to view the Dual File List display or press Del to change back to the Single display. (This works only if one of the windows is active; if the DOS prompt is highlighted, this does not work.)

Note that the current list display setting (either Single List or Dual List) can be recorded for subsequent sessions with Shell. There will be more on saving the configuration of Shell later.

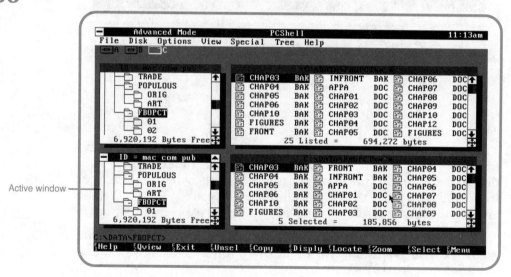

Figure 4.8   Dual File List display.

> ▶ **Tip:** To open a second set of windows quickly and read the directory on another drive, press Ctrl-Alt-<drive letter>, where "drive letter" corresponds to the drive you want to view (A, B, etc.). Press Tab to move highlight between windows.

Shell Menus

In addition to the Help menu, Shell offers six pull-down menus where you can access the program's commands. Additionally, you can access the most common commands using the shortcut (function keys), as displayed in the message bar at the bottom of the Shell screen. These menus are:

87

- ▶ File
- ▶ Disk
- ▶ Options
- ▶ View
- ▶ Special
- ▶ Tree

These menus, and the commands contained within them, are described here. This section provides just an introduction to the PC Tools Shell commands and does not explain how to use them in practice. Subsequent chapters detail, according to function, the use of Shell commands.

The Shell File Menu

The File menu, shown in Figure 4.9, contains the following commands used for running a program, exiting the Shell, and managing individual files:

Open—runs the program in which the selected file was created and loads the file into the program.

Run—lets you run a program from Shell.

Print—prints the selected file or the displayed file list.

Search—hunts through a selected file and looks for a specified string of characters.

View File Contents—displays the contents of a file.

Move—transplants a file to another directory or disk.

Copy—creates a duplicate of a file. Copies can be made anywhere in the same disk or directory as the original or in another disk or directory.

Compare—matches two files to see if they are the same or different. Each dissimilarity can be viewed individually.

Delete—erases selected files from disk.

Rename—changes the DOS name of a file.

Change File—opens a submenu that offers the following options:

> **Edit File**—lets you view a file (program or document in ASCII form) and edit it character by character.
>
> **Hex Edit File**—lets you view a file (program or document) in hexadecimal form and edit it byte by byte.
>
> **Clear File**—erases a file and wipes away all data on disk. This prevents reclaiming the erased file or viewing its remnants.
>
> **Attribute Change**—alters certain information attached to each file created by DOS, including the time and date of creation or last edit and whether or not the file can be edited or erased.

Locate—hunts through all or portions of your disks to find specified files.

Verify—checks the integrity of a file, either a program file or data file, to determine if it can be used.

Undelete—reclaims accidently deleted files.

Secure—lets you protect files with a password.

Select All Toggle—selects all files in the current directory.

Exit—closes Shell.

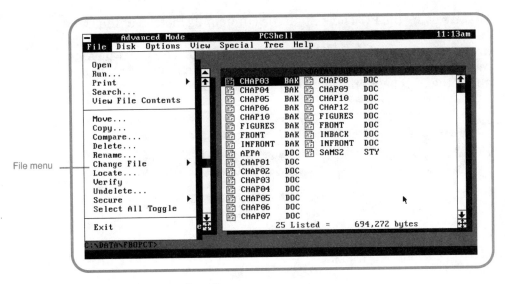

File menu

Figure 4.9   The File menu.

Some of the Shell commands under the File menu are duplicates of those that DOS provides, as detailed in Table 4.4.

Table 4.4   Equivalent File Menu DOS Commands

PC Shell Command	Equivalent DOS Command
Copy	COPY
Move	No direct command
Compare	COMP or FC
Find	FIND
Rename	REN
Delete	DEL or ERASE
Verify	VERIFY
View	TYPE

By using the PC Tools Shell file commands instead of the DOS commands, you are provided with convenient "fill-in-the-blanks" prompts, such as the one shown in Figure 4.10. You don't have to remember the special syntax DOS requires of its commands or worry about the effects of entering a command incorrectly.

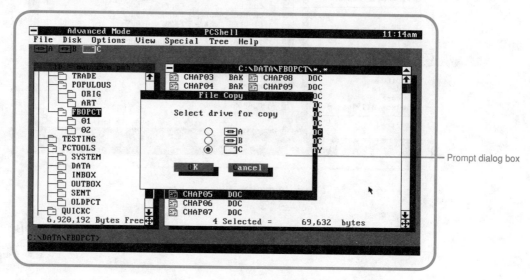

Figure 4.10   The Prompt dialog box provides prompts for entering additional information.

The Shell Disk Menu

Just as the File menu manages files, the Disk menu governs operations that apply to entire disks or disk directories. The Disk pull-down menu is shown in Figure 4.11 and contains these commands:

Copy—duplicates the entire contents of one disk onto another disk. The copy includes visible and hidden files.

Compare—matches two disks and indicates whether they are the same or different. You can optionally view the differences, if any.

Rename Volume—changes the name that you (or someone else) previously gave to a disk.

Search—hunts through the entire disk and looks for a specified string of characters.

Verify—quickly scans the disk and determines if all the data on it is readable.

Format Data Disk—initializes or renews the format of a floppy disk, preparing it for new data.

Make Disk Bootable—writes system information and the COMMAND.COM file onto a disk to make it bootable. *Bootable* means you can use the disk to start up your computer.

Directory Maintenance—displays the Directory Maintenance screen that lets you manage the directories on a disk. You can use this screen to add, delete, rename, and move directories in a directory tree.

Park Disk Heads—positions the read/write heads of a hard disk drive over an unused portion of the disk surface to prevent the heads from crashing down and destroying data. With the heads parked, you can safely move your computer.

Sort Files in Directory—lets you change the order in which the files on the current directory are stored.

91

Disk Information—provides a rundown of important facts about a disk, such as its capacity, number and size of bad sectors, and number of files.

View/Edit—lets you look at the data anywhere on a disk and, optionally, edit it.

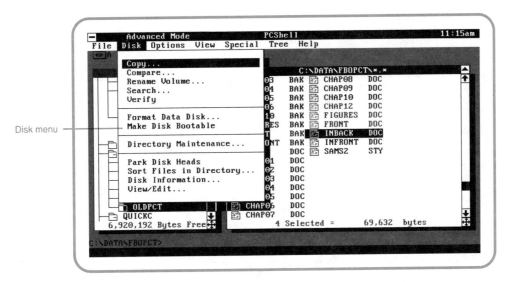

Figure 4.11   The Disk menu.

As with the File menu, some of the Shell commands under the Disk menu are similar to ones DOS provides (see Table 4.5).

Table 4.5   Equivalent Disk Menu DOS Commands

PC Shell Command	Equivalent DOS Command
Copy Disk	DISKCOPY
Compare Disk	DISKCOMP
Search Disk	FIND
Rename Volume	LABEL
Verify Disk	CHKDSK
View/Edit Disk	No direct command
Format Data Disk	FORMAT
Make System Disk	FORMAT /S
Disk Info	CHKDSK (only partial information as that given with Disk Info command)
Park Disk	SHIPDISK (can cause damage to some non-IBM hard disk drives)
Directory Maintenance	
Add	MKDIR
Rename	None
Delete	RMDIR
Prune and Graft	None

92

The Shell Options Menu

The Options menu (see Figure 4.12) lets you control several features of Shell that tell Shell how to present information and how to interact with you, the user:

Confirmation—lets you specify whether you want a prompt to warn you before Shell carries out a command. You can turn the following three options on or off:

Confirm on Delete—displays a prompt that warns you before deleting a file.

Confirm on Replace—displays a prompt warning you that you are about to replace a file on disk with another file of the same name.

Confirm on Mouse Operations—displays a prompt telling you the consequences of the mouse operation you're about to perform.

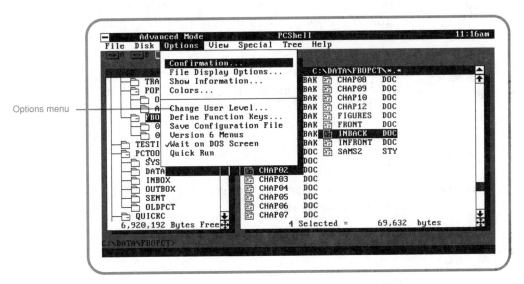

Options menu

Figure 4.12   The Options menu.

93

File Display Options—lets you select how you want the files in the File List window sorted (by name, extension, time, or date) in ascending or descending order (ascending is A, B, C or 1, 2, 3; descending is Z, Y, X or 10, 9, 8). You can also specify the type of information you want displayed for the files: the size of the file, the date and/or time the file was created, the files' attributes, and the number of clusters the file consumes on disk.

Show Information—provides a rundown of important facts about the selected file, such as its size and the actual amount of space it takes up on disk.

Colors—lets you change the colors of the various screen elements in Shell.

Change User Level—lets you change the user level to Beginner, Intermediate, or Advanced, giving you more or fewer options on each menu. More about this later in the chapter.

Define Function Keys—lets you assign different commands to the function keys that are displayed at the bottom of the screen.

Save Configuration File—records the changes you make in the Options menu for the next time you use Shell.

Version 6 Menus—lets you use the menus that were available in PC Tools 6.0. This is useful if you're accustomed to using the menus in version 6.0, but if you select this option, many of the commands in this book will not work as described.

Wait on DOS Screen—pauses Shell, so you can read the last screen displayed by another program. This is useful if you run programs from the Shell. When you quit the program to return to Shell, Shell resumes operations automatically, often preventing you from seeing the last screen that the other program displays. With this option, you can pause the screen before the transition.

Quick Run—tells the Shell to run the program quickly, without freeing up memory first.

The Shell View Menu

The View menu, shown in Figure 4.13, gives you control over the appearance of the PC Shell screen. You can use this menu to turn certain windows on or off and to configure the screen to make it easier to use.

Single File List—is the default setting; it displays one directory tree and one file list.

Dual File Lists—displays a split screen containing two directory trees and two file lists.

Program/File Lists—displays a split screen containing a directory tree, file list, and Program menu.

Program List Only—displays only the Program menu, discussed later in this chapter.

Viewer/File Lists—displays a split screen containing a directory tree, file list, and file viewer (in which you can view the contents of a file).

Custom List Configure—lets you set up a custom screen. The first four options let you turn the following windows on or off: Tree List, File List, Program List, and View Window. Background Mat lets you turn the screen background on or off; if you turn it off, you can see the screen that is beneath PC Shell. DOS Command Line lets you display the DOS prompt, so you can enter DOS commands directly at the prompt. Viewer Config lets you display the viewer window horizontally (across the screen) or vertically (up and down). Window Style controls the layout of the windows; Tiled butts the edges of the windows up against each other, whereas Cascaded lets the windows lie on top of one another.

Hide All Lists—removes all lists and the menu bar from screen, so you can work at the DOS prompt or work with any underlying programs.

Set Date/Time—lets you set the date and time on your computer.

Refresh—tells PC Shell to reread a disk. If you add or delete a directory, the change may not appear immediately on screen. This option refreshes the screen to show any changes.

Filters—screens the file list to display a specific group of files or to select a group of files.

Unselect Files—lets you quickly unselect all selected files.

95

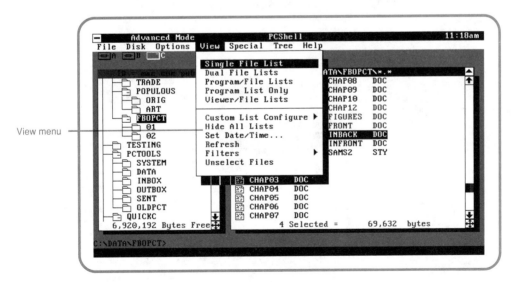

View menu

Figure 4.13   The View menu.

The Shell Special Menu

The Special menu, illustrated in Figure 4.14, contains several utilities that provide important information about your computer system.

System Info—checks the hardware configuration of your computer and provides information about the size of your hard drive, the floppy drives available, the amount of RAM in your computer, and more.

DeskConnect—lets you connect two computers, so you can transfer files between them.

File Map—displays a map of the currently selected file, as it resides on a hard or floppy disk.

Disk Map—displays a map of the current disk, showing parts used and still available, along with important areas like bad sectors.

Memory Map—displays a list of programs loaded into memory and how much RAM is taken up by each.

Remove PC Shell—dislodges PC Shell from active memory in your computer, assuming you loaded Shell in memory-resident mode. If PC Shell is not running in memory-resident mode, this option is not listed.

96

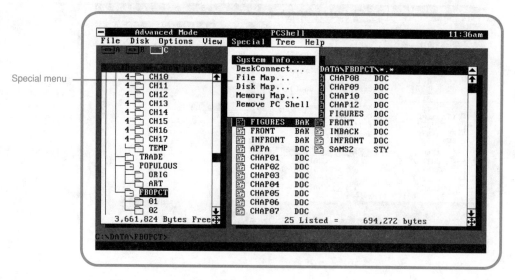

Special menu

Figure 4.14   The Special menu.

The Shell Tree Menu

The Tree menu is new to PC Tools 7. This menu gives you more control over your Directory Tree window, allowing you to collapse and expand branches at the touch of a key (or mouse button). You can then remove the directories you're not working with from the display, removing the clutter.

Expand One Level—lets you see the subdirectories one level below the current directory. If you collapsed part of your directory tree, you can use this command to expand it.

Expand Branch—shows all subdirectories at all levels below the current directory.

Expand All—expands the entire directory tree, so all directories and subdirectories are displayed.

Collapse Branch—hides all subdirectories under the current directory, so you see only the current directory.

97

> ▶ **Tip:** Note the characters +, *, and – next to the commands. These keys let you enter the corresponding commands directly from the keyboard, so you don't have to access the Tree menu. Just highlight the directory you want the command to affect and then press + to expand it one level, * to expand the entire branch, or – to collapse the branch. You can also use the mouse by clicking on the directory icon if it contains a + or – as shown in Figure 4.15.

The Shell Program Menu

In addition to six pull-down menus, Shell offers a Program menu, which lists programs (as well as batch files) you may want to run directly from Shell. To display the Program menu, press F10 or click on F10 Menu in the message bar (you could also select one of the Program List commands from the View menu). Depending on how you installed the PC Tools programs and what software is already contained in your hard disk, the menu will already be filled with a number of program groups, as shown in Figure 4.16.

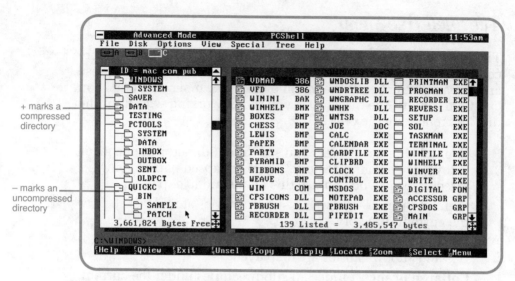

+ marks a compressed directory

– marks an uncompressed directory

Figure 4.15 You can expand a collapsed directory by pressing +, or collapse a directory by pressing –.

> **Tip:** You can toggle between the Program menu and the Shell by pressing F10 or clicking on F10 Menu in the message bar.

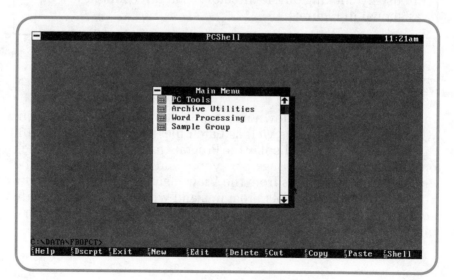

Figure 4.16 The Program menu.

The Program menu automatically includes the PC Tools program group. If you select that group, a submenu opens, displaying the following programs and program subgroups:

Recovery Tools—DiskFix, File Fix, Undelete, and Unformat.

System Tools—Compress, FileFind, System Information, Directory Maintenance, and View.

Security Tools—PC Secure, Data Monitor, and Wipe.

Setup Tools—Install, PC Configuration.

CP Backup—The PC Tools hard disk backup program.

Commute—The PC Tools remote computing program.

Desktop Manager—PC Tools Desktop.

These programs are discussed in more detail in later chapters.

Note that many of the PC Tools programs (Compress, Backup, Format, Secure, and DiskFix) are really stand-alone applications you can run without Shell. You may run any of these programs, as listed in Table 4.6, by entering its file name at the DOS prompt or selecting it from the Program menu. (Refer to the appendix for more details.)

99

Table 4.6   Program Menu Name and File Name

Program Menu Name	PC Tools Stand-Alone Program
DiskFix	DISKFIX.EXE
File Fix	FILEFIX.EXE
Undelete	UNDEL.EXE
Unformat	UNFORMAT.EXE
Compress Disk	COMPRESS.EXE
FileFind	FF.EXE
System Info	SI.EXE
Directory Maintenance	DM.EXE
View	VIEW.EXE
PC Secure	PCSECURE.EXE
Data Monitor	DATAMON.EXE
Wipe	WIPE.EXE
Install	INSTALL.EXE

(continued)

Table 4.6   (continued)

Program Menu Name	PC Tools Stand-Alone Program
PC Config	PCCONFIG.EXE
CP Backup	CPBACKUP.EXE
Commute	COMMUTE.EXE
Desktop	DESKTOP.EXE

During the installation of PC Tools, the software searches for common programs such as Lotus 1-2-3, dBASE, Microsoft Word, WordPerfect, and WordStar, automatically adding these to the Program menu. The Program menu may contain a program group, for example, called "Word Processing Programs." You can readily add, remove, or edit the listed programs as explained in Chapter 7 "Running Programs WITH Shell."

100

As with any command in a Shell menu, you can select any of the programs in the Program menu with either the keyboard or the mouse. (The exact procedure for using the keyboard and mouse with the PC Tools programs is explained fully in Chapter 2, "Getting Started with PC Tools.")

Variable User Levels

PC Shell allows you to select one of three user levels: Beginner, Intermediate, or Advanced. These user levels determine the contents of the pull-down menus. Only a handful of the most critical commands are listed in the menus under the Beginner user level. The number of commands increases as you select Intermediate or Advanced.

Table 4.7 shows the commands provided in each of the three modes. After you become proficient with Shell, you'll probably want to select Advanced Mode, as it allows you to use all of the commands PC Tools offers.

Table 4.7   PC Shell User Level Commands

Menu/Command	Beginner	Intermediate	Advanced
File Menu			
Open	X	X	X
Run	X	X	X
Print		X	X
Sear**c**h		X	X
View File	X	X	X
Move	X	X	X
Copy	X	X	X
Comp**a**re	X	X	X
Delete		X	X
Re**n**ame	X	X	X
Chan**g**e File		X	X
Locate	X	X	X
Verif**y**		X	X
Undelete		X	X
Se**c**ure			X
Select All Toggle	X	X	X
E**x**it	X	X	X
Disk Menu			
Copy	X	X	X
C**o**mpare	X	X	X
Rename Volume		X	X
Search		X	X
Verify		X	X
Format Data Disk	X	X	X
Make Disk **B**ootable	X	X	X
Directory **M**aintenance	X	X	X

(continued)

101

Table 4.7 (continued)

Menu/Command	Beginner	Intermediate	Advanced
Disk Menu (continued)			
Park Disk Heads		X	X
Sort Files in Directory		X	X
Disk Information			X
View/**E**dit			X
Options Menu			
Confirmation	X	X	X
File Display Options	X	X	X
Show Information	X	X	X
Colors	X	X	X
Change **U**ser Level	X	X	X
Define Function **K**eys	X	X	X
S**a**ve Configuration File	X	X	X
Ver**s**ion 6 Menus	X	X	X
Wait on DOS Screen	X	X	X
Quick Run	X	X	X
View Menu			
Single File List	X	X	X
Dual File List	X	X	X
Program/**F**ile Lists	X	X	X
Program List Only	X	X	X
Viewer Menu			
Single File Lists	X	X	X
Custom List Configure	X	X	X
Hide All Lists	X	X	X
Set Date/**T**ime	X	X	X
Refresh	X	X	X
Fi**l**ters	X	X	X
Unselect Files	X	X	X

Menu/Command	Beginner	Intermediate	Advanced
Special			
System Info	X	X	X
DeskConnect	X	X	X
File Map			X
Disk Map			X
Memory Map			X
Remove PC Shell	X	X	X
Tree Menu			
Expand One Level	X	X	X
Expand Branch	X	X	X
Expand All	X	X	X
Collapse Branch	X	X	X

103

The following steps describe how to change the user level:

1. Pull down the Options menu and select Change User Level. A dialog box appears, prompting you to select a user level.
2. Select one of the three user levels: Beginner, Intermediate, or Advanced.
3. Press Enter or select OK to accept your changes.

The currently set user level is shown in the upper left corner of the PC Shell screen.

Using the DOS Command Line

If you prefer entering some commands at the DOS prompt, Shell can accommodate you. To display the DOS command line, pull down the View menu and select Custom List Configure. From the submenu that appears, select DOS Command Line. The DOS prompt appears in its usual position—the lower left corner of the screen.

To enter a command at the prompt, you must first activate the DOS command line. To do so, press the Tab key until the line is highlighted (the cursor will appear after the prompt), or click on the line with the left mouse button. You can then enter a command in the usual way—type it and press Enter. Shell will temporarily exit to DOS, where your command will be executed. After the command is finished, press any key to reenter Shell. If you have the Wait on DOS Screen option (on the Options menu) set to off, Shell automatically restarts, without waiting for you to press a key.

User-Definable Function Keys

To further customize the PC Tools screen, you can define your own shortcut function keys. For example, you can define a function key, say F2, to format your floppy disks. Then, whenever you want to format a disk, instead of pulling down the Disk menu and selecting **F**ormat Data Disk, you can simply press F2.

Shell lets you redefine seven of the ten function keys. Function keys F1, F3, and F10 are not redefinable.

To redefine a function key:

1. Pull down the Options menu and select Define Function **K**eys. The Define Function Keys dialog box appears, as in Figure 4.17.
2. On the left side of the dialog box that appears, select a function key to redefine (choose any key except F1, F3, or F10).
3. On the right side of the dialog box, select an action, such as Copy File or Rename File.

Repeat Steps 2 and 3 for each function key you want to redefine. When done, select **U**pdate to accept the changes or **C**ancel to quit without saving.

*Figure 4.17   The Define Function Keys dialog box lets you
customize the keys.*

Running Shell on a Network

PC Tools can be used on a network as long as certain measures are followed.

▶   The PC Tools programs should be installed in a write-protected directory on a Novell NetWare, IBM PC LAN, or compatible network server.

▶   The PC Tools server directory should be included in the PATH statement executed with the system administrator's AUTOEXEC.BAT file.

▶ The AUTOEXEC.BAT file for each user should include an environment variable specifying where the program should place all user-specific files. The variable should indicate a directory where the individual user has read and write privileges, such as:

```
SET PCTOOLS=C:\MYTOOLS
```

for a directory called MYTOOLS on drive C:.

▶ All of the drives on the network (real and virtual) that can be accessed by the user will appear on the drive line above the file and directory list windows.

▶ All of PC Shell's commands are available on the network except for Directory Sort, Disk Info, Disk Map, File Map, Rename Volume, Search Disk, Undelete File, Verify Disk, Format Data Disk, Make System Disk, and View/Edit Disk.

The PC Tools manual includes additional specifics on setting up the program on network systems. You'll find more information about using PC Tools on a network in Chapter 13.

Saving the Shell Configuration

The Save Configuration File command (in the Options pull-down menu) lets you save certain changes you've made to Shell and its windows. The settings are stored in the file PCSHELL.CFG. If this file is damaged or erased, Shell will return to its original defaults. You can purposely erase the PCSHELL.CFG file if you want to return to the factory settings and start over.

To save a new configuration, choose the Save Configuration File command from the Options menu. Shell pauses a moment while it updates the PCSHELL.CFG file. If you don't manually save the configuration, Shell will remind you to do it when you exit the program.

What You Have Learned

In this chapter, you learned the basics of PC Shell and how to use the PC Shell interface to enter commands. You also learned,

▶ The /R parameter loads Shell in memory-resident mode.

▶ Shell displays the root directory and subdirectories of the currently selected disk in a Tree window.

▶ Shell displays the files contained within the currently selected directory in a File List window.

▶ If you have a mouse, you can select multiple contiguous files with the drag-select technique.

▶ To change the current drive, press Ctrl-<drive letter> or click on the drive letter with the mouse.

▶ The File menu contains those commands used for running a program, exiting PC Shell, or managing individual files.

▶ The Disk menu controls operations that apply to entire disks or disk directories.

▶ The Options menu lets you control the presentation of Shell's windows and the data contained within them.

▶ The View menu lets you display various windows in Shell and display additional elements on the PC Shell screen.

▶ The Special menu contains miscellaneous PC Tools commands and features.

▶ The Program menu lists programs you can run directly from Shell.

107

Managing Files with Shell

In This Chapter

▶ *Copying selected files*
▶ *Safely renaming and deleting files*
▶ *Using Shell commands for DOS functions*
▶ *Viewing, editing, and printing files*
▶ *Locating any file, anywhere*
▶ *Securing sensitive files*

PC Shell performs all of the file functions offered by DOS, but Shell is much easier and quicker to use. Shell actually helps you work faster, and because you can see exactly what you're doing at every instant, you're less likely to make mistakes. But, even if you do, PC Tools can help you fix them.

This chapter discusses file management using Shell; Chapters 6 and 7, respectively, detail how to manage disks and run programs with Shell.

List Files Display

In Chapter 4, "Understanding PC Shell," you learned how Shell displays the files within a subdirectory in the File List window. This window is the main gateway to Shell's file management functions. (If you haven't read Chapter 4 yet, do so now and learn how to move around inside Shell and select files and directories with the keyboard or mouse.)

Normally, Shell displays only file names in the File List window. Assuming the File List window is full size, you can view about 48 files at one time, or roughly 16 files in each of three columns. The three columns wrap from left to right, as shown in Figure 5.1.

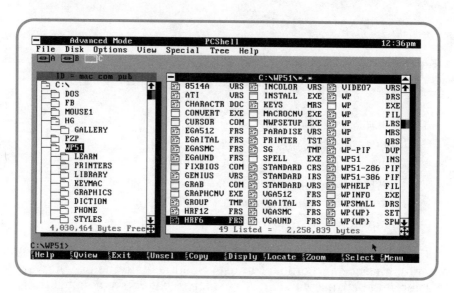

Figure 5.1 *When displaying more than one row of files at a time, the file list wraps from the bottom of the row on the left to the top of the row on the right.*

Files that won't fit in the window can be scrolled into view from the lower right corner of the window. As files scroll into view in the lower right corner, files at the beginning of the list scroll out of view in the upper left corner.

You can change the File List Display to list the files in a different order or to list additional information about the files, including file size and time/date of creation or last edit. The more information you display, the fewer files you can see in one window. To sort the list in a different order or display additional information, use the File Display Options command from the Options menu, as described in the following Quick Steps:

Q Setting File Display Options

1. Pull down the Options menu.

2. Choose File Display Options.   The dialog box shown in Figure 5.2 appears. The currently selected options are shown in the dialog box.

3. Under Sort By, select **N**ame, **E**xtension, **S**ize, or **D**ate/Time.   This tells Shell what element to use when performing the sort. You can select only one option.

4. Under Sort Direction, select Ascending or Descending.   Ascending order is A B C . . . or 1 2 3 . . . . Descending order is Z Y X . . . or 10 9 8 . . . .

5. Under What to Display, select **S**ize, **D**ate, **T**ime, **A**ttribute, and/or Number of Clusters.   You can select more than one option. This tells Shell the type of information to display for each file.

6. Select OK to save the settings or **C**ancel to cancel the changes you've entered.   If you select **OK**, the File List window is updated to show the effects of the new settings. □

111

Figure 5.3 shows a File List window displaying the files in ascending order by name, including sizes and attributes.

> ▶ **Tip:** The order in which Shell displays files is entirely independent of the order in which files are recorded on the disk, or the order in which files are displayed when you ask for DIRectory while in DOS. PC Tools provides additional features and commands for physically sorting files on a disk (the Compress program) and for sorting directories (the Sort Files in Directory command in the Disk menu).

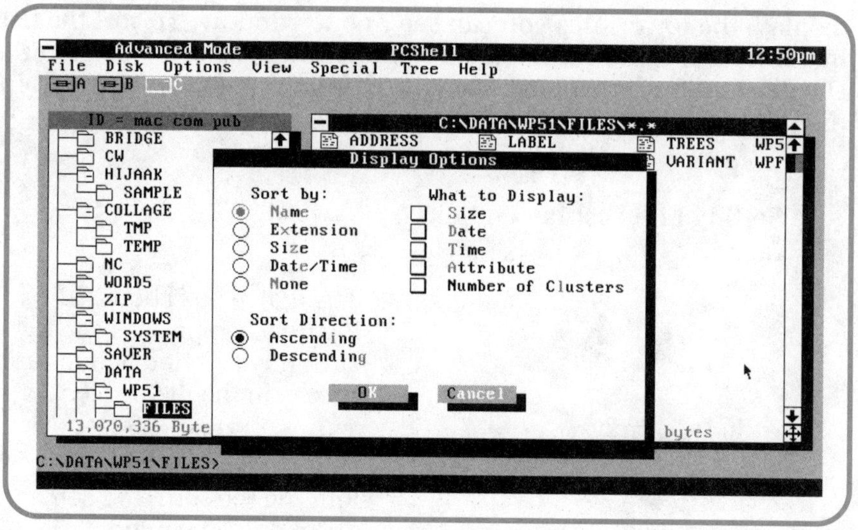

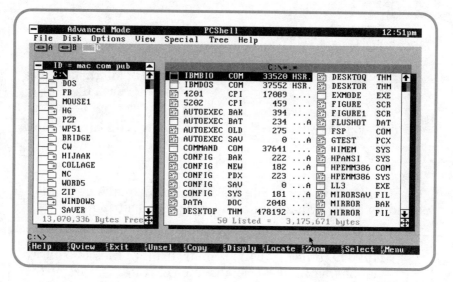

Figure 5.2   The Display Options dialog box.

112

Figure 5.3   File display with attributes and sizes.

Changes you make in the Display Options dialog box are recorded in the PCSHELL.CFG configuration file. Should this file be damaged or erased, Shell will revert to the factory display setting, which is file name and extension only, with no sorting.

Copying Files

One of the most common tasks while operating a computer is copying files. Shell lets you copy files to any disk or directory quickly and easily. And because the available drives and directories are displayed on-screen, you never have to worry about typing the wrong path.

Shell handles file copying differently depending on whether you are copying files within a single disk and directory or to a different disk and/or directory. These techniques will be discussed separately.

Copying to the Same Directory and Disk

Copying a file to the same disk and directory is useful if you want to edit a file to see if you can improve it. If editing the copy makes it worse, you can then use the original, unchanged file. Making a copy of a file in the same directory and disk is no more difficult than the other techniques, but the copy must be given a different name from the original. The following Quick Steps give this procedure:

113

 Copying a File to the Same Directory/Disk

1. If you haven't done so already, select the disk and directory that holds the file you want to copy.

2. Highlight the file to copy in the File List window.

   Selects the file to copy.

3. Pull down the File menu and select Copy.

   The dialog box in Figure 5.4 appears, prompting you to specify a destination for the copy.

4. Select the same drive that contains the source file.

5. Select a subdirectory for the copy, if any. In this case, it will be the same subdirectory that contains the original file.

   Another dialog box appears, as in Figure 5.5, prompting you to enter a new name for the file.

6. Enter a new name and/or extension for the copied file.

Shell provides the original file name, so you can edit it or merely add a distinguishing character (like BUDGET1 to a file named BUDGET) to supply the new name. You can also change the extension (for example, use .NEW for the new file).

7. Select OK.

Copies the file to the same directory under the new name. ☐

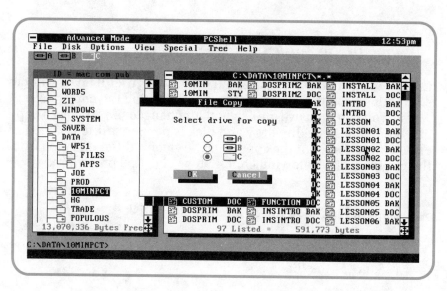

Figure 5.4   The File Copy dialog box prompting you to enter the target drive.

If you select more than one file for copying, Shell will ask that you provide a new name for each one. Unfortunately, you cannot perform "wild-card copies" where you indicate a group of files to copy with a wild-card character (? or *) and include the wild card in a "group destination" file. However, DOS can perform a wild-card copy with its COPY command:

```
COPY *.DOC *.BAK
```

Should you need to perform a copy procedure such as this (it's not that common, in any case), you can always enter the command at the DOS prompt (assuming it's displayed).

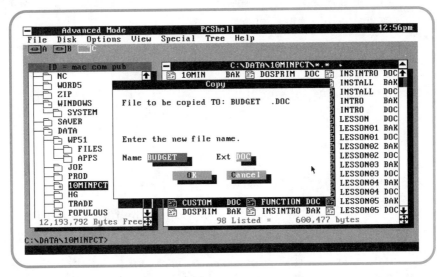

Figure 5.5   PC Tools lets you rename the copied file in case a disk or directory already contains a file with the same name.

▶ **Tip:** After you copy a file, Shell remembers the destination disk you selected, so it automatically selects it for the next copy. However, Shell always asks you to select a destination directory. If you plan on making copies of several files, it's best if you copy them all at once.

Copying Files to a Different Subdirectory or Disk

Copying files to a different subdirectory or disk involves the same basic procedures as those outlined previously, except you don't need to provide a new name for the copy. The following Quick Steps explains how to copy files to a different subdirectory or disk:

Copying Files to a Different Subdirectory or Disk

1. If you haven't done so already, select the disk and directory that holds the file(s) you want to copy.

2. Select the file(s) to copy from the File List window.

   Identifies the source file(s).

3. Pull down the File menu and select Copy.

   A dialog box appears, prompting you to select a destination for the copied file(s).

4. Select the drive to which you want to copy the selected file(s).

5. Select the directory where you want the copies stored.

   Copies the file(s) into the new disk/subdirectory. □

116

Shell flashes a dialog box that informs you that the file(s) is being copied. If your computer is equipped with a fast hard disk drive, the dialog box will remain on the screen only momentarily.

Fast File Copying with a Mouse

If you have a mouse, you can quickly copy one or more files by dragging them from directory to directory. Copying files using a mouse is best done with the Dual List Display. A quick way of displaying the Dual List Display is to press the Ins key. (See Chapter 6 for more on Dual and Single File List display.) Use the following Quick Steps to copy files with a mouse:

Fast Mouse File Copying

1. In one list, select the disk and directory that contains the file(s) you want to copy.

   Sets the source directory.

2. In the other list, select the disk and directory where you want the copies sent.

   Sets the destination directory.

3. Select the file(s) to copy by clicking on them with the left mouse button.

   Selects the file(s) to copy.

4. Point to any one of the file(s) you selected and hold down the left mouse button.

5. Drag the mouse pointer so the message box is in the destination File List window.

As you drag the mouse, the Copy Files message box appears, as shown in Figure 5.6 telling you that *x* number of files will be copied.

6. Release the mouse button.

Copies the file(s) for you automatically. ☐

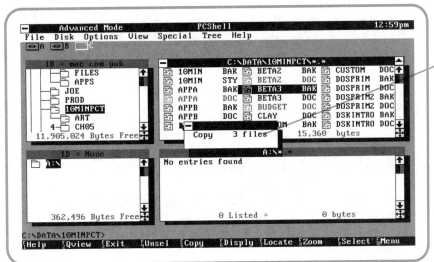

Copy Files
message box

Figure 5.6   Copying files in Dual List Display using the mouse.

▶ **Tip:** You can also drag the file(s) directly into a subdirectory in the Tree window, as shown in Figure 5.7. This requires that you copy the file(s) within the same drive and that both source and destination subdirectories are visible in the Tree window.

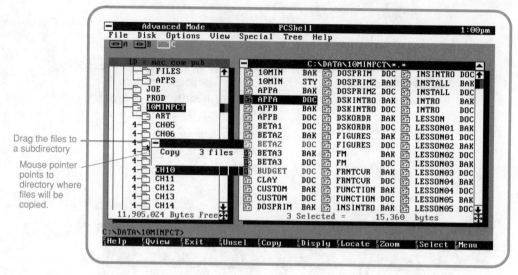

Drag the files to a subdirectory

Mouse pointer points to directory where files will be copied.

Figure 5.7   Copying file(s) from the File List window directly into a subdirectory.

Using the Keyboard with the Dual List Display

You may copy files with the Dual List Display when operating Shell from the keyboard. The procedure is the same as a Single List Display, except that Shell asks you to confirm that you want to use the second path (second list) as the target. Select **OK** to confirm.

Name Conflicts

If you try to copy a file to a disk or directory that already contains a file with the same name, Shell asks if you want to replace it or quit. Shell displays the same dialog box whether you are copying one file or many.

▶ Press the **R**eplace File button to replace only the indicated file.

▶ Press the Replace **A**ll button if you are copying many files and want to replace them all at once.

▶ Press the Skip **F**ile button if you are copying many files and want to skip the current one.

▶ Press the **S**kip All button to skip all files.

▶ Press the **C**ancel button to cancel the copy.

Moving Files

Moving a file is similar to copying a file, except that the original is erased and only the copy remains. As with the Copy command, Shell lets you move files to any disk or directory. But unlike Copy, you cannot move a file within the same subdirectory on the same disk. (What use would that be?) Therefore, you need only concern yourself with moving between subdirectories and disks. The following Quick Steps summarize this procedure:

 Moving a File to a Different Subdirectory or Disk

1. If you haven't done so already, select the disk and directory that holds the file you want to move.

119

2. Highlight the file to move in the File List window.

    Selects the file to move.

3. Pull down the File menu and select Move.

    A dialog box appears, asking you to specify the drive where you want the file moved.

4. Select the drive where you want the file sent.

5. Select the subdirectory in which you want the file stored.

    Moves the file to the designated disk and directory. □

Shell flashes a dialog box that informs you that the file is moved. If your computer is equipped with a fast hard disk drive, the dialog box will remain on the screen only momentarily.

Fast Mouse File Moving

If you have a mouse, you can quickly move one or more files by dragging them from one subdirectory to another. File moves with the mouse are best performed with the Dual File Lists. If a single list is displayed, press the Ins key to display two lists, and then take the following steps:

Q **Fast Mouse File Moving**

1. In one list, select the drive and directory that contains the file(s) you want to move.	Sets the source directory.
2. In the other list, select the drive and directory where you want the file(s) moved.	Sets the destination directory.
3. Click on the files you want to move.	Selects the file(s) to move.
4. Hold down the Control (Ctrl) key.	Indicates a Move File operation.
5. Move the mouse pointer to one of the selected files, and hold down the left mouse button.	
6. Hold down the left mouse button, and drag the message box into the destination File List window.	The Move Files message box appears, as shown in Figure 5.8, telling you that *x* number of files will be moved. As you drag the mouse, the message box moves.
7. Release the mouse button.	Confirms the Move File operation, and reminds you that the original file will be erased. □

120

> ▶ **Tip:** You can also drag the files directly into a subdirectory in the Tree window. This requires that you move the files within the same drive and that both source and destination subdirectories are visible in the Tree window.

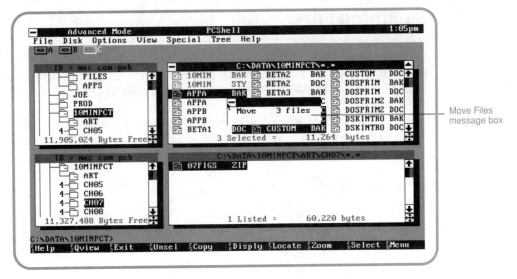

Figure 5.8   *Moving files in Dual List Display using the mouse.*

121

Name Conflicts

If you try to move a file to a disk or directory that already contains a file with the same name, Shell asks if you want to replace it or quit. Shell displays the same dialog box whether you are moving one file or many.

▶ Select **R**eplace File to replace just the indicated file.

▶ Select Replace **A**ll if you are moving many files and want to replace them all at once.

▶ Select Skip **F**ile if you are moving many files and want to skip the current one.

▶ Select **S**kip All to skip all files.

▶ Select **C**ancel to cancel the move.

Renaming Files

The Rename File command in the File menu functions the same as
the DOS REN (or RENAME) command. But, as usual with PC Tools,
the Shell command is much easier to use. Shell makes it fairly easy
to rename groups of files at one time, even if the file names are greatly
dissimilar. Use the following Quick Steps to rename a file:

 Renaming a File

1. Select the file(s) you wish to
   rename.

   Specifies the file(s) that will
   be affected.

2. Pull down the File menu and
   select Rename.

   The File Rename dialog
   box appears, as shown in
   Figure 5.9.

3. Enter the new name and/or
   extension for the file(s).

4. Select Rename to rename the
   file(s) or select Cancel to quit
   without renaming.

   If you selected Rename, PC
   Shell renames the file(s).

122

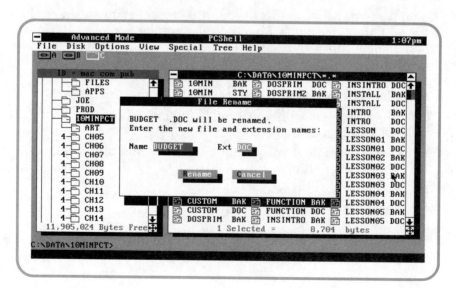

Figure 5.9   The File Rename dialog box.

If you select more than one file, Shell asks you if you want to perform a Global or Single file rename:

▶ The Global rename feature changes the names of files using wild-card characters (? and *) in place of one or more character in the file name. Selecting Global displays the dialog box in Figure 5.10. To use the Global rename feature, type the name and/or extension you want to change. For example, if you want to add the .TXT extension to all selected files, enter the * wild card in the Name field and `txt` in the Ext field.

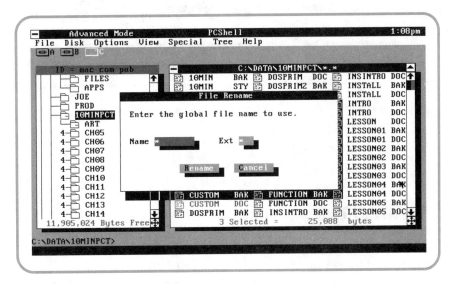

123

Figure 5.10   The dialog box shown when renaming many files all at once (the Global option).

▶ The Single rename feature changes the names of files one at a time. You are prompted for the new name for each file in turn, as illustrated in Figure 5.11.

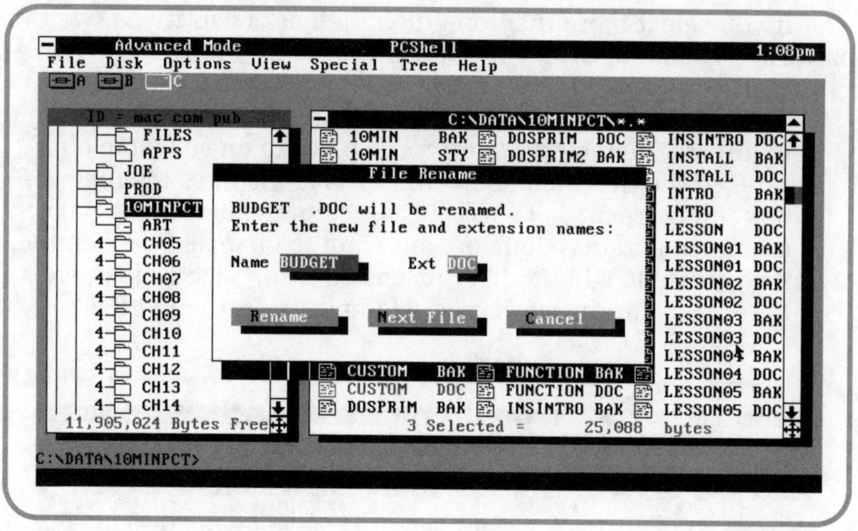

Figure 5.11   *The dialog box shown when renaming many files one at a time.*

Deleting Files

Files you no longer need should be deleted so that they don't take up precious disk space. (This is true whether your hard disk has 10M of storage space or 100M; sooner or later, you'll need that room.) The following Quick Steps explains how to erase unneeded files from disk:

Erasing a File

1. Select the file(s) you want to delete.

   Specifies the file(s) that will be erased. Make sure the selected files are the ones you want to delete.

2. Pull down the File menu and select **D**elete.

   Tells Shell to delete the selected files. A warning box appears, telling you that you're about to delete the selected file(s).

3. Select **D**elete to confirm the
operation, or select Cancel to
quit without deleting file(s).

Shell carries out the
command.

□

If you have selected more than one file, Shell presents the dialog
box shown in Figure 5.12. You can:

▶ Select **D**elete to erase the indicated file.
▶ Select **N**ext File to keep the indicated file and move to the
next one.
▶ Select Delete **A**ll to erase all files. (Be careful!)
▶ Select **C**ancel to stop.

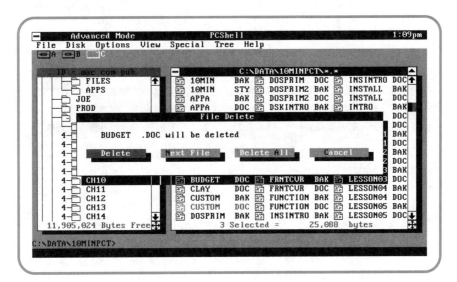

*Figure 5.12   When more than one file is selected, PC Tools
displays this dialog box so you can selectively delete files, or
erase them all at once.*

⊘ **Caution:** If you delete a group of files by mistake, don't
panic. Don't turn off your computer. And don't copy or
move files. Skip ahead to Chapter 9, "Recovering Lost Files and
Damaged Disks," to find out what to do.

Verifying Files

The Verify File command checks the integrity of a file and makes certain that the entire file can be read from the disk. Verify works on one file or many.

To verify a file:

1. Select the file(s) you want to verify.
2. Pull down the File menu and select Verify. Shell checks the file and looks for possible problems.

If Shell can't find anything wrong with the file, it displays the dialog box shown in Figure 5.13. (When verifying many files, each of the selected files that passed the test will be displayed.)

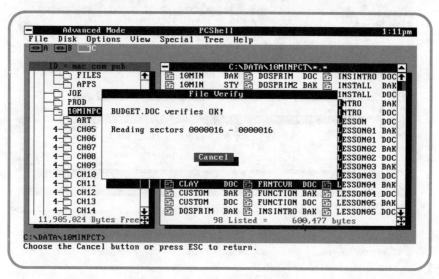

Figure 5.13   A file verified as OK.

However, if Shell detects a problem with a file, it will indicate the error and the logical sector that contains the error. You may be able to repair the file using the advanced file restoration techniques outlined in Chapter 9, "Recovering Lost Files and Damaged Disks."

Comparing Files

You may have occasion to compare two files to see if they are the same. The Compare command in the File menu does this for you quickly and painlessly.

There are many ways to use the Compare command, depending on whether you are checking files that are in the same directory or in separate directories or disks. The steps that follow describe the two most straightforward methods of using the Compare command in these two contexts.

Comparing Files in the Same Directory

Follow these steps for comparing two files in the same directory:

127

1. Change to the drive and directory that contains the files you want to compare.
2. Select one of the files you want to compare.
3. Pull down the File menu and select Compare. Shell prompts you to specify a drive.
4. Select the same drive you selected in Step 1. A dialog box appears, asking if the two files have the same or different names.
5. Select **D**ifferent. A message box appears, telling you to select a directory.
6. Select the same directory you selected in Step 1. The File Compare dialog box appears, as shown in Figure 5.14.
7. Type the name and extension of the second file you want included in the comparison.
8. Select **O**K. Shell compares the two files and determines whether the two are the same or different.

Comparing Files on Different Disks and/or Directories

The following steps explain how to compare two files contained in different directories or on different disks:

1. Pull down the View menu and select **D**ual File Lists. This splits the screen.
2. In the first list, select the first of the two files to compare.
3. In the second list, select the second of the two files to compare.
4. Pull down the File menu and select Compare. A dialog box appears asking if you want to compare files with matching or different names.
5. If the selected files have different names, select **D**ifferent. If they have the same names, select **M**atching.
6. Verify that you are using the second path (the second list) as the target by clicking the **O**K button.

For Different Names only,

7. Enter the name of the second file in the name and extension editing fields provided.
8. Select **O**K.
9. Verify that the file names for the comparison are correct, and select Co**m**pare.

Shell now checks the two files against one another and determines whether the two are the same or different.

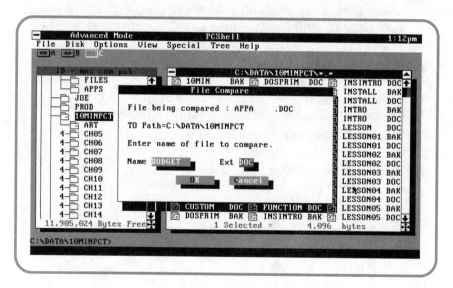

Figure 5.14   The File Compare dialog box displays the names of the two files that will be compared.

Viewing, Editing, and Printing Files

DOS users have long suffered with the TYPE command, which quickly scrolls a text document on the computer screen. TYPE provides no means to freeze the display, so you can go forward or back one line at a time. Likewise, printing and editing files require some arcane DOS commands (like COPY FILENAME.DOC PRN:) or using (horrors!) the DOS EDLIN file editor.

Relax. Shell offers its own features for viewing, editing, and printing files. While you'll most likely use these abilities to work with text documents, you can also edit any file type, including program files. (Be careful!) What's more, you can directly view dBASE (II and III) and Lotus 1-2-3 (1A and 3) documents in their proper format.

129

Viewing a File

Viewing a file lets you see its contents, but not all files are easy to decipher. There are three basic types of files you'll encounter on the PC:

▶ *ASCII text documents.* Straight text documents without control codes or other special characters. They are created by some word processors, as well as the capture files generated by telecommunications programs. README files distributed with many programs are formatted in straight ASCII. Shell displays these in the same manner as a word processor displays text in its editing screen, as illustrated in Figure 5.15.

▶ *Binary text documents.* Documents that have been stored with control codes and special formatting codes. These are created by most applications programs, including word processors, electronic spreadsheets, and data managers. With the exception of the document file listed in the next section, you see the text of the document interspersed among unintelligible codes when viewing a binary document, as shown in Figure 5.16.

▶ *Program files.* Files that consist almost entirely of binary characters and little (if any) intelligible text (refer to Figure 5.17).

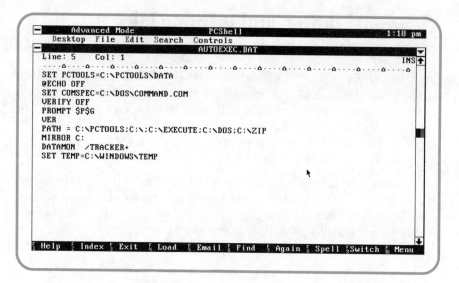

Figure 5.15   Sample ASCII text file as seen with the File View command.

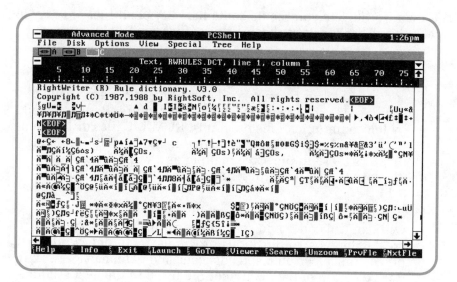

Figure 5.16   Sample binary text file as seen with the File View command.

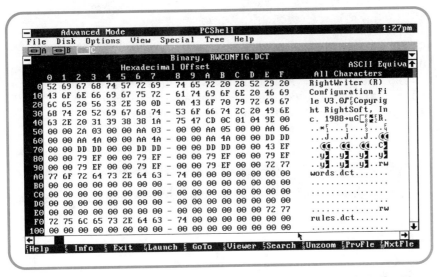

*Figure 5.17   Sample binary-only file as seen with the File View
command.*

Use the following Quick Steps when you want to view a file from Shell:

 Viewing a File

1. Highlight the file you want to   Selects the file to view.
   view.
2. Select F2 Qview.   The View window appears. □

Use the cursor keys to scan forward and backward through the
file. When you are finished, close the window. (Press Escape or F3,
or click in the window's close box with the mouse.) The View
window provides some shortcuts and options:

▶ Press the Home, End, Page Up, and Page Down keys to move
through the document quickly.

▶ If you have selected two or more files, select F10 NxtFle to view
the next file or select F9 PrvFle to view the previous file.

▶ **Tip:** You can display a special View window in a portion
of the PC Shell screen by selecting **V**iewer/File Lists from
the View menu. You can then view a file in the Viewer window
simply by selecting it in the File List window.

Special View Filters

PC Shell incorporates *filters* to display the contents of over 30 different types of document files in their original format. Shell automatically senses that you are using one of the supported document formats and selects the appropriate filter for you. An example of a viewed WordPerfect document is shown in Figure 5.18.

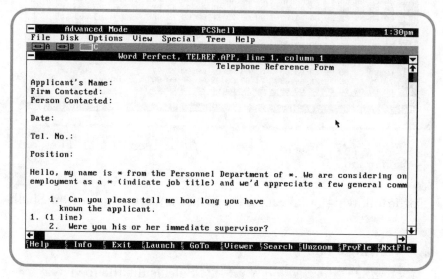

Figure 5.18   A WordPerfect document displayed in proper format using File View.

Shell comes with the following file filters (additional filters may be packaged with later releases of PC Tools; check the README.TXT file).

Viewers for Word Processing Programs	ASCII
	Text (default)
	DCA Final Form
	DCA Revisable Form
	DisplayWrite
	Microsoft Word
	Microsoft Works
	Microsoft Windows Write
	MultiMate
	WordPerfect
	WordPerfect 4.2
	WordStar (5.5)

	WordStar 2000
	XyWrite
Viewers for Database Programs	dBASE II and III
	Microsoft Works
	Paradox
	Microrim Rbase
Viewers for Spreadsheet Programs	Borland Quattro
	Borland Quattro Pro
	Lotus 1-2-3 (1A and 3)
	Lotus Symphony
	Microsoft Works
	Microsoft Excel
	Microsoft Excel Ver. 3
	Mosaic Twin
Viewers for Miscellaneous File Types	LZH
	Binary
	PAK
	SEA
	ZIP
	ZOO
	PC
	PCX

133

Shell will display the file in binary format if the file has a .COM, .EXE, .OBJ, .BIN, or .SYS file extension. If the file is in one of the formats listed above and has an extension of .TXT or .BAT, Shell will display it in text mode. You can select a different viewer format as long as the Viewer window is active:

1. Press F6 or click on `F6 Viewer` in the message bar. A list of available viewer formats appears.
2. Select the format you want to use from the list.

Editing a File

If you feel so inclined, you can edit files, even binary documents and programs, with Shell. Of course, changing the contents of program files can lead to disastrous consequences if you don't know exactly what you're doing. It is not the purpose of this book to explain program editing, hexadecimal code, and other technical topics. If you'd like to learn more about these subjects, check out the many programming books now available and refer to the *PC Tools Data Recovery* and *DOS Utilities* manual.

However, you may find the Text Editing feature useful for editing batch files, such as AUTOEXEC.BAT. Shell offers two methods of editing files: Edit File and Hex Edit File.

► The *Edit File command* runs the Desktop word processor (Notepads) and displays the contents of the selected file on the Notepads editing screen. This gives you the power of a full-featured word processor. (For more information about Notepads, refer to Chapter 12.)

► The *Hex Edit File command* displays the contents of a file in hexadecimal format. You see everything contained in the file, including nulls (hex 00) and special characters. You can use the Hex Edit command to change each byte of a file, but be careful.

The following steps describe how to edit an existing file and create a new file:

134

1. Select the file you want to edit.
2. Pull down the File menu and select Change File. The Change File submenu appears offering the two edit options.
3. Select **E**dit File to edit a text file, or select **H**ex Edit File to edit a hexadecimal file.
4. If you selected **H**ex Edit File, a dialog box appears, allowing you to create a copy of the selected file, so you can edit the copy without affecting the original. To create a copy, type a name and/or extension for the new file and select **O**K. Otherwise, select **O**K without typing a new name.
5. If you selected **E**dit File, Shell runs the Desktop Notepads program and loads the selected file into Notepads.

   If you selected **H**ex Edit, the contents of the file appear in the Edit File window. Press F7 to display the cursor so you can start editing. You can then use the cursor keys to move around.
6. To make changes, position the cursor at the point where you want to edit and begin typing. Use the Delete and Backspace keys to remove characters you don't want. If you wish to overwrite existing characters, press the Insert (Ins) key so that the INSERT indicator in the window goes out.
7. Save the document when you are done with the changes (select F5 Save or (in Desktop) pull down the File menu and select **S**ave).

The Shell File Editor (for Hex Edit) works like almost any other word processor and is fairly self-explanatory. That is, type a character to enter it at the cursor, press the Tab key to add a tab, press Enter to start a new line, and so forth. Table 5.1 lists the editing keys you can use in the file editor; these same keys work in Notepads.

Table 5.1   File Edit Editing Keys

To	Press
Delete character under cursor	Delete
Erase character to left of cursor	Backspace
Move down one line	Down Arrow
Move up one line	Up Arrow
Move left one character	Left Arrow
Move right one character	Right Arrow
Move to beginning of line	Home
Move to end of line	End
Move to start of file	Ctrl-Home
Move to end of file	Ctrl-End
Move to start of window	Home, Home
Move to end of window	End, End
Move up one window	Page Up
Move down one window	Page Down

Printing a File

The Print File command makes a paper copy of one or more selected files. Shell does not provide elaborate printing features, however; you are limited to printing to the LPT1 device only (unless you've redirected LPT1 to another port using the DOS MODE command). Document formatting is also limited. Still, the Print File command serves its duty well in making quick copies of text and binary documents. Use the following Quick Steps to print a file from Shell:

Printing a File

1. Highlight a file to print. (You may also select multiple documents if desired; the remaining steps are the same for single or multiple files.)

   Selects a file to print.

2. Pull down the File menu and select **P**rint.

   The Print submenu appears.

3. Select **P**rint File.

   The File Print dialog box appears, as shown in Figure 5.19.

4. Select a printing format.

   Formats the document as straight text, as text with special print options, or as a "sector dump" in ASCII and hex format.

5. Press the **P**rint button when you are done making your selection.

   Initiates printing.

136

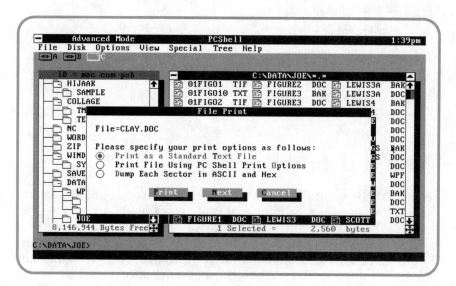

Figure 5.19   The File Print dialog box.

If you selected the "Print File Using PC Shell Print **O**ptions," an additional dialog box, illustrated in Figure 5.20, appears. Here, you may select the number of lines per page, the margins, and other formatting variables. The options are self-explanatory. Make the desired changes, and press the **P**rint button.

> ▶ **Tip:** If you are using a laser printer, such as the Hewlett-Packard LaserJet Series II, you should select Yes for the "Want to eject last page?" option. This ensures that the last page of the document is ejected from the laser printer, thus saving you the hassle of doing it manually.

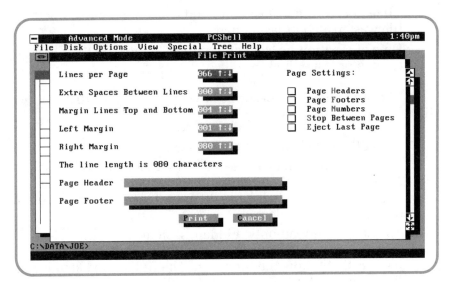

137

Figure 5.20   The File Print Options dialog box.

Changing File Attributes

Each file created on the PC carries with it certain attributes, special characteristics that the computer can use during some of its operations. These attributes are:

Read only—Indicates whether the file can be both read and written to (read only off) or just read (read only on).

Hidden—Indicates whether the file is visible (hidden off) in a normal DOS DIRectory or invisible (hidden on). Note that Shell lists hidden files.

System—Indicates whether the file is reserved for system use (system on) or regular application use (system off).

Archive—Indicates if the file has not been recently backed up using any of several types of disk backup programs, including PC Tools and DOS Backup. When archive is on, the file is new or has been edited and should be backed up in the next backup session. When archive is off, the file has already been backed up and needn't be again.

Time of creation or last edit—Indicates the time of day the file was created or last edited.

Date of creation or last edit—Indicates the date the file was created or last edited.

138

The following steps describe how to change the attributes of a file:

1. Select the file(s) you want to change.
2. Pull down the File menu, select Change File, and then select Attribute Change. Shell presents the dialog box shown in Figure 5.21 (yours will look different depending on the file or files you have selected).
3. To change the read-only, hidden, system, or archive attributes press R, H, S, or A, respectively or click on the periods that follow the file name. The first period stands for R, the second for H, third for S, and the fourth for A.
4. To change the time, position the cursor at the beginning of the Time field (keyboard or mouse) and enter a new time from the keyboard.
5. To change the date, position the cursor at the beginning of the Date field (keyboard or mouse) and enter a new date from the keyboard.
6. When you are done changing the attributes, select the **Up**-date button or select **C**ancel to cancel all changes.

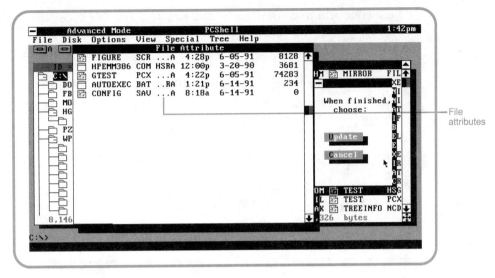

Figure 5.21   File attributes for selected files (only those files currently selected are shown).

Getting File Information

Shell provides some interesting tidbits about files in its File Information dialog box.

To look at information about a file:

1. Select a file.
2. Choose the Show Information command from the Options menu. A dialog box like the one in Figure 5.22 appears.

Here's what the information in the More File Information box means:

File name—The name of the file.

Extension—File extension, if any.

File Path—Location of file in directory tree.

File Attributes are—Indicates if file is read only, hidden, system, and/or archive.

Last time file accessed—Time of day and date of creation or last edit. (Note: The word *accessed* is misapplied here, as you can access, but not change, a file, and it won't be up-dated.)

The file length is—Actual size of file, in bytes.

Total clusters occupied—The number of disk clusters consumed by the file. A *cluster* is a unit of space on a disk. (See Chapter 9 for more details on clusters.)

Starting cluster number—The physical disk cluster containing the first bytes of the file.

Total files indirectory—Total number of files contained in the subdirectory holding the selected file.

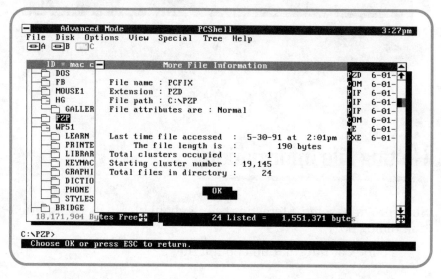

Figure 5.22   Interesting tidbits about the file in the More File Information dialog box.

Locating Files

How many times have you created a file, safely recorded it on your hard disk, then promptly forgotten the exact name of the file or which subdirectory you saved it in? If you're like most PC users, this has happened plenty of times. Shell offers a nifty way to search for files by file name, extension, and contents and to view the location and names of all the files that match your search specifications. Once a file has been located, you can open it, delete it, copy it, and more.

To find a file, change to the drive that contains the file you want to search for (if you're not sure which drive contains the file, you'll have to search each of them). Pull down the File menu and select Locate. The FileFind screen appears, as shown in Figure 5.23. Use the following options on this screen to enter the specifications for the search:

▶ Drives displays a screen that lets you specify the directories you want to search. If you started FileFind by selecting Locate from the File menu, you cannot use this screen to change drives.
If you ran FileFind by entering `FF` at the DOS prompt or by running it from the F10 Program menu, you can use this screen to change drives or select multiple drives.

▶ Filters lets you narrow the search by searching for files according to their size, the date they were created or changed, or the file's attributes. For example, if you know that the file you're looking for was edited last week, you can enter a range of dates that corresponds to that week.

▶ File Specification is a text box that lets you specify the name of the file you're looking for. If you don't know the exact name of the file, you can use the wild-card characters * and ?:

.—searches through all files in the disk.

.—searches through all files just in the root directory.

\wp51*.exe—searches only through files with extension .EXE in WP51 directory.

. -.bat—searches only through files in current directory with any extension except .BAT.

▶ Containing lets you search the *contents* of files for a specific character string (a word, phrase, or any combination of characters). Ignore Case, tells FileFind to disregard the capitalization in the entry. Whole Word tells FileFind to find the exact text you enter. For example, if you type `bird`, FileFind will not find `birdseed`.

▶ Groups lets you save the search specifications for files you frequently search for. To create a search group, select Edit from the Groups dialog box, and then select New. The next time you want to search for the same group of files, you can select the group from the group list.

141

▶ **V**iew is used after the files are located. To view a file, high-light its name in the matching files window (at the bottom of the screen) and press Alt-V or click on the **V**iew button.

▶ Go To is used after you select a file from the matching files screen. It lets you exit the FileFind window and return to the directory where the selected file is stored.

When you're done typing your entries and making your selections on the FileFind screen, press the Start button to start the search. PC Shell searches the specified drive and directory and displays the names of the files that match your search instructions. When the search is complete, a dialog box appears, asking if you want to return to the Shell. Select **OK**. This returns you to the Shell with the Located Files window displayed, as in Figure 5.24.

To effectively use FileFind, you don't have to take advantage of all the options. You can usually find what you're looking for by typing an entry in the Specification box. The following Quick Steps lead you through the process:

142

Q Locating Files by Name

1. Change to the drive that contains the file you want to find.

2. Pull down the File menu, and select Locate.

   The FileFind screen appears.

3. Type the name of the file you're looking for.

   You can use the wild-card characters * and ?. For example, to find all files with the .DOC extension, type `*.doc`. Use * in place of a group of characters or ? in place of single characters.

4. Select Start.

   PC Shell searches all directories on the specified drive and displays the names of the files that match your search instructions. When the search is complete, a dialog box appears, asking if you want to return to Shell.

5. Select **OK**.

This returns you to Shell with the Located Files window displayed. ☐

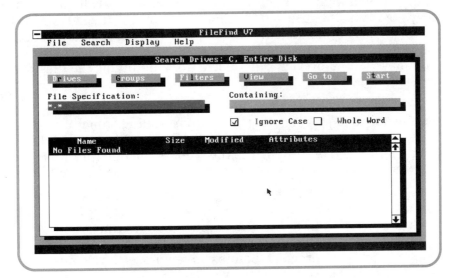

Figure 5.23   FileFind lets you specify the types of files you want to find and the drives and directories you want to search.

143

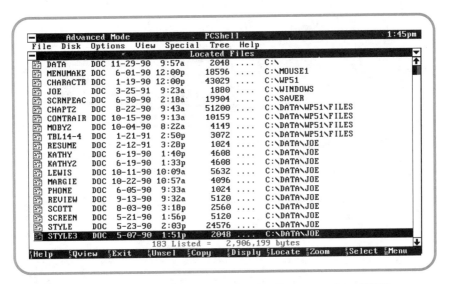

Figure 5.24   Found files that contain the extension .DOC indicated in the Located Files window.

Securing Sensitive Files with PC Secure

Although you want complete control over your files at all times, you may not want other users to have the same control. If you have files that contain confidential information, for example, you may want to prevent others from reading that information. If you're on a network, you may want to prevent other users from modifying the files you create.

PC Tools includes a program called PC Secure that locks files or directories to prevent other users from reading or modifying the files. The program scrambles the contents of the file in a seemingly random manner, *encrypting* the file. Unless the other user has the key (the password), he or she cannot gain access to the file (*decrypt* it).

You can run PC Secure from the DOS prompt, by entering pcsecure at the prompt, or from within Shell by selecting **Se**cure and then **E**ncrypt File from the File menu. The first time you run PC Secure, a message box appears telling you that this is the first time you're running the program. Before you can proceed, you must enter a master key password. This password will unlock any file with any password you use in the future; if you forget a password, you can use the master key password to unlock the file. Select **OK** to continue. A dialog box appears, as in Figure 5.25, prompting you to type a master key password.

144

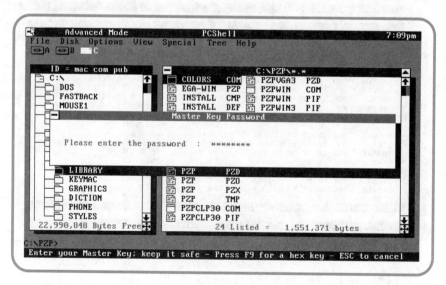

Figure 5.25   Before you can use PC Secure, you must create a master key password.

You have two choices here. You can create an alphanumeric key or a hexadecimal key:

Alphanumeric Key. This consists of any string of letters, numbers, or punctuation marks between 5 and 32 characters long. PC Secure treats uppercase and lowercase characters differently (*f* is not the same as *F*). Type the password; the characters you type appear as asterisks on-screen. Press Enter and you're asked to type the password again. Retype the password and press Enter. The key is created.

Hexadecimal Key. This consists of a combination of letters (a-f or A-F, case doesn't matter) and numbers (0-9); the password must be 16 characters long. To create a hexadecimal key, press F9 and then type the password; the characters you type appear on-screen. Press Enter and the key is created; you don't have to confirm it.

(Note: It's a good idea to write this password down and store it in a safe location.)

145

What happens next depends on whether you're running PC Secure from Shell or from the DOS prompt. If you're running the program from Shell, PC Secure assumes that you want to encrypt the highlighted (selected) file, and it prompts you to enter a password; press Esc to abort the operation. If you're running the program from the DOS prompt, you'll be greeted with the PC Secure opening screen, shown in Figure 5.26.

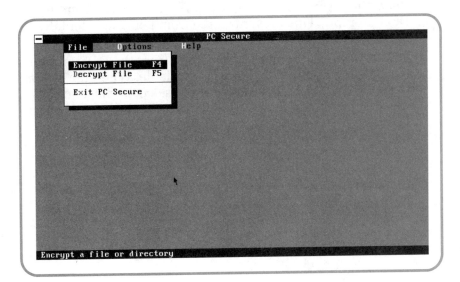

Figure 5.26   The PC Secure opening screen.

Before encrypting files, take a look at the PC Secure settings to make sure the encryption method is set as desired. If the PC Secure opening screen is displayed, pull down the Options menu. If you're in Shell, pull down the File menu, select **S**ecure, and then select **S**ettings. Although the screen will look different, depending on how you're running PC Secure, you'll see the following settings, which you can change:

Full DES Encryption (Full Encryption). DES stands for Data Encryption Standard. The Full Encryption option provides greater file security than quick encryption.

Quick Encryption. This option offers less security than full encryption, but it runs two to eight times faster.

No Encryption. Choose this option when you want to use other PC Secure features without encrypting a file. This is available only if you run PC Secure from Shell.

Compression. Condenses the encrypted file so it uses less disk space.

One Key. This option allows you to use the same password for an entire session. For the first file you encrypt, PC Secure will prompt you to enter a password. For subsequent files, PC Secure will use the same password.

Hidden. (Available only if you run PC Secure from the DOS prompt.) Choose this option if you want the file not to appear in a DOS directory listing. You will still be able to see the file's name in PC Shell.

Read Only. (Available only if you run PC Secure from the DOS prompt.) This prevents a file from being accidentally deleted or modified.

Delete Options. If you run PC Secure from the DOS prompt, the Delete Original File option is available. When the option is on, PC Secure makes a copy of the selected file, encrypts the copy, and then deletes the original file. When this option is off, PC Secure makes a copy of the selected file, encrypts the copy, and adds the extension .SEC to the encrypted copy. The original file remains intact. If you run PC Secure from Shell, you're given three delete options: No Delete, Quick Delete (which deletes the file just as you would delete it from Shell), and DOD Delete (which wipes out the file on disk according to Department of Defense security standards).

146

Expert Mode. This option disables the master key password. If you forget the password you used to lock a file, you won't be able to use your master key to open the file.

Save Configuration. (Available only if you run PC Secure from the DOS prompt.) Choose this option to save the settings you just entered for future encryptions.

Once you've entered the settings you want to use, you can run PC Secure from the Shell or from the DOS prompt to encrypt files.

Running PC Secure from the Shell

You run PC Secure from the Shell the same way you enter any file-management commands from the File menu. First you select the files you want to encrypt; then you select the command that you want to execute. The following steps explain:

1. In the File List window, select the file or files you want to encrypt.
2. Pull down the File menu and select Secure. The Secure submenu appears.
3. Select **E**ncrypt File. A dialog box appears, prompting you to enter a password.
4. *To use an alphanumeric password,* type the password, press Enter, type the password again, and type enter. Don't use the same password you used for your master key.

   To use a hexadecimal password, press F9, type the password and press Enter. Don't use the same password you used for your master key.

PC Secure starts encrypting the file, and displays the progress box shown in Figure 5.27. Wait until the encryption is complete.

To decrypt files, select the files you want to decrypt, pull down the File menu, select Secure, and then select **D**ecrypt File. You'll be prompted to enter a password. Type the password and press Enter. As long as the password is correct, PC Secure starts decrypting the file. You'll be told when decryption is complete.

147

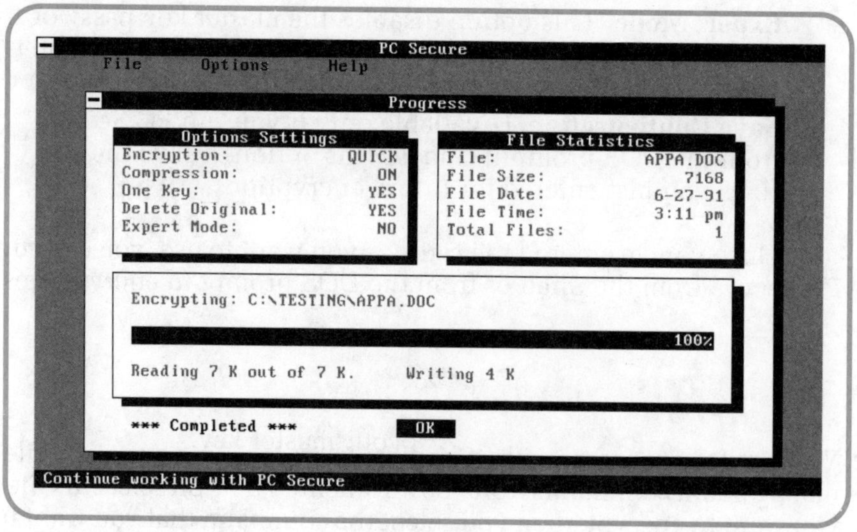

Figure 5.27   As PC Secure encrypts a file, it displays the progress.

Running PC Secure from the DOS Prompt

PC Secure runs a little differently when you run it from the DOS prompt, because you must select the files you want to encrypt from within PC Secure. You won't have the convenient file-selection options you have available in Shell:

1. Change to the drive and directory that contains PC Tools. If you installed PC Tools to run from any directory, this step is not necessary.

2. Type pcsecure and press Enter. You can add either of the following parameters to the PCSECURE command:

    /G—destroys the original (nonencrypted) file according to government (Department of Defense) standards for file security.

    /M—allows you to encrypt a file several times to require two or more people with different passwords to decrypt a file. The passwords will have to be entered in the proper order.

This starts PC Secure, and you'll see the screen displayed in Figure 5.26.

3. Pull down the File menu and select **E**ncrypt File. The File Selection dialog box appears as in Figure 5.28.

4. In the Drives list, select the letter of the disk that contains the files you want to encrypt.

5. In the Directories list, select the directory that contains the files you want to encrypt. To move up the directory tree, select the [. .] entry.

6. In the Files list, select the files you want to encrypt.

7. Select **E**ncrypt. A dialog box appears prompting you to enter a password.

8. *To use an alphanumeric password*, type the password, press Enter, type the password again, and type enter. Don't use the same password you used for your master key.

   To use a hexadecimal password, press F9, type the password and press Enter. Don't use the same password you used for your master key.

   PC Secure starts encrypting the files, and shows the progress of the operation as you saw in Figure 5.27.

149

To decrypt files, perform the same steps, except in Step 3 select **D**ecrypt File instead of **E**ncrypt File. When you enter the password, you won't be prompted to confirm it; PC Secure will initiate the decryption process.

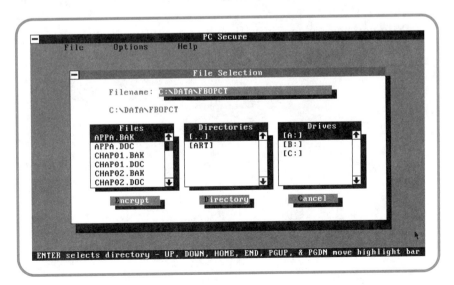

Figure 5.28   When you run PC Secure from the DOS prompt, you must select the files you want to encrypt from the File Selection dialog box.

What You Have Learned

This chapter discussed using Shell to manipulate and maintain the files on your hard disks and floppy diskettes. You also learned:

▶ The default setting of List Files window displays just the file name, but you can add auxiliary information, including file size and attributes.

▶ You can copy one or more files from disk-to-disk or directory-to-directory using the Copy command on the File menu.

▶ Shell warns you if you attempt to copy or move one or more files into a disk or directory that already contains files with the same name.

▶ Shell always double-checks if you want to delete a file by presenting a warning dialog box before completing the command.

▶ The Verify command checks the integrity of a selected file to make sure your computer can read the file.

▶ Shell lets you change file attributes, including read-only, hidden, system, and archive settings.

▶ You can locate any file on a disk with the Locate command (from the File menu).

▶ You can run FileFind from the DOS prompt by typing `ff` and pressing Enter.

▶ You can secure sensitive files by encrypting them.

Managing Disks with Shell

In This Chapter

▶ *Displaying the contents of disks*
▶ *Copying floppy disks*
▶ *Verifying and comparing disks*
▶ *Formatting data and program disks*
▶ *Maintaining directories*

Program and document disks are no longer obscure entities with lives of their own. PC Shell helps you tame your disks and puts you in control. Rather than use arcane DOS commands, you'll use Shell's pull-down menus to format and copy disks, verify the contents of disks, maintain subdirectories in your hard disk, and more.

Disk Display

Shell can display the contents of either one or two disks at a time. With the Single File List display, you can view the contents of just one disk. With Dual File Lists, you can view the contents of two disks at the same time. You change displays with the appropriate commands in the View menu, as the following Quick Steps explain:

To View the Contents of One Disk

1. Press Alt-V or click on View in the pull-down menu bar.

   The View menu appears.

2. Select **S**ingle File List.

   Two windows appear: the Directory Tree window on the left and the File List window on the right.

3. To change disk drives, hold down the Ctrl key and press the letter of the drive you want to use or click on the drive icon as shown in Figure 6.1.

   The directory tree for the selected drive appears in the Directory Tree window. A list of files in the current directory appears in the File List window.   □

152

> ⊘ **Caution**: Before changing to a floppy disk drive (A or B), make sure you have a formatted disk in the drive.

Selected drive —

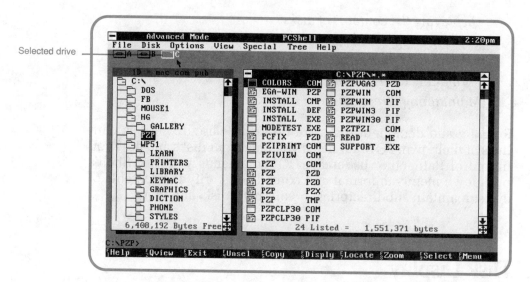

Figure 6.1   The icon for the currently selected drive appears highlighted.

To View the Contents of Two Disks

1. Press Alt-V or click on View in the pull-down menu bar.

   The View menu appears.

2. Select **D**ual File Lists

   Two sets of windows appear, each set containing a Directory Tree window and a File List window. Both sets display the contents of the same disk. You can move from window to window by pressing Tab or Shift-Tab or by clicking inside the window with your mouse.

3. To display the contents of a different disk in one set of windows, switch to either window in the set.

4. Hold down the Ctrl key and press the letter of the drive you want to use or click on the drive icon as shown in Figure 6.1.

   The directory tree for the current drive appears in the Directory Tree window, as shown in Figure 6.2. A list of files in the current directory appears in the File List window.   □

153

Active window ─

```
─  Advanced Mode              PCShell                      2:22pm
 File  Disk  Options  View  Special  Tree  Help
 ⟷A  ⟷B  ▭C
─   ID = None        ▲        A:\*.*                           ↑
 🗁 A:\                ↑   No entries found
                      ↕
           362,496 Bytes Free↕      0 Listed =       0 bytes ↕

    ID = mac com pub        C:\PZP\*.*
 🗀 DOS              ↑   ▭ COLORS    COM 🗎 PCFIX    PZD 🗎 PZP      PZX↑
 🗀 FB                   🗎 EGA-WIN   PZP ▭ PZIPRINT COM 🗎 PZP      TMP
 🗀 MOUSE1               🗎 INSTALL   CMP 🗎 PZIVIEW  COM 🗎 PZPCLP30 COM
 🗀 HG                   🗎 INSTALL   DEF ▭ PZP      COM 🗎 PZPCLP30 PIF
   🗀 GALLERY            ▭ INSTALL   EXE 🗎 PZP      PZD 🗎 PZPVGA3  PZD
   🗀 PZP                ▭ MODETEST  EXE 🗎 PZP      PZO ▭ PZPWIN   COM↕
        6,408,192 Bytes Free↕       24 Listed =   1,551,371 bytes
 A:\>
 §Help  §Qview  §Exit   §Unsel  §Copy   §Disply §Locate §Zoom   §Select §Menu
```

Figure 6.2 Dual File Lists display with top list currently selected.

> **Tip:** A quick way of displaying Dual File Lists is to press the Ins key. To return to the Single File List display, press Del. To display two file lists and select a different drive for the second list with a single step, hold down the Ctrl key, hold down the Alt key, and press the letter of the drive you want to activate.

Refreshing the Tree

Recall that the directory tree is the directory path on a given disk (usually a hard disk). The tree starts at the root directory, displayed as the first item in Shell's Tree window, and branches out into many subdirectories.

It takes a few moments for Shell to register the organization of the tree and present it in the Tree window, so the program doesn't do it all the time. Normally, Shell rereads the tree every day, unless you've set a new option for the /TRn parameter, as described in Chapter 4, "Understanding PC Shell."

This can become a problem when you've added or deleted subdirectories, because Shell won't immediately recognize the change. If you suspect that you are viewing an old rendition of the directory tree, pull down the View menu and select **R**efresh. This command forces Shell to examine the tree structure and update the Tree window.

Similarly, the effect of copying and moving files between directories and disks may not be immediately updated in the File List window. For example, you may copy a set of files to a new disk, but the File List window won't immediately show the added files. You can counter this problem in one of two ways: Choose the Refresh command, or select another directory (or disk) and then reselect the old one. The files should now be updated.

Copying Disks

Even if your computer is equipped with a hard disk drive, you'll still need to make copies of floppy disks occasionally. For example, you

154

may need to make a clone of a data disk for distribution to the branch offices in your company, or you may need to make backup copies of a new program you purchased, to protect the originals from damage.

Shell offers a convenient and nearly foolproof method of copying disks (especially compared to the DOS DISKCOPY command). You can use Shell to copy disks using one drive or two. When using two drives, both must be the same size and type. You can't copy from a 5-1/4" drive to a 3-1/2" drive or from a low-density to a high-density drive, for example.

The instructions that follow assume you are using Shell from a hard disk drive. Before you begin, make sure you have a blank disk of the same size and capacity of the original disk you want to copy. The blank disk does not need to be formatted. Also, write-protect the original disk to prevent it from getting damaged during the copying process. To write-protect a 5-1/4" disk, put a write-protect sticker over the square notch on the side of the disk. For a 3-1/2" disk, slide the write-protect tab so you can see through the "window." The following Quick Steps give the procedure for copying a floppy disk using one drive:

155

 Copying with One Disk Drive

1. Insert the disk you want to copy in the drive (A or B), and close the drive door, if it has one.

2. Pull down the Disk menu and select **Copy**.

   The Disk Copy dialog box shown in Figure 6.3 appears.

3. Choose the drive you want to use for copying the disk and then select **OK**.

   An identical dialog box appears, asking you to select the target drive.

4. Select the same drive you selected in Step 3 and select **OK**.

   Tells Shell to use the same drive for the source and target

   Shell does not assume you've placed the original disk in the drive already and asks you to do it now.

5. Press the **OK** button to go on.

   Shell starts reading the disk and storing it in your computer's memory. As it reads, Shell displays the progress.

6. Remove the source disk from the drive and insert the target (blank) disk. Press the **OK** button to continue.

After reading the source disk, Shell prompts you to insert the target disk.

Shell copies the data from your computer's memory to the target disk.

□

Depending on the available memory in your computer, the capacity of the disks, and how you loaded Shell, the program may not be able to read the entire contents of the disk in one pass. If necessary, swap the source and target disks in and out of the drive as requested by Shell.

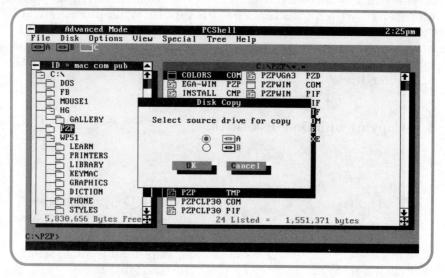

Figure 6.3   Choose the source and then the target drive in the Disk Copy dialog box.

▶ **Tip:** You don't need to format a disk before using it to store a copy of another disk. Shell will automatically sense whether the disk is properly formatted and will format it during the copying process. However, if you are using disks of questionable quality, you may want to preformat them using Shell before copying files to them. Shell will report any errors during disk formatting.

During copying, Shell provides a progress indicator, as illustrated in Figure 6.4. During the copy operation, Shell indicates the current status of each sector of the disk.

▶ F means formatting track.

▶ R means reading track.

▶ W means writing track.

▶ E means an error reading or writing the track.

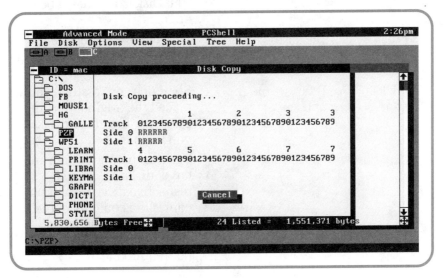

157

Figure 6.4   During copying, Shell provides a progress status report.

▶ **Tip:** When using Shell in memory-resident mode, you may want to provide a little more memory to the program so that single-drive copies go faster and with fewer disk swaps. When loading Shell into the computer, use the /RL (resident, large) parameter, as described more fully in Chapter 4. Using this parameter won't consume more memory when Shell is inactive, but it will minimize disk swapping.

Copying with Two Disk Drives

1. Place the source disk (the one you want to copy) in one drive.

2. Place the target disk (the one you want to copy to) in the other.

   We'll assume the source is placed in drive A, and the target in drive B.

3. Pull down the Disk menu and select **C**opy.

   The Disk Copy dialog box appears.

4. Choose drive A for the original (source) disk and select **OK**.

   An identical dialog box appears, asking you to select the target drive.

5. Select drive B for the blank (target) disk and select **OK**.

   Shell does not assume you've placed the original disk in the drive already and asks you to do it now.

6. Press the **OK** button.

   Verifies that the source and target disks are in their respective drives. Shell now copies the contents of the source disk to the target disk. Disk swapping is not required. □

Verifying and Comparing Disks

Although Shell does a good job ensuring that the copies it makes of disks are error-free, you may want to verify the integrity of your copied disks with the Verify and Compare commands. You don't need to limit these commands to when you've copied disks. You can (and should) routinely verify your data disks to be sure the information stored on them is still reliable. Likewise, you may need to compare two disks against each other occasionally to determine if they are exact duplicates.

Verifying a Disk

The Verify command in the Disk menu scans the entire contents of the disk—including files, subdirectories, and unused space—to make sure the data is readable.

To verify a disk:

1. Insert the disk you want to verify in the desired drive.
2. Activate the drive (hold down the Ctrl key and press the letter of the drive or click on the icon for the drive you want to verify).
3. Pull down the Disk menu and select **Verify**.
4. After Shell pauses to inform you that the disk is about to be verified, press **O**K to continue or **C**ancel to quit.

If Shell finds an error in a sector not previously marked as "bad," it displays the sector number containing the error, as shown in Figure 6.5. Shell will also indicate if the error is within the data portion of the disk or occurs within the DOS system area (which represents a greater danger, as the entire contents of the disk may be threatened).

159

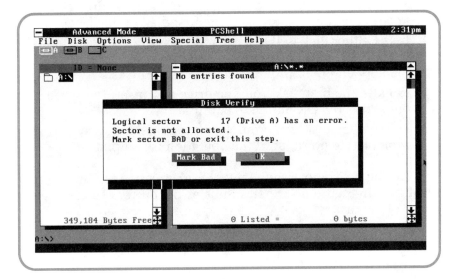

Figure 6.5   Shell has found sector 17 contains an error, as shown in the Disk Verify dialog box.

In the lucky instance when the error occurs in a formatted but unoccupied (unused) portion of the disk, Shell marks the spot as "bad" so data will never be written there. If the error occurs in a used portion of the disk, Shell asks if you want to mark the sector as bad so that data can be rerouted around the problem.

Comparing Two Disks

The Compare Disk command in the Disk menu checks two disks against one another. You can compare disks using one disk drive or two. When using two drives, both must be the same size and type. For example, you can compare two 5-1/4" 360K disks, but not a 5-1/4" disk against a 3-1/2" disk.

To compare disks with one disk drive:

1. Pull down the Disk menu and select Compare. A dialog box appears, as in Figure 6.6, prompting you to select the drive you want to use for the source.
2. Select A or B to specify the source drive and select OK. An identical dialog box appears asking you to specify the target drive.
3. Select the same drive you selected in Step 2. A dialog box appears, telling you to insert the first disk in the drive.
4. Insert either disk in the drive and press the OK button. Shell reads as much of the disk as it can into your computer's memory and then prompts you to switch disks.
5. Remove the first disk from the drive and insert the second one. Press the OK button to continue.
6. Follow the on-screen prompts, swapping disks when prompted to do so, until the operation is complete.

During the comparison, Shell provides a progress indicator, as illustrated in Figure 6.7. Shell indicates the current status of each sector of the disk.

▶ R means reading track.
▶ C means comparing track.

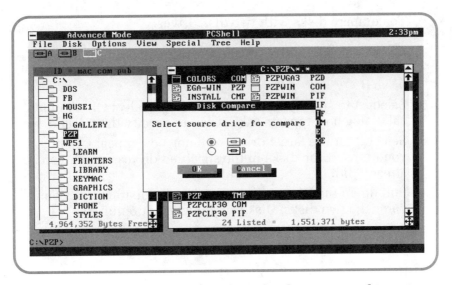

Figure 6.6   Choose the same drive for the source and target drives.

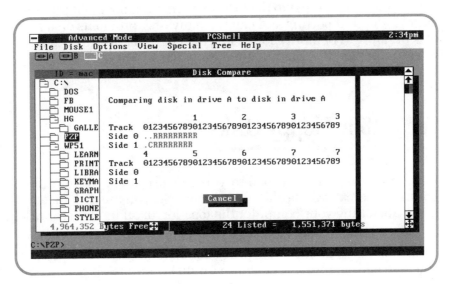

Figure 6.7   During Compare, Shell provides a progress status report.

To compare disks with two disk drives:

1. Place one disk in drive A and the other disk in drive B. We'll assume the source is placed in drive A, and the target in drive B.

2. Select A to specify the source drive and select **O**K. An identical dialog box appears asking you to specify the target drive.

3. Select B for the target drive. A dialog box appears, telling you to insert the disks in the specified drives, which you already did.

4. Pull down the Disk menu and select **C**ompare. Shell compares the two disks. Disk swapping is not required.

Performing a Surface Scan

162

Another method of verifying a disk is to perform a surface scan using the PC Tools DiskFix program. DiskFix analyzes the surface of the disk in a similar manner to the Verify Disk command, but it provides more in-depth reporting and can fix many disk problems on a hard disk or floppy. For more about using the PC Tools DiskFix program, refer to Chapter 10, "Maintaining Your Disks."

Formatting Floppy Disks

Disks must be formatted before you can use them to hold data. Formatting creates a file allocation table (FAT) on the disk that acts as a map, telling your computer the location of all its storage areas.

Formatting a disk using the DOS FORMAT command can be dangerous. If you enter the wrong command at the wrong prompt, you may end up formatting your hard disk, completely wiping out the data it contains. PC Tools offers a safer way that forces you to select the disk you want to format and warns you if the disk you're about to format contains data. It also allows you to format in such a way that if you format a disk by mistake, you may be able to unformat the disk and recover the lost files.

> ▶ **Tip**: If you chose, during the installation process, to have your DOS FORMAT program replaced with PCFORMAT, the DOS FORMAT file has been renamed FORMAT!.COM so that it won't be used when you type FORMAT at the DOS prompt. You can still use the old DOS FORMAT program by entering FORMAT! at the DOS prompt. The Installation program adds a batch file named FORMAT.BAT that starts the PC Format program. When you enter FORMAT at the DOS prompt, the PC Format program starts, and you'll see the screen shown in Figure 6.8.

Formatting a Floppy Disk with PC Format

You can access PC Format from within the PC Tools Shell program or directly from the DOS prompt. Here, we assume you're formatting a floppy disk. For information on formatting a hard disk (a more advanced topic), refer to Chapter 10.

163

PC Format automatically senses the type of floppy disk drives contained in your computer and—depending on the drive type—allows you to select from among several possible media formats. Table 6.1 lists the drive types and formats supported by Shell.

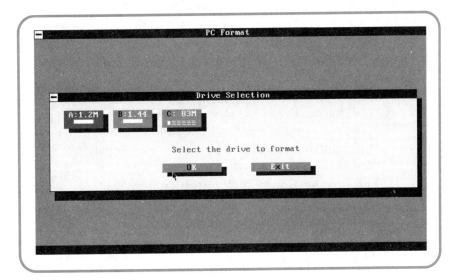

Figure 6.8   The PC Format opening screen.

Table 6.1 Drive Types and Formats Supported by Shell

Disk Size	Type	Storage Capacity
5-1/4"	Single-sided	160K
5-1/4"	Single-sided	180K
5-1/4"	Double-sided	320K
5-1/4"	Double-sided Double-density	360K
5-1/4"	Double-sided High-density	1.2M
3-1/2"	Double-sided Double-density	720K
3-1/2"	Double-sided High-density	1.4M

To determine the type of disks you have, look at the manufacturer's label on the disks or on the box that the disks came in. The two most common types of disks are DSDD and DSHD. *DSDD* stands for double-sided double-density, and is the same as low-density (LD). *DSHD* stands for double-sided high-density, which stores about twice as much information.

To run PC Format from Shell:

1. Insert the blank disk you want to format into the external drive you want to use: A or B.
2. Pull down the Disk menu and select **F**ormat Data Disk. The Format Disk screen appears, as you saw in Figure 6.8.
3. Select A or B, and then select **OK**. A dialog box appears, as in Figure 6.9, prompting you to enter format instructions.
4. Select the type of format you want to perform:

   Safe format. This is the default option. It's also the safest option. If you perform a safe format on a disk that contains data, you usually get the data back, as long as you don't store any other files on the disk.

   Quick format. To quickly format a previously formatted disk so it can be unformatted.

   Full format (floppy disk only). To format more thoroughly but allow the disk to be unformatted.

   Destructive format (floppy disk only). To format and erase all data on a disk for security purposes. Choose this option only if you want to make sure that no one (including you) can recover the information from the disk.

5. To make the disk bootable, select Install System Files (see next section, "Making a Bootable Disk").

6. If you ran the Mirror program on the disk previously, you can select Save Mirror Info to save that information, giving you a better chance of recovering files.

7. Specify the storage capacity of the disk you want to format. Table 6.1 shows available storage capacities.

8. To label the disk, select Label and type a label (up to 11 characters). A label indicates what's on the disk. If you access the disk in PC Shell, the label appears at the top of the Directory Tree window.

9. Select OK to start the process. The Validating Drive message box appears for a moment. Then,

   If the disk you're trying to format has files on it, PC Shell displays a warning box like the one in Figure 6.10. Select OK to go ahead with the format or Cancel to quit.

   If the disk does not have files on it, you'll see the Formatting dialog box (see Figure 6.11).

10. Wait until the formatting is complete, and then select OK.

165

> ▶ **Tip:** At any time during the format process you can stop Shell by pressing the Escape key.

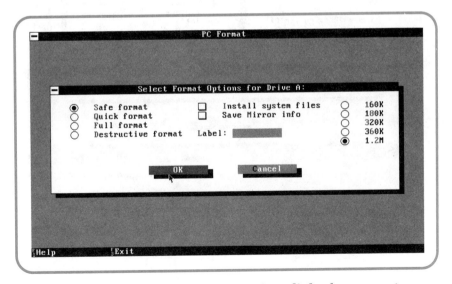

Figure 6.9   The Select Format Options dialog box prompts you to enter formatting instructions.

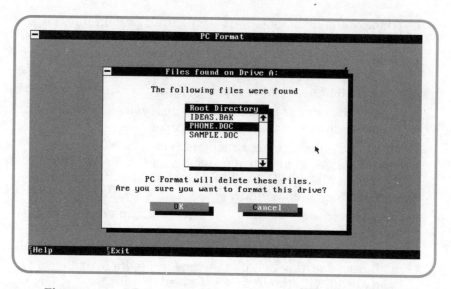

Figure 6.10 *PC Format warns you before formatting a disk that contains data.*

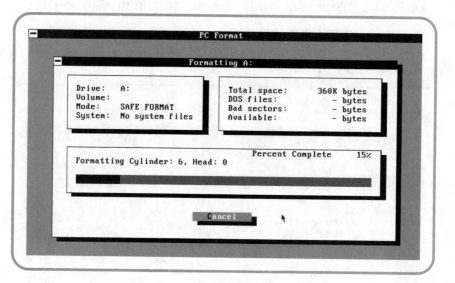

Figure 6.11 *The Formatting dialog box keeps you abreast of the progress.*

> ▶ **Tip:** You don't have to format disks from within Shell; you can run PC Format from the DOS prompt. To start the program, change to the drive and directory that contains the PC Tools program files, usually C:\PCTOOLS. (If you installed PC Tools to run from any directory prompt, you don't have to change directories.) Type `pcformat` and press Enter. You can then proceed from Step 3 in the format process just described.

Shell provides a status report during formatting. Sectors formatted correctly are shown as a dot; uncorrectable errors are shown as an E. Shell will attempt to format and verify troublesome sectors several times before it assigns an error. Unlike the DOS FORMAT command, PC Format continues with the formatting process even when errors occur.

After formatting is complete, Shell provides you with some important information about your disk, including total bytes of disk space and bytes in bad sectors. If you want to format another disk, remove the one that's in the drive, replace it with a fresh one, and repeat the format process. Otherwise press the **C**ancel button to quit.

167

> ▶ **Tip:** Did Shell report an error during disk formatting? Although Shell may uncover a bad sector or two on a disk, it's not totally unusable. The bad sectors are "locked out" from use, so your computer won't try to store information on them. The disk won't have as much free space on it, but at least you won't have to throw the whole thing away. However, you should avoid using a disk with sector errors to hold hard disk backup data or to store a backup copy of another disk.

Making a Bootable Disk

A *bootable disk* starts your computer. During disk formatting, you have the option of installing system files; selecting this option copies the required boot files to the disk. You can then use the disk to boot your computer. Because you have a hard disk, you probably won't need to make many bootable disks. The boot files take up valuable disk space that you'll probably want to use to store other information.

It is a good idea to have at least one bootable floppy disk on hand in case something happens to your hard disk that prevents it from booting your computer. But if you made the Recovery disk during the PC Tools installation process, you already have a bootable floppy disk.

Renaming a Disk

Your computer considers disks as "volumes" and allows you to name the volumes for record-keeping purposes. Both Shell and DOS permit you to provide the name when you format the disk; Shell goes one step further and lets you easily add or change the name at any time.

The following steps describe how to rename a disk:

1. Place the disk you want to rename in a disk drive.
2. Select the drive you want to rename.
3. Pull down the Disk menu and select **R**ename Volume.
4. Shell provides you with a dialog box for entering a new name, as shown in Figure 6.12. The old name, if any, is displayed above the new volume label entry box. Type in a new name (up to 11 characters).
5. Press the **R**ename button when you're done.

> ▶ **Tip:** Get into the habit of naming your disks, but exercise care to use different and descriptive names. For example, if one of your data disks is used to store backups of your Lotus 1-2-3 worksheets, call it something like LOTUS1, with the anticipation that you'll be creating other Lotus worksheet disks in the future—LOTUS2, and so on.

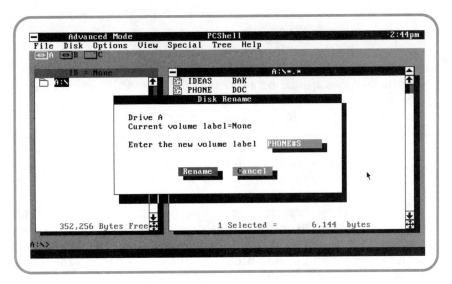

Figure 6.12   The Disk Rename dialog box.

Directory Maintenance

While subdirectories allow you to store files in centralized locations on a hard disk, they can be difficult to manage. For example, take the seemingly simple task of renaming a subdirectory. Unfortunately, DOS doesn't currently allow it, so if you want to rename a subdirectory, you have to create a new one. Once that's accomplished, you have to move the files from the old directory to the new one.

Shell offers a series of directory maintenance tools to help smooth your trials with DOS subdirectories. You can:

▶ Add a new subdirectory.

▶ Rename a subdirectory.

▶ Delete a subdirectory.

▶ Prune and graft (move) subdirectories.

▶ Modify certain attributes of a subdirectory.

> ⊘ **Caution:** With the exception of adding a new subdirectory, you should avoid using the directory maintenance commands when using Shell in memory-resident mode while another DOS application is loaded into memory. Otherwise, the application may not be able to track the changes you make, leading to possible loss of data.

All of the directory maintenance commands are located in a separate Directory Maintenance program, which you can run from Shell or from the DOS prompt. Either way you run the program, you'll see the Directory Maintenance screen shown in Figure 6.13. To access this screen from Shell, pull down the Disk menu and select Directory **M**aintenance. To access this screen from DOS, type dm at the DOS prompt and press Enter. The horizontal bars on the left of the screen represent the relative size of each directory.

170

You can display the directory tree for a different drive the same way as you do in Shell: Hold down the Ctrl key and press the letter of the drive whose tree you want to view or click on the drive's icon just below the pull-down menu bar.

Adding a New Directory

You can add a new directory anywhere in the directory tree of your hard disk. (Of course, you can also add directories to a floppy disk, although few PC users do so.)

To add a new directory:

1. Change to the drive on which you want to add a directory.
2. Highlight the drive letter or the directory under which you want the new directory to appear.
3. Select F4 Make. The Make Directory dialog box appears, prompting you to name the new directory.
4. Type a name for the new directory (up to eight characters for the base name and three characters for the extension), and then select **O**K. The directory appears under the drive or directory you highlighted in Step 2.

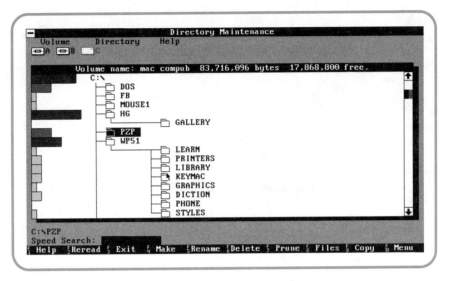

Figure 6.13   The Directory Maintenance screen.

> ▶ **Tip:** If the new directory did not appear in Step 4, select
> `F2 Reread`. This tells the Directory Maintenance program
> to look at the directory structure again, in much the same way
> as the Refresh command on Shell's View menu.

Renaming a directory

You can rename any directory using the Rename command.

To rename a directory:

1. Highlight the directory whose name you want to change.
2. Select `F5 Rename`. The Rename Directory dialog box appears
   as in Figure 6.14.
3. Type the new name and an optional extension for the directory, and then select **OK**.

The renamed directory may not be immediately visible in the
directory tree until you force Directory Maintenance to reread the
tree as discussed earlier.

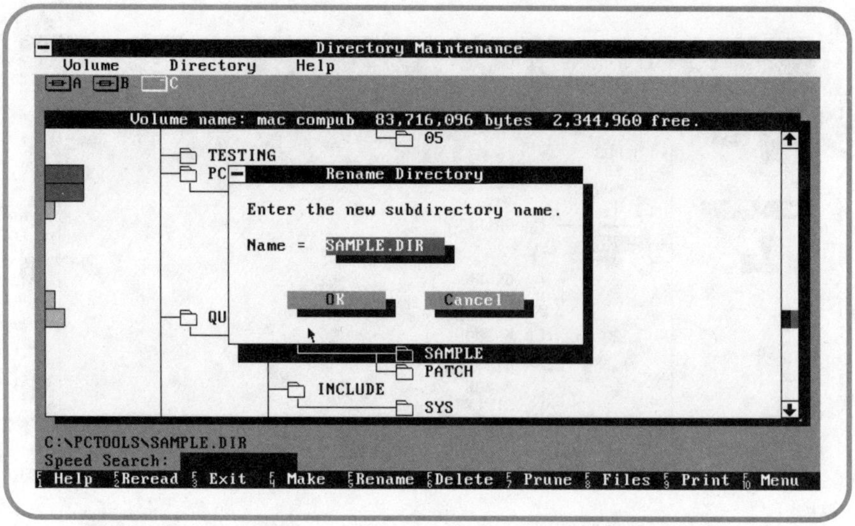

Figure 6.14   The Directory Rename dialog box.

172

Deleting a directory

Delete directories you no longer need so that they don't clutter up
your hard disk. Before you can delete a directory, you must empty
it of all files and delete any of its directories. For obvious reasons, you
cannot delete the root directory.

To delete a directory:

1. Highlight the directory you want to delete.
2. Select F6 Delete. The Delete Directory dialog box appears,
    prompting you to confirm the deletion.
3. Select OK to delete the directory or Cancel to cancel the
    operation.

The deleted directory may remain in the directory tree until you
force Shell to reread the tree, as explained earlier.

Prune and Graft

Prune and graft lets you move the contents of a directory including
all files and any subdirectories listed under it to another location in
the directory tree.

To prune and graft a directory:

1. Highlight the directory you want to move. This directory and any of its subdirectories will be included in the move.
2. Select F7 Prune. The highlighted directory and all its subdirectories (if any) are highlighted.
3. Use the Up and Down Arrow keys or your mouse to drag the directory to its new location in the tree. If you drag it to another directory, the moved directory becomes a subdirectory of the directory you moved it to. If you drag the directory to the top of the tree, it appears as a directory under the root directory, as in Figure 6.15.
4. Press Enter or select F7 Graft to graft the directory to its new location. A dialog box appears, prompting you to confirm the operation.
5. Select **O**K to confirm the graft or **C**ancel to quit.

173

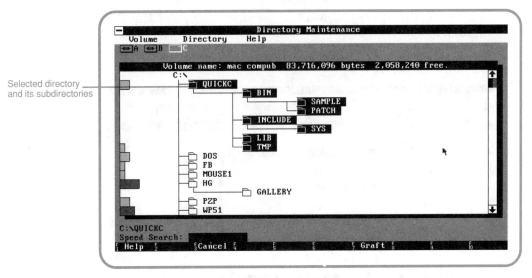

Selected directory and its subdirectories

Figure 6.15   Move the pruned directory to the directory under which you want it to appear.

Modify Directory Attributes

Like files, directories have certain attributes that describe important characteristics about them. Shell allows you to modify a directory's attributes in order to hide the directory and its contents or protect the directory by treating it as a system directory, preventing others from accessing it.

Hidden—Indicates whether the directory is visible (hidden off) in a normal DOS DIRectory or invisible (hidden on). Note that Shell lists hidden directories.

System—Indicates whether the directory is reserved for system use (system on) or regular application use (system off).

The following steps describe how to modify directory attributes:

1. Highlight the directory whose attributes you want to change.
2. Pull down the Directory menu and select Modify **A**ttributes. the Modify Attributes dialog box appears, as in Figure 6.16, allowing you to make your selections.
3. Select the attributes you want to set, and then press the **OK** button.

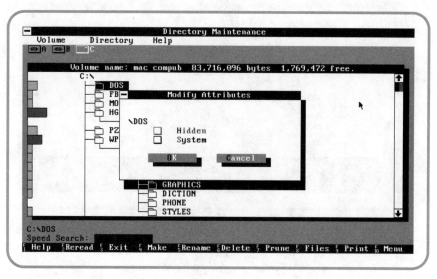

Figure 6.16   The Modify Attributes dialog box.

Disk Information

The Disk Information command, located on the Disk menu, provides information about the currently selected disk, including size, number of files, number of directories, sectors per track, and more. The Disk Information dialog box, shown in Figure 6.17 (yours will be different, depending on the drive you select), is intended mainly to keep you abreast of the condition of your disks. You can also use it when recovering damaged disks, as described in Chapter 10, "Maintaining Your Disks."

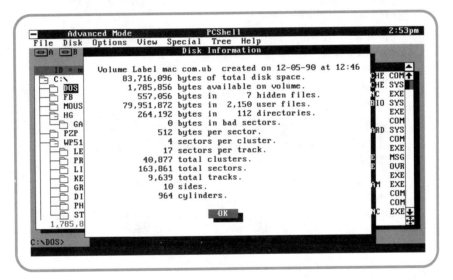

Figure 6.17   Useful information about a disk. The information contained in the sample illustration is for an 82M hard disk.

The following Quick Steps tell you how to get disk information:

 Getting Disk Information

1. Select a disk to check.

2. Pull down the Disk menu and   The Disk Information
   select Disk Information.   window appears.

3. When you're done looking at   Returns you to Shell.
   the Disk Information box,
   press the **O**K button.

175

Sorting Files

Nothing's worse than a jumble of files. The Sort Files in Directory command, found on the Disk menu, helps you put your files in order. You can sort by any of five fields, in either ascending or descending order. The sorting procedure also sorts directories.

To sort a disk or directory:

1. Select the disk and/or directory whose files you want to sort.
2. Pull down the Disk menu and select Sort Files in Directory. The Directory Sort dialog box appears, prompting you to enter sorting instructions.
3. Select a field for sorting, either name, extension, size, date/time, or select number (works only with files you previously selected).
4. Indicate whether you want the sorting to be in ascending or descending order.
5. Press the Sort button when you are done.
6. Shell asks how you want to review the results of the sort, as illustrated in Figure 6.18.

    The View option sorts the files in the Shell window only. It does not sort the files on disk. This is similar to the File Display Options command on the View menu. The Update option sorts the files on the disk. The Resort option returns you to the previous dialog box, where you can select another sorting field.

If you've re-sorted the root directory of your hard disk or floppy disks, the order of the files and directories will not be updated until you force Shell to reread the drive. Simply reselect the drive you sorted and the changes are updated.

Printing Disk and Directory Contents

The Print command, on the File menu, opens a Print submenu that gives you the options of printing the selected file(s) or printing the current file list. You can use the Print File List command to build a master disk/subdirectory catalog to help you easily find files stored on archive disks. This command is also useful if you share disks with other users; a printout of the names of the files included on the disk can be very helpful.

Before printing a list of files in a directory, make sure that your printer is on and that it is on-line.

To print the directory's contents:

1. Select the disk and directory whose file list you want to print.
2. Pull down the File menu and select **P**rint. The Print submenu appears.
3. Select Print File **L**ist.

Shell informs you that printing is in progress. If an error occurs (the printer wasn't ready, for instance), you have the option of quitting or trying again.

177

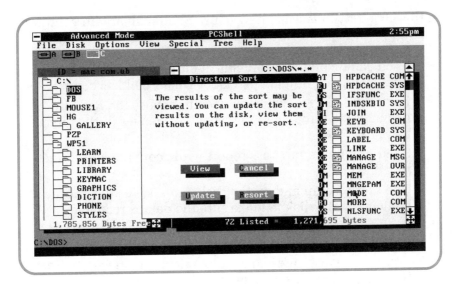

Figure 6.18   The Directory Sort dialog box.

Saving a Contents List in a File

Shell doesn't offer a way to send the listing to a file, rather than directly to the printer. But with a separate utility, such as PRN2FILE (available through PCMAGNET on CompuServe), you can intercept data sent to a printer and capture it in an ASCII text document. Once the data is captured, you can format and edit it with any word processor or with the Notepads editor in the PC Tools Desktop. Make a text-file copy of all your directories or disks and save them in a master catalog file. You can then use the file (with the proper formatting, of course) with a data management program to pinpoint quickly the location of a particular document. This technique is particularly handy when cataloging a collection of floppy disks.

What You Have Learned

In this chapter you learned how to use Shell to maintain your hard and floppy disks. You also learned:

▶ Shell can display the contents of either one or two disks at a time, using the **S**ingle File List or **D**ual File Lists commands.

▶ From time to time, you may need to choose the Refresh command to force Shell to recognize changes in the directory structure.

▶ Shell provides a progress report while copying and formatting disks.

▶ The Verify command on the Disk menu scans the entire contents of the disk to make sure the data is readable.

▶ Shell can format any PC standard floppy disk size and capacity that your floppy disk drive can handle.

▶ You can make a disk bootable by selecting the **I**nstall system files option before starting the formatting process.

▶ You can sort files in the disk directory using the Sort Files in Directory command.

Running Programs with Shell

In This Chapter

- ▶ *Running program files*
- ▶ *Opening document files*
- ▶ *Running programs from the program menu*
- ▶ *Customizing the program menu*

Imagine the convenience of running a program at the touch of a key. Or how about choosing a document and automatically launching the program that created it? Using Shell takes the place of typing program names at the DOS prompt, making it easy to start all your programs. You can even choose to open a selected document when you start a program, saving you the trouble of doing it manually. You can use Shell as a way station for all your programs—running a program and then returning to Shell when you're done.

Shell as a Way Station

Shell is a substitute for starting your PC programs from the DOS prompt. Instead of returning to DOS when you quit your programs, you are returned to Shell, where you can start another program or perform some file and disk maintenance with Shell's other functions.

If you want to make Shell your permanent program launcher, you should have it run automatically when you start your computer. If Shell is not set up to run automatically, you can change the setup:

1. Exit any programs that are currently running and display the DOS prompt.
2. Change to the drive and directory that contains the PC Tools program files. This is usually C:\PCTOOLS.
3. Type `install` and press Enter. The PC Tools Program Configuration screen appears, as in Figure 7.1.
4. Select PC **S**hell. The PC Shell Configuration screen appears, as in Figure 7.2.
5. Select **R**un PC Shell to run PC Shell automatically on startup. If you want Shell to run in memory-resident mode, select **L**oad PC Shell. A check mark appears in the box next to each selected option.
6. Select **OK** to return to the main Configuration screen.
7. Select E**x**it. A dialog box appears, telling you that you're about to exit the configuration program.
8. Select S**a**ve Configuration to put a check mark in the box, and then select **OK**. Another dialog box appears asking if you want to reboot at this time.
9. Select **R**eboot if you want the changes to take affect immediately, or select Return to **D**OS if you want the changes to take affect the next time you boot your computer.

> ▶ **Tip:** You can run two other programs in addition to PC Shell at the same time. Load PC Shell in memory-resident mode, but don't run it. Run one of your other programs. At this point, you can hot-key back and forth between Shell and the other program using Ctrl-Esc. To run a third program, return to the Shell and then use one of the methods discussed next to run the program. You won't be able to hot-key into and out of the third program, but you will be able to access data in that program.

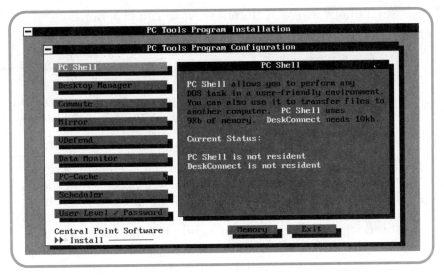

Figure 7.1   Use the PC Tools Program Configuration screen to change the PC Tools setup options at any time.

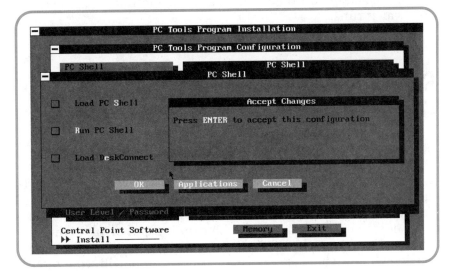

Figure 7.2   To run the Shell in memory-resident mode, you can choose Run PC Shell at startup, Load PC Shell at startup, or both.

Shell offers several different ways to run programs:

▶ From the DOS prompt. If the DOS prompt is displayed (at the lower left corner of your screen), you can run the programs from the DOS prompt as you normally would.

▶ The Run command on the File menu lets you run a program as you would from the DOS prompt. When you select this command, a dialog box opens, allowing you to enter the DOS command required to run the program.

▶ The Open command on the File menu lets you run a program by selecting the program's executable file from the File List window. (The *executable file* is the file that starts the program.) If you select a data file instead of a program file, this command runs the associated program and then loads the data file into the program.

▶ The program menu contains a list of programs that you can run by selecting a program from the menu. The PC Tools Installation program adds many programs to the menu automatically, but you can add a program to the menu if it's not listed or edit the program's command line to change the way it runs.

Running Programs from the DOS Prompt

Before you can run programs from the DOS prompt in Shell, you must make sure the DOS command line is displayed and active. To display the line, pull down the View menu, select **C**ustom List Configure, and then select **DOS** Command Line. This puts a check mark next to the DOS Command Line option and displays the DOS prompt. To activate the DOS command line, press the Tab key until the line is highlighted or click on the DOS prompt with your mouse.

Once the command line is active, you can change directories at the prompt and enter the commands required to run the program as you normally would.

Using the Run Command

The Run command, located in the File menu, lets you start any program or batch file located on a hard or floppy disk. This command displays the Run DOS Command dialog box that allows you to enter a command the same way you would enter the command at the DOS prompt. Follow these simple procedures to use the Run command:

 Running a Program with the Run Command

1. Pull down the File menu and select **R**un.

   The Run DOS Command dialog box appears.

2. Type the command required to run the program.

   For example, if Microsoft Word is stored in the C:\WORD5 directory, you might type `c:\word5\word` to run the program.

3. Select **OK** to enter the command.

   Assuming the command is correct, Shell runs the program. □

183

Using the Open Command

The Open command, located just above the Run command on the File menu, provides a more powerful tool for running programs. You simply select the file that executes the program from the File List window and then "open" the file. The following Quick Steps give this procedure:

Running a Program with the Open Command

1. Change to the drive and directory that contains the program you want to run.

2. In the File List window, highlight the program or batch file (.COM, .EXE, or .BAT extension) that initiates the program.

   Tells Shell which file starts the program.

3. Pull down the File menu and select **O**pen.

The Open File dialog box appears as in Figure 7.3.

4. Type any parameters required by the program. (This step is optional.)

Parameters are switches that tell the program how to operate. For example, you may have used the /r parameter to run PC Shell in memory-resident mode. Refer to the program's documentation to determine available parameters.

5. Select **O**pen.

This opens the selected file, starting the program. □

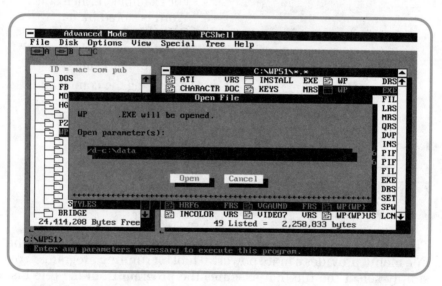

Figure 7.3   *The Open File dialog box.*

To bypass the File menu and enter the Open command directly, try one of the following shortcuts:

▶ Highlight the program or batch file and press Ctrl-Enter.

▶ If you're using a mouse, double-click (with the left button) on the desired program or batch file.

Starting a Program and Loading a Document

Although the Open command is designed to open programs and batch files, you can also use it to start a program and load a document at the same time. Normally, Shell won't let you open a nonprogram or nonbatch file (for example, a .TXT document file created by a word processor), unless you've "associated" the document type to one of your programs on your hard disk. Shell monitors the file extensions of documents, so when you open a document, it finds the program that goes with it, starts the program, and loads the document. See the section in this chapter entitled "Associating Document Files with Programs" for more information.

Running Programs from the Program Menu

185

When you first installed PC Tools, the INSTALL program automatically inserted the PC Tools programs (Compress, PC Format, CP Backup, etc.) in the Shell program menu (this menu consists of the Main menu and several submenus). During the installation, INSTALL also searched through your hard disk for other recognizable application programs and added them, either individually or in groups, to the program menu. For example, if INSTALL found WordStar, WordPerfect, and Microsoft Word, they would be included in a group called Word Processing. You could then select Word Processing from the Main menu to view a list of programs on the Word Processing submenu. Several of the PC Tools programs are similarly grouped, as shown in Figure 7.4.

To display the Main program menu, press F10. The Directory Tree and File List windows disappear, and the Main program menu appears in the middle of the screen. Pressing F10 again turns the Main program menu off and redisplays the Directory Tree and File List windows. If you'd like to display a split screen, with the Directory Tree and File List windows on top and the Main program menu on the bottom, pull down the View menu and select Program/File Lists.

Notice in Figure 7.4 that one of the letters in each of the program groups is highlighted. As in the rest of Shell's menus, these highlighted letters represent quick-keys you can use to select one of the program groups or items from the menu. If you select a group, a submenu appears as in Figure 7.5, showing a list of subgroups or a list of programs in the group. You can then select another group or program.

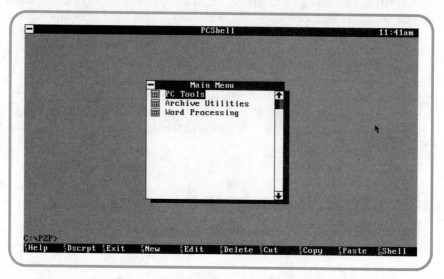

Figure 7.4 *The Main program menu lists programs and program groups.*

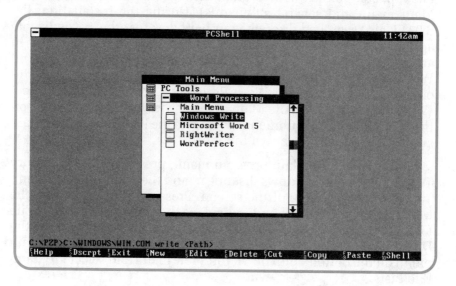

Figure 7.5 *Selecting a group opens a submenu containing a list of subgroups or a list of programs in the group.*

The program menu is meant to list the programs you use most often, thus freeing you from hunting them down in the File List window and starting them manually with the Open command. Shell keeps track of the location and other important tidbits (as explained in the next section) of each program listed in the program menu.

To use the program menu, merely choose a program listed on it. There's no need to indicate parameters; these are included with the program entry in the menu and are entered automatically.

Adding Programs to a Program Menu

You can add programs or program groups to a program menu at any time. The following Quick Steps lead you through the process:

 Adding a Program Group

187

1. Start at the program menu on which you want the group's name to appear, as in Figure 7.5.

   You can add a program group to the Main program menu or to one of its submenus.

2. Select **F4 (New)**.

   The New Menu Item dialog box appears, as in Figure 7.6.

3. Select Group and then OK.

   The Program Group Information dialog box appears, as in Figure 7.7.

4. Type a title for the group and press Enter.

   The title can be as long as like, but it's best to keep it under 25 characters. You can type a caret (^) before the letter you want to appear highlighted.

5. To protect the group with a password, type a password (up to 10 characters), and press Enter.

   If you add a password, you'll have to enter it whenever you want to access the program group.

6. Select OK to add the group to the menu.

□

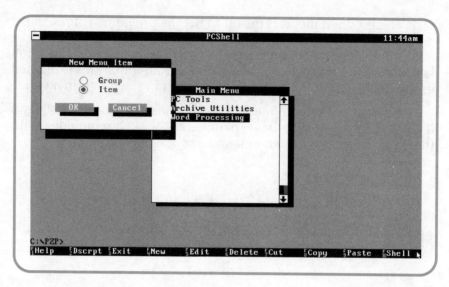

Figure 7.6   The New Menu Item dialog box prompts you to add a program group or item.

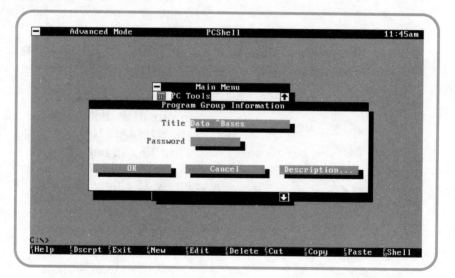

Figure 7.7   The Program Group Information dialog box lets you create a new program group.

Q Adding a Program to a Group

1. Select the group in which you want the program listed.

2. Select `F4 (New)`. The New Menu Item dialog box appears.

3. Select Item and then **OK**.

The Program Item Information dialog box appears, as in Figure 7.8.

4. In the Program Title box, type the name of the program and press Enter.

You can type a caret (^) before the letter you want to use to select the program, but don't use the same letter for more than one program.

5. In the Commands box, enter the path to the directory that contains this program's program files, followed by the name of the file that runs the program.

For example, if you have WordPerfect in a directory called WP51 on drive C, you would type `c:\wp51\wp.exe`. You can add parameters by typing / and then the parameters you want to use.

6. In the Startup Directory box, enter a path to the directory that contains the data files you created using the program.

For example, if you store WordPerfect document files in C:\WP51\FILES, type `c:\wp51\files`.

7. Select **OK** to accept the information you just entered.

The name of the new program appears on the program menu. You can now run the program from the Shell. □

189

Editing a Program in a Program Menu

If you add a program to the menu and it doesn't run as expected, or if you'd like to change the way it runs, you can edit its Program Item Information screen. To do so, highlight the program's name and select `F5 (Edit)`. This displays the Program Item Information dialog box, where you can enter any changes.

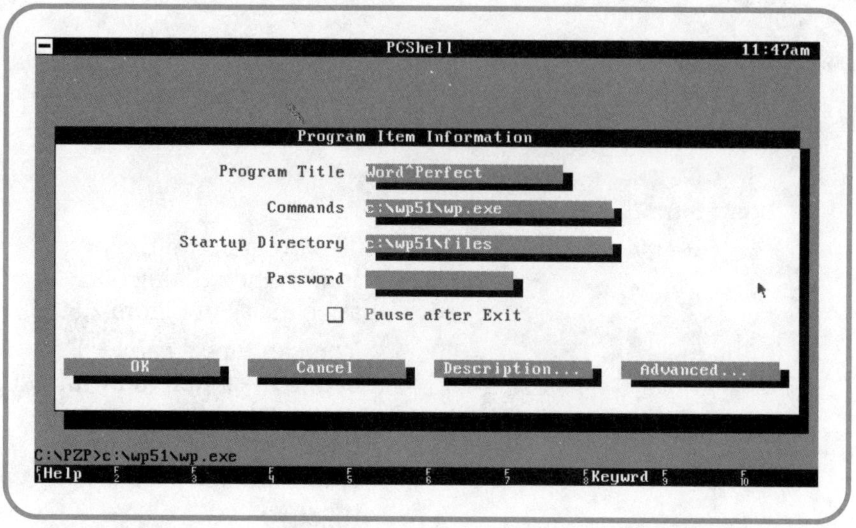

Figure 7.8 The Program Item Information dialog box prompts you to enter the information needed to run the program.

Using Advanced Program Options

At the bottom of the Program Item Information box is a button labeled **A**dvanced. If you select this option, you'll see the Advanced Program Item Information dialog box, shown in Figure 7.9. This dialog box lets you enter advanced instructions about how you want the program to run:

User Prompt. Tells Shell to pause and display a prompt before starting the program. For example, if you run the program from a floppy disk, you can display a prompt telling you to insert the floppy disk before continuing. Fill in the user prompt (up to 128 characters) as desired. Leaving this field blank skips the user prompt, and Shell immediately runs the application once you select it from its program menu.

File Associations. A file association is a document (data) file that was created using the designated program. You can indicate one or more file associations in this field (up to 128 characters). Most file associations will be documents with particular name extensions, such as *.TXT and *.DOC. For more information, refer to the following section, "Associating Document Files with Programs."

Keystrokes. These are keys that Shell automatically "presses" for the selected application when you first start it. This field is helpful if you need to press a series of keys to start an application all the way or to load a document into the program. This is an advanced topic; see the DOS Shell/ File Manager manual for more details on how to program with keystrokes.

Quick Run. Selecting this option causes Shell to run the application without freeing up memory. Normally, keep this option off so Shell frees up some of its memory for use by your applications.

Exit to DOS after Application. Goes to DOS when the application is terminated instead of going back to Shell. With this option off, the program returns to Shell, bypassing the DOS prompt.

Force Launch with Selected File. Runs the program and loads the file you selected in the File List window. If the program allows, you can have the selected file loaded along with the program even if the file is not associated with the program. With this off, Shell ignores selected document files and loads the program clean.

191

Don't Clear Screen before Launch. Normally, Shell clears the screen before running a program to clean the screen and remove any characters unique to PC Shell. If your other program is losing characters when you run it from Shell, try turning this option on.

This is a PC Tools Application. This indicates that the program is a PC Tools program, thus allowing Shell to run the program more quickly.

> ▶ **Tip:** Shell records the programs contained in the program menu in the PCSHELL.CFG file. If this file is erased or damaged, your list of programs will be lost. Therefore, it's a good idea to keep a backup (on a floppy disk) of the PCSHELL.CFG file, in case something should ever happen to the original.

After a program has run, you will be returned to Shell. You will probably be requested to press a key to reenter Shell. If you're using the mouse, just press one of the mouse buttons to reactivate Shell.

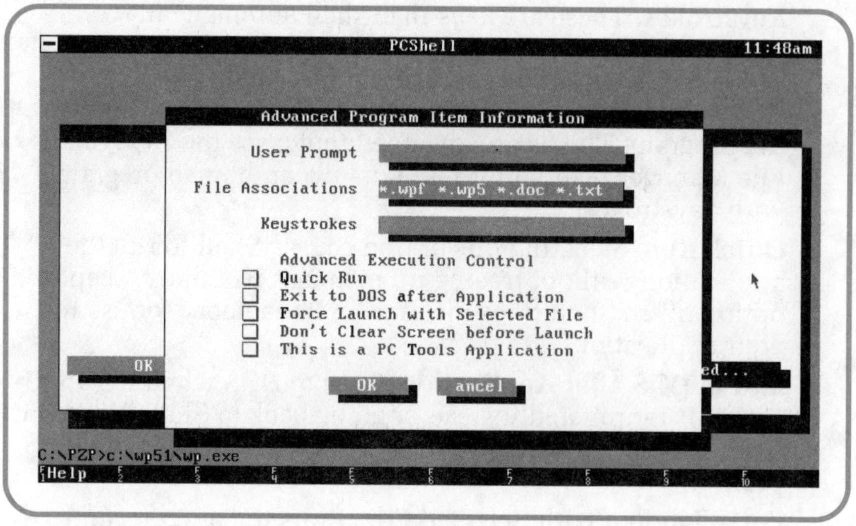

Figure 7.9   *The Advanced Program Item Information dialog box lets you customize a program's operation.*

192

Using Program Descriptions

At the bottom of both the Program Group and Program Item Informa-tion boxes is a button labeled **D**escription. Pressing this button allows you to enter a description for the program group or program. To see what these descriptions look like, return to the Main program menu, and select F2 Dscrpt. Press the Down Arrow key to highlight Archive Utilities. The Main program menu now shows the pro-gram group on the left, and a description of the group's function on the right, as in Figure 7.10.

Associating Document Files with Programs

One of the most useful features of Shell is that you can run a program by selecting (from the File List window) a data file that you created using the program. For example, you can associate a file having the extension .DOC to the Microsoft Word program. With a single command, you can then run Word and load a selected document file into the program.

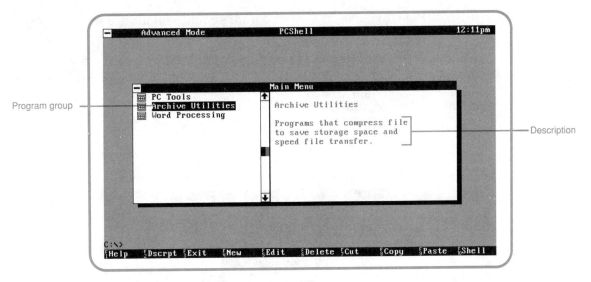

Program group

Description

Figure 7.10 *You can add descriptions to programs and program groups to indicate the function of each group and program.*

193

Running a program and loading a document requires that you provide a file extension association in the Advanced Program Item Information dialog box, as detailed in the previous section. When you run a file with a particular extension, Shell automatically runs the associated program and loads the document.

> **Tip:** Specifying a file extension may not be enough. If you find that you cannot open a data file with its associated program, add the variable *<path>* to the end of the command line in the program's Information dialog box. For example, after `c:\word5\word.exe`, you would press the Spacebar and then type `<path>`, as in Figure 7.11. This inserts the selected file's path and name at the end of the command line.

Note that you may not be able to open a document file with all programs. The program you're running must accept a file name as a command-line parameter. For example, if you can type

`<PROGRAM><FILENAME.TXT>`

at the DOS prompt to Run the program and automatically load the file, then you can use the File Association feature of Shell to enter a similar command. If the program does not allow for this, you cannot do it in Shell. Refer to the individual program's documentation to see if file names are allowed as command line options.

Once a file is associated with a particular program, you can run the program and load the document file with a single command:

1. Highlight the document file you want to load.
2. Pull down the File menu and select **O**pen. Shell runs the program and loads the selected document file into it.

194

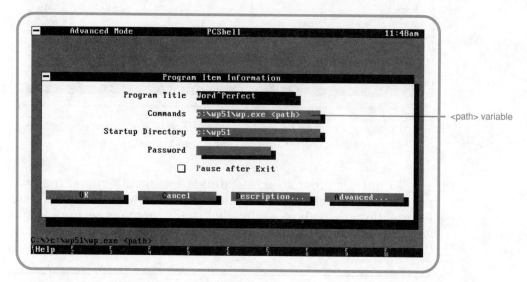

Figure 7.11   *You may need to add the <path> variable to specify the associated file's location.*

Shared File Associations

Some of the programs in your program menu may share the same file associations. While no harm will come to your computer or files if this occurs, Shell will associate a given file association only with the first program it finds in the menu that recognizes the extension.

For example, suppose you have WordStar, WordPerfect, and Microsoft Word on your hard disk. During installation, INSTALL will enter the .DOC extension in the file association fields for all three programs. Regardless of which program created the file in the first place, Shell will start the first program in the list when you select a .DOC document. If you want to run another program when you select a certain file, move the programs in the program menu as discussed later in this chapter, or use a unique file extension for naming files created in each program.

Deleting a Program from a Program Menu

If a program menu contains programs that you never run from the Shell, you may want to delete their names from the menu.

To delete a program, perform the following steps:

1. Display the menu that contains the program whose name you want to delete.
2. Highlight the program name you want to delete.
3. Select F6 Delete. A dialog box appears, asking you to confirm the deletion.
4. Select **D**elete to delete the program name or **C**ancel to cancel the operation.

Moving a Program in a Program Menu

If you don't like the position of one of the programs on the menu, or if the program's position is causing problems with file associations, you can move the program. To do so, highlight the program's name and select F7 Cut. The program's name disappears, but is stored in a temporary location. Move the highlight to the name of the program or group above which you want the cut program to appear. Select F9 Paste. The name of the program appears in its new location.

What You Have Learned

In this chapter you learned how to use PC Shell to run your applications. You also learned:

195

▶ You can run any program from the Shell as if you're running it from the DOS prompt by selecting the Run command from the File menu or by typing the command at the DOS prompt.

▶ The Open command allows you to run a program by selecting its executable program file from the File List window.

▶ The Open command also lets you run a program and load an associated document file into the program with a single command.

▶ A keyboard shortcut for the Open command is: Select a program or batch file to run, and press Ctrl-Enter.

▶ A mouse shortcut for the Open command is: Double-click on the program or batch file you want to run.

▶ The program menu is for programs you often use.

▶ You can add a program or program group to the program menu at any time.

▶ The Program Information screen lets you enter the information Shell needs to run the program. You can edit the program information at any time.

▶ By associating document files to programs, you can run a program and load its document file with a single command.

196

Backing Up Your Hard Disk

In This Chapter

▶ *Backup strategies*
▶ *Configuring CP Backup for your computer*
▶ *Backing up an entire hard disk*
▶ *Backing up a portion of a hard disk*
▶ *Restoring files in case of data loss*

Consider the following nightmare: You finished a week-long project, saving the files on your computer's hard disk. The next day, when you return to print the files, you find the hard disk has "crashed." The contents of the disk, the files, everything is gone. Not only must you re-create a week's worth of data, you have to rebuild your hard disk and reinstall all your programs, a task that in itself can take several days.

This scenario is often described to promote the benefits of making backups—a copy of the files stored on your hard disk. The scenario is a common one because it occurs often. In fact, odds are that something like it will happen to you sooner or later. But with backup files stored safely on floppy disks, on a tape drive, or on a separate location on your hard drive, you can recover from such a catastrophe.

The Central Point Backup (or CP Backup) utility makes it easy to back up your hard drive. You simply select the drives, directories, and files you want to back up from a list, and enter specific instructions by selecting options from the various menus.

Backup Strategy

Backup programs are worthless if you don't have a *backup strategy*— a plan that ensures the backup copies are up-to-date. For best results, you should back up your entire hard disk at least once a week, and back up any files that change during the day at the end of the day.

Central Point Backup (a stand-alone program you can access from within Shell, from the DOS prompt, or from Windows) lets you back up just a portion of the hard disk, or just those files that were changed or created since the last backup. That makes daily backups much more palatable. Instead of spending 10 to 30 minutes to back up an entire 30M hard disk, you spend only a few minutes backing up the work you've done for that day.

Backup Types

Central Point Backup offers five types of backups. To understand the different types, you must understand how *archive bits* work. What's an archive bit? It's a code attached to each file. Whenever you create or edit a file, the archive bit is set (on), indicating that the file is not backed up. When the file is backed up, by any backup program, the archive bit turns off. The backup program then knows which files were changed or created since the last backup. This becomes important in deciding which of the following backup methods to use:

Full. Archives all the files on the hard disk or, optionally, just those files and subdirectories you manually selected. During a full backup, CP Backup ignores the setting of the archive bit. (It backs up everything, no matter how the archive bit is set.) After the backup is complete, the program resets the archive bit to *off* to indicate that the files were backed up.

Full Copy. Functions the same as full backup, except that the settings of the archive bit do not change after the backup is complete.

Incremental. Backs up only those files with the archive bit set (recently edited or created). When the backup is complete, the program resets the archive bits. If you have

previously performed a full backup, incremental backups
will be appended to the end of the full backup. This means
that you have one set of backup disks.

Separate Incremental. Functions the same as incremental
backup, except that the backed up files are not appended to the
full backup. You end up with two sets of backup disks: a set for
the full backup and a set for each of the incremental backups.

Differential. Archives only those files that were changed
since the last full backup. The archive bit is not reset after
the backup is complete.

Establishing a Backup Strategy

A backup strategy is a consistent routine for backing up your hard
disk. Without an effective backup strategy, you might as well not
even back up your hard disk. For example, if you back up the hard
disk only occasionally, the backed-up (original) files will probably
be seriously out of date; any changes you made or files you created
since then will be lost for good. You can't restore what you haven't
backed up.

199

An ideal backup strategy is one full backup every week—say
every Friday before you go home for the weekend—plus a partial
(incremental) backup at the end of each day. While that may seem
like a lot of extra work, it really isn't. Few hard disks are over 40M
(under DOS 3.X hard disk partitions are limited to 32M), and few
hard disks are filled to capacity. On average, it will take you between
15 to 20 minutes to back up your hard disk using the full backup
method. That's required only once a week. The incremental backups
take only a few minutes.

If you don't use your computer daily, there's no reason to back
up its hard disk every day. As a rule of thumb, though, if you use your
computer on any particular day, back up your work.

Estimating Diskette Requirements

Central Point Backup crams hard disk data onto diskettes. The
number of diskettes you need to back up your hard disk depends on
several variables:

▶   The amount of data stored on the hard disk. (Note: The
    capacity of the hard disk is not important; you may have less
    than 10M of data on a 40M disk.)

▶ The capacity of the diskette, such as 360 or 720K or 1.44M.

▶ The setting of the Compression option within Central Point Backup. The amount and effect of the compression depends on the speed of your computer and the format of the data on your hard disk. You can select Compression to minimize the number of diskettes or to minimize time.

When you start a hard disk backup, CP Backup estimates the number of diskettes you need to complete the task. In my experience, the estimate is high; the program usually accomplishes the task with fewer diskettes. CP Backup will provide you with its estimate before you actually start the backup process, so you can stop it if you don't have enough diskettes on hand. The diskettes do not have to be formatted, but if they are, the process will go faster.

On average, using 1.44M or 1.2M media (which is preferred, as it takes fewer diskettes and speeds up the process), you need about one diskette for every 1.5M of hard disk data. Accordingly, a hard disk with 15M will require approximately ten 1.44M or 1.2M diskettes.

After you make the first backups of your hard disk using the full and incremental methods, you can better estimate the number of diskettes you'll need for your weekly and daily backups. If you're going to make separate incremental backups, you'll need a single set of diskettes for the weekly backups and a separate set for each daily backup. For instance, if your hard disk requires 20 diskettes for a weekly (full) backup, and two diskettes for each of the daily (incremental) backups, you'll need 30 diskettes to fill the quota. (This assumes you'll be making five daily backups per week.)

Label the sets so you can readily identify them. Write WEEKLY on the weekly full-backup diskettes, and MONDAY, TUESDAY, etc., for each set of daily incremental-backup diskettes. (You'll number the disks during the backup process.) If you plan on appending the incremental backup to the full backup, you need not worry about keeping separate sets of disks.

A Note on Diskette Quality

For obvious reasons, don't skimp on the quality of diskettes used for hard disk backup. Though you'll be using plenty of diskettes to maintain a weekly and daily backup schedule, you'll reuse these diskettes, so the expenditure is one-time-only.

200

If your computer is equipped with high-density 3 1/2" or 5 1/4" floppy disk drives (1.44M and 1.2M capacity, respectively), purchase only high-density disks for them. High-density disks cost a little more than double-density, but you'll actually save money because you'll need only a half or a third as many disks.

A Preview of Central Point Backup

The CP Backup program looks and works much the same as a dialog box in PC Shell. As shown in Figure 8.1, the CP Backup screen consists of a menu bar at the top (with five menus: File, Action, Options, Configure, and Help), several buttons that display additional dialog boxes, and a few pull-down lists. You select commands, files, and other items in CP Backup the same as you do in Shell. The Windows version, shown in Figure 8.2 is a little more graphic, but it offers the same options. We'll discuss any differences between the two versions where those differences arise.

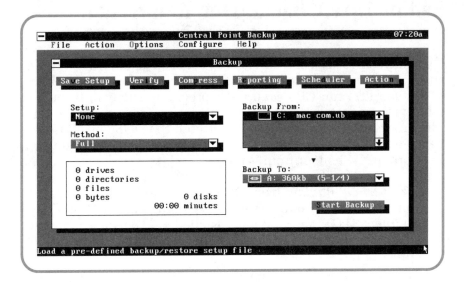

Figure 8.1   The CP Backup screen.

If at any time you need help on a particular topic, look to the message bar at the bottom of the screen. If that doesn't tell you what you need to know, press F1 to view context-sensitive help, or use the Help menu.

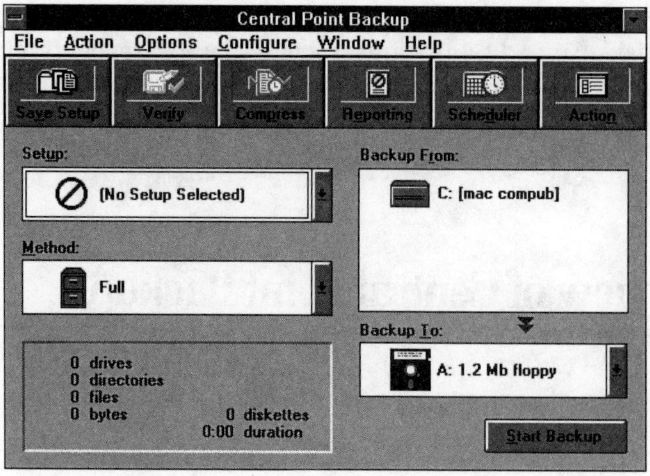

Figure 8.2   *The Windows version of CP Backup has a different look but offers the same options.*

Setting Up CP Backup for Your System

If you haven't used CP Backup before, you need to tell it a few things about your computer and the way you want to perform the backups. When you first run CP Backup, the program leads you through a setup process that configures the backup program for your system. The process is basically the same for both the DOS and Windows versions, although you'll take different steps to start CP Backup from DOS, from PC Shell, or from Windows.

To start CP Backup from DOS, change to the drive and directory that contains the PC Tools program files (for example, C:\PCTOOLS). If you installed PC Tools to run at any directory prompt, you can skip this step. Type `cpbackup` and press Enter.

To start CP Backup from Windows, display and activate the PC Tools program window. (Refer to Chapter 3 for information on activating windows.) Double-click on the CP Backup icon or highlight the icon and press Enter.

To start CP Backup from PC Shell, press F10 to display the Main program menu. Select the PC Tools program group. Select CP **B**ackup.

> ▶ **Tip:** If you run CP Backup from Shell and receive an `Out of Memory` error message, exit Shell and remove it from memory, and then run CP Backup from the DOS prompt or from Windows.

No matter how you start CP Backup, you'll see a CP Backup welcome screen indicating that you must set up the program. To continue with the setup:

1. Select **OK**. A dialog box appears, asking if you're backing up to a tape drive. A *tape drive* is a special drive used especially for backups.

2. If you don't have a tape drive, select **No** Tape. If you have a tape drive, select **S**earch or **Y**es. The program tests your drives, and then displays the Define Equipment dialog box, as in Figure 8.3.

3. Check the information displayed to make sure the drive types are correct. This is the *drive* type NOT the *disk* type. If you're unsure, accept the displayed settings. You can change the settings later if the backup test fails.

4. Select **OK**. The Choose Drive & Media dialog box appears, as in Figure 8.4.

5. Select the capacity of the disks or tape you plan to use for storing the backups. The disk capacity may be lower than the drive capacity, but don't choose a high-capacity disk, if you have a low-capacity drive or if you're using low-capacity disks.

   If you choose the same capacity for each of two floppy drives, select **T**wo Drive Backup. This allows you to switch disks in one drive while CP Backup is writing information onto the disk in the other drive.

6. Select **OK**. The Backup Confidence Test dialog box appears, indicating your equipment will be tested to see how fast it can perform a reliable backup.

7. Select **C**ontinue. A warning box appears, telling you to insert a blank disk in the drive you're using for the backup operation.

8. Insert a blank disk, or a disk that contains information you will never again need, into the specified drive. Make sure the disk has the same capacity as the capacity you specified in Step 5.

203

9. Select **OK** to continue. The Backup Progress dialog box appears as in Figure 8.5.

CP Backup backs up randomly selected files from the current directory and stores the backup on the tape or floppy disk. It then compares the backed up files (on the tape or disk) to the original files on the hard disk, to determine if they match. This test is performed at various speeds to determine the fastest speed at which your computer can make reliable backups. When the test is finished, the results are displayed. CP Backup automatically sets the backup speed to the highest speed at which your computer passed the test:

High Speed—uses the special controller circuitry (called *DMA*, for *direct memory access*) in your computer to read data from the hard disk while writing it to the floppy disk. Of course, your computer must be equipped with a compatible DMA controller. Most PC compatibles have the required controller.

Medium Speed—bypasses the DMA circuitry of the computer. CP Backup reads information off the hard disk and writes it onto the floppy disk in two distinct steps.

Low Speed—setting should be used when backing up to a device other than a floppy disk and when backing up within a network.

204

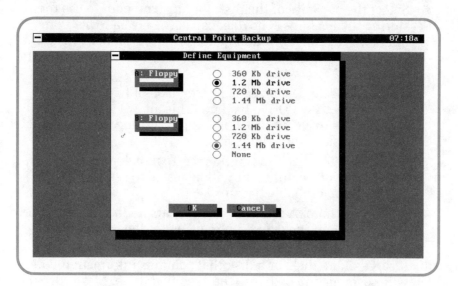

Figure 8.3   Specify the types of floppy drives you have in the Define Equipment dialog box.

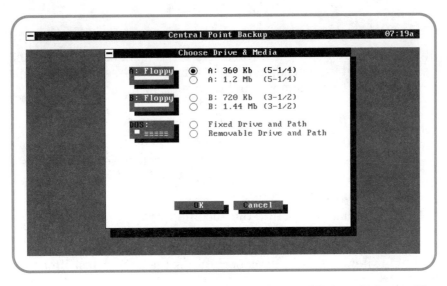

Figure 8.4   Specify the size and capacity of floppy disks you'll use to store the backups in the Choose Drive and Media box.

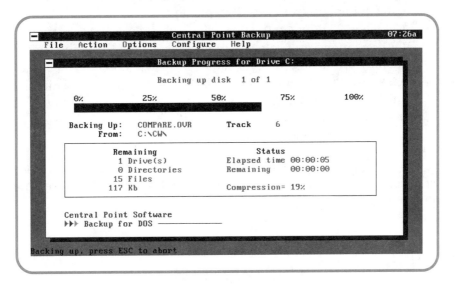

Figure 8.5   CP Backup performs a backup test in the Backup Progress dialog box.

Fail the Test?

If your computer can't pass the test at any speed, or if it passes the test but only at low speed, make sure all memory-resident programs are unloaded from memory, and then retest your computer:

1. Start CP Backup as explained earlier, and select **B**ackup.
2. Pull down the Configure menu and select **B**ackup Speed.
3. Select the speed you want to test and select **T**est. The Backup Confidence Test box appears.
4. Select **C**ontinue to continue.
5. Insert a blank disk into the specified drive, and select **OK**.

If your computer still can't pass the test, try changing the following items, one at a time, performing the backup test after each change:

▶ If you're running Backup from Shell, try quitting Shell and unloading it from memory (with the KILL command). Then run CP Backup from the DOS prompt.

▶ If you're running CP Backup on a network, pull down the Options menu and select **T**ime Display. This turns the time display off during the backup.

▶ Make sure the backup media setting matches the capacity of the disk you're using.

▶ Test at a lower speed. If you initially tested at high speed, test at medium or low speed.

This may seem like a lot of work now, but if you can get your computer to perform reliable backups at high speed, you'll save time in the long-run.

Additional Backup Options

Even though you can use CP Backup right now, you'll probably want to set additional options before you begin. The following is a list of options you can choose from:

- ▶ Backup Method
- ▶ Reporting
- ▶ Compress
- ▶ Verify
- ▶ Media Format
- ▶ Format Always
- ▶ Error Correction
- ▶ Virus Detection
- ▶ Save History
- ▶ Overwrite Warning
- ▶ Time Display

Backup Method

207

The Backup Method command lets you set the type of backup process you desire, either full, full copy, incremental, separate incremental, or differential. These options are described earlier in the section entitled "Backup Types."

 Setting the Backup Method

1. Click on the Method box or press Alt-M.

   This pulls down the Method list, as in Figure 8.6.

2. Select the backup method you want to use.

   This closes the list, but your selection appears in the Method box. ☐

The last backup method displayed in the Method pull-down list is Virus Scan Only. With this method selected, CP Backup will not actually back up the hard disk. Instead, CP Backup scans all the files on the hard disk for viruses. If it finds a file that contains a virus, you're given the option of renaming the file to exclude it from the backup.

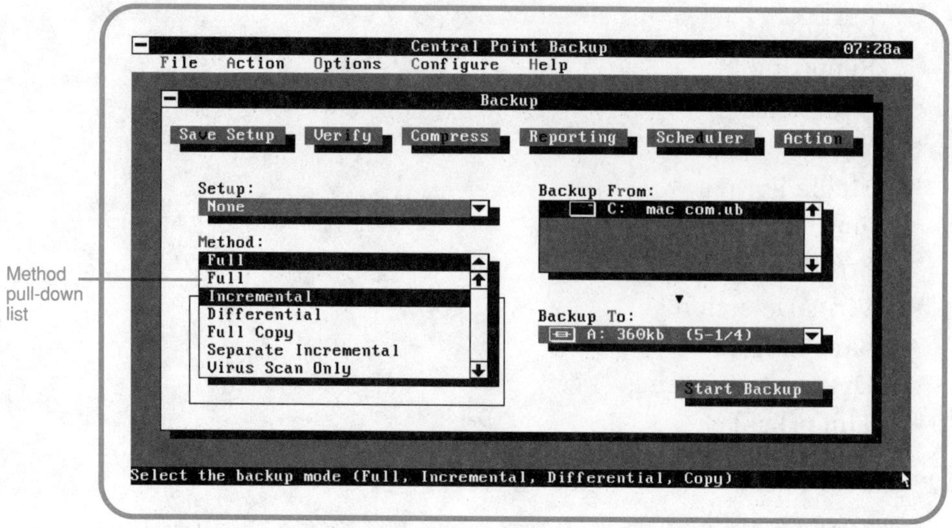

Figure 8.6   *Select a backup method from the Method pull-down list.*

208

Compress

The Compress button opens a dialog box that lets you select optional compression when backing up data. You have a choice of compression to minimize the number of diskettes, compression to minimize time, or no compression.

Minimize Space. Reduces the number of diskettes required to make the backup (generally 10 to 60 percent, depending on the type of data stored in your computer).

Minimize Time. Reduces the time required to make the backup. Time compression depends almost entirely on the speed of the processor in your computer. You'll enjoy little time compression if your PC or compatible is equipped with a slower 8088 or 8086 microprocessor; time compression is improved with faster 80286 and 80386 computers.

None. Turns off all compression.

The following steps describe how to set the Compression option:

1. Press the Compress button. The Compress dialog box appears.
2. Select Minimize **S**pace, Minimize **T**ime, or **N**one, as desired.
3. Press the **O**K button to return to CP Backup or press the **C**ancel button to cancel any changes.

Verify

The Verify command checks the integrity of the data recorded on the backup diskettes. You have three choices: When **F**ormatting, **A**lways, or **N**one. Verification lengthens the backup process.

209

> **When Formatting**. Checks the trustworthiness of the diskette when first formatted immediately prior to backing up the hard disk. Works with the High Speed option.
>
> **Always**. Checks the backup data after it has been recorded on the diskette.
>
> **None**. Turns off all verification.

The following steps describe how to set the Verify option:

1. Press the Verify button. The Verify dialog box appears.
2. Select When **F**ormatting, **A**lways, or **N**one, as desired.
3. Press the **O**K button to return to CP Backup or press the **C**ancel button to cancel any changes.

Media Format

CP Backup uses two types of diskette formatting procedures: standard and nonstandard. The *standard format* uses regular DOS disk formatting, which allows DOS to read the media. The *nonstandard format* uses a unique format employed only by CP Backup. The nonstandard format uses less disk space, but requires CP Backup to read the diskettes; you won't be able to access the disk in DOS. If you want to use the same disk later to store data files, you'll have to reformat it using PC Format.

By default, the standard DOS format is used. To use the nonstandard CPS format,

1. Pull down the Options menu and select Media **F**ormat.
   A dialog box appears, showing the formatting options.
2. Select CPS **F**loppy Format.

CP Backup offers similar options for backing up to tape drives. The QIC compatible format is the standard for tape drives. This format makes the backup copies compatible with other backup programs. The CPS tape format makes the backup compatible with backups created with previous versions of PC Tools.

Format Always

By default, CP Backup formats diskettes only when they need to be formatted. For example, if you insert a blank, unformatted diskette into the floppy drive during the backup process, CP Backup will format the disk before storing any backup files on it. The Format Always command tells CP Backup to format the diskette regardless of whether or not it's already formatted. Backups take considerably longer when the Always option is set, but better data integrity is ensured.

To set the Format Always option (turn it on and off), pull down the Options menu and select Format **A**lways. A check mark appears next to the command when the option is turned on.

Virus Detection

The Virus Detection option tells CP Backup to scan the files you're backing up for over 500 known viruses. If CP Backup finds a file that contains a virus, a dialog box appears, allowing you to rename the file. If you choose to rename the file, CP Backup excludes the file from the current backup. As you'll see in Chapter 11, you can then eliminate a virus from your hard disk by removing all files from the disk and then restoring virus-free files from your untainted backups.

Error Correction

When the Error Correction option is set, CP Backup uses a special error-correction protocol to recover from numerous types of errors that can occur on a disk. Error correction lengthens the backup process, but it can be well worth it. To turn on error correction, choose the **E**rror Correction command from the Options menu. A check mark appears by the command when the option is turned on.

Reporting

The Reporting options let you create a report on the progress of the backup process. If you choose to make a report, you can send it to a printer or to a disk file. The following list describes the Reporting options:

> **None**. Cancels reporting.
>
> **Report to Printer**. Sends the report to the printer. CP Backup requires that the printer be connected to the LPT1 parallel printer port.
>
> **Report to File**. Sends the report to a file on disk.

211

The following steps describe how to set the Report option:

1. Press the **R**eporting button. A dialog box appears, asking you where you want the report sent. See Figure 8.7.
2. Select **N**one, Report to **P**rinter, or Report to **F**ile.
3. Press the **O**K button to return to CP Backup or press the **C**ancel button to cancel any changes.

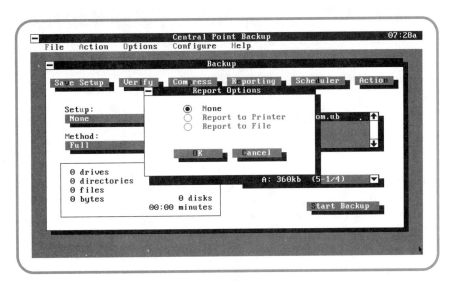

Figure 8.7   The Report Options dialog box.

Overwrite Warning

The Overwrite Warning option lets you control the alert messages provided by CP Backup. The Overwrite Warning option is turned off or on; when the default is on, the Overwrite Warning command in the Options menu is shown with a check mark. The Overwrite warning serves two purposes:

▶ Alerts you that CP Backup is about to overwrite a previously used backup diskette (see Figure 8.8).

▶ Alerts you that existing files will be overwritten during a restoration.

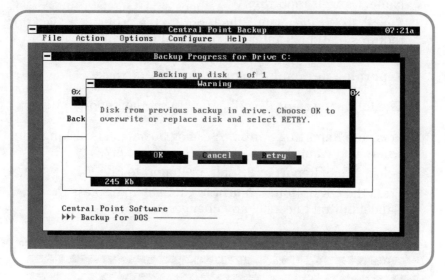

Figure 8.8   Warning dialog box displayed when using a diskette used in an earlier backup.

Time Display

The Time Display option toggles the time display during backup. It is turned off or on. When it is on, the Time Display command in the Options menu is shown with a check mark.

Save History

Whenever you perform a backup, CP Backup creates a history file that contains an index of all the files included in the backup. When you restore files, the first thing CP Backup does is read the backup history to determine which files were included in a specific backup operation. During the high and medium speed backups, the history file is stored in two places: on the last floppy disk of the backup set (or on the tape) and on the hard disk (in the directory that contains the CP Backup program files). At low speeds, or when you have the Save History file option off, the history file is stored only on the last floppy disk of the backup set or on the tape.

To turn the Save History option on or off, pull down the Options menu and select Save **H**istory. A check mark next to the option indicates Save History is on.

CP Backup's Defaults

213

Table 8.1 lists the backup options and their defaults. Unless you require otherwise, you should consider the defaults as the recommended setting.

Table 8.1   CP Backup Default Options

Option	Default
Backup Method	Full
Reporting	None
Compress	Minimize Time
Verify	Verify When Formatting
Media Format	DOS
Format Always	Off
Error Correction	On
Virus Detection	Off
Save History	On
Overwrite Warning	On
Time Display	On

Backing Up All Files on a Hard Disk

With the CP Backup program configured and the desired options selected, you can now back up your hard disk. If this is the first time you've backed up the drive, you should use the full backup method and back up everything on the disk.

During the backup process, CP Backup will prompt you to insert Disk Number *xx* into the drive. Write this number on the diskette so that you can readily identify it. If and when you need to restore the hard disk with previously backed up data, you'll be prompted to insert one or more of these numbered diskettes into the drive.

The following Quick Steps provide a simple procedure you can follow to back up your entire hard disk:

214

 Performing a Full Backup

1. Pull down the Action menu and select Backup From.

   The Backup From Directory dialog box appears as in Figure 8.9.

2. Select the disk(s) you want to back up. To select more than one disk, press the Allow Multiple Drive Backups button and select OK.

3. Select the Backup To box.

   A list of the available floppy drives and their capacities appears.

4. Select the drive and type of disk you're using from the list.

   The Fixed Drive option lets you back up to a different hard drive in your system. This is not recommended, however, because the backup copies take up valuable disk space and may suffer damage if your hard disk crashes.

5. Select Start Backup.

   The Name Backup Set dialog box appears, as in Figure 8.10.

6. Type a description for the backup set (up to 30 characters), and press Enter.

   For example, type
   `full backup drive c:`

7. Press the **OK** button to continue.

   A message appears, telling you to insert a disk into the specified drive.

8. Insert a disk, and select **OK**, if necessary.

   If CP Backup thinks the disk contains information, it displays a warning message.

9. If a warning message appears, select **OK** to override the warning, or switch disks and select **Retry**.

   The backup process begins, and the progress is displayed, as shown in Figure 8.11.

10. Switch disks when prompted.

    As you remove a backup disk, write a number on it to keep the disks in order.   □

215

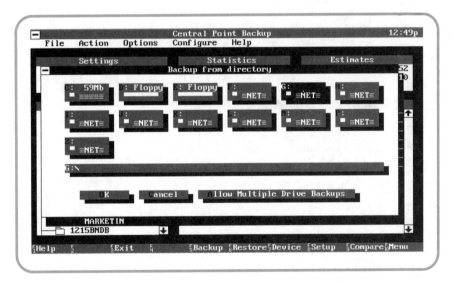

Figure 8.9   The Backup from Directory dialog box.

▶ **Tip:** If you're running CP Backup for Windows, you can continue working with your other Windows programs. CP Backup will work in the background and prompt you to switch disks as needed.

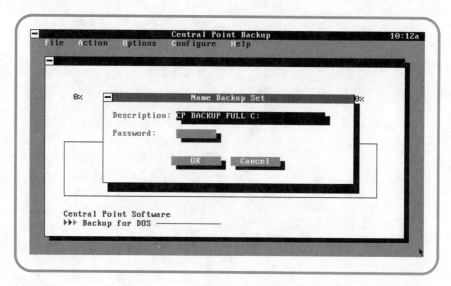

Figure 8.10   Assign a unique name to each set of backup disks.

216

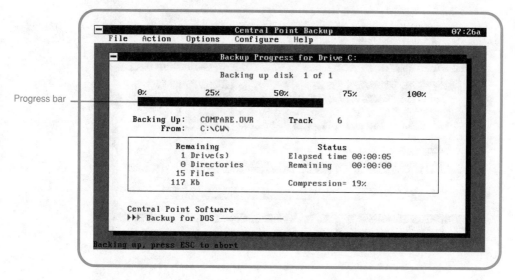

Figure 8.11   The progress of the backup is displayed.

When the backup is complete, store the backup diskettes in a safe place. If possible, store the diskettes in a fireproof safe or file cabinet. Do not remove the diskettes from the premises because you need ready access to them: for an emergency restoration and for the next backup at the end of the day or week.

Backing Up Modified Files

Now that you have a backup copy of all the files on your hard disk, you can perform daily, incremental backups to copy only those files that have changed since the full backup. You can perform two types of incremental backups: incremental and separate incremental. Incremental appends (attaches) the incremental backup to the last disk of your full backup, so you need only one set of backup disks. Separate incremental stores the incremental backup on a separate set of disks. The following steps assume you want to append the incremental:

 Performing an Incremental Backup

1. Pull down the Action menu and select Backup From.

    The Backup From Directory dialog box appears as in Figure 8.9.

2. Select the disk(s) you want to back up. To select more than one disk, press the Allow Multiple Drive Backups button.

3. Select the **M**ethod box and press Enter, or click on the down arrow to the right of the box.

    A list of backup methods appears.

4. Select **I**ncremental.

5. Select **S**tart Backup.

    A dialog box appears, telling you to insert the last floppy disk used in the full backup.

6. Insert the last floppy disk you used to back up the selected drive, and press Enter.

    CP Backup backs up all files since the last backup and all new files and stores the files on the last floppy disk in the set.   □

217

Backing Up Selected Directories and Files

You don't have to back up all the files on your hard disk. For example, you may have two or three directories that contain the data files you create. Because the files in these directories change more often than program files change, you may want to back up your data files daily and back up your program files once a month or whenever you add or modify a program.

With selective backups, you choose the directories and files you want to back up. You can also use the following commands to help you include or exclude directories or groups of files:

▶ Subdirectory Inclusion

▶ Include/Exclude Files

▶ Attribute Exclusions

▶ Date Range Selection

Choosing Directories

By default, CP Backup does not display a Directory Tree and File List window like those in PC Shell. However, you can view and use a similar display by highlighting a drive in the Backup From box and pressing Enter or by clicking on the drive. The screen changes to show the selected drive's directory tree and file list, as in Figure 8.12. If the directory tree and file list do not appear, press Enter again or click on the drive.

Selected subdirectories and files are shown highlighted in the Directory Tree and File List windows. Initially, all directories and files are selected.

To deselect all subdirectories and select them individually:

1. With the current selection on the root directory (c:\), press Enter or click the left mouse button. This deselects all subdirectories and files.

2. With the cursor keys or right mouse button, scroll through the directory tree until you reach the subdirectory you want to include.

3. Press Enter or click the left mouse button to select the subdirectory.

4. Repeat Steps 4 and 5 until you have selected all subdirectories to back up.

If you make a mistake and select a subdirectory you didn't mean to include, highlight the subdirectory and press Enter again or click on it with the left mouse button.

If you're using a mouse, you can select several subdirectories at once by dragging over them. Position the mouse cursor on the first directory you want, press and hold the right mouse button, press and hold the left mouse button, and drag the mouse to the last directory in the series. Release both mouse buttons.

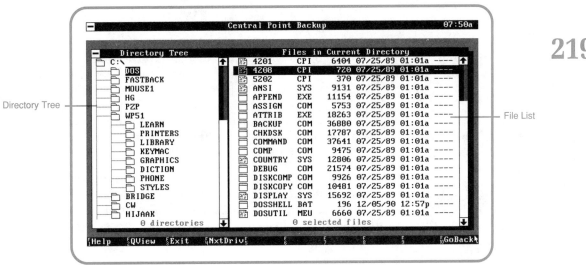

Directory Tree

File List

Figure 8.12   Select the directories and files you want to back up.

▶ **Tip**: If you want to back up more than half the directories, you can use the same procedure to exclude directories. After displaying the directory tree, don't start by deselecting the entire tree. Instead, scroll through the tree and select those subdirectories you want *excluded* from the backup. Press Enter or the left mouse button to deselect them.

You can select or unselect individual files the same way. To select a file:

1. With the current selection on the root directory, press Enter or click the left mouse button. This deselects all subdirectories and files.

2. With the cursor keys or right mouse button, scroll through the directory tree until you reach the subdirectory that contains the files you want.

3. Press the Tab key or click inside the File List window.

4. With the cursor keys or right mouse button, scroll through the directory list until you reach the files you want to back up.

5. Press the Enter key or click the left mouse button to select a file.

6. Select another file or press the Tab key to reactivate the Directory Tree window and select another subdirectory. Repeat Steps 2 through 5 until you've selected all the files you want to
back up.

220

If you make a mistake and select a file you didn't mean to include, highlight the file and press Enter again or click the left mouse button.

If you're using a mouse, you can select several files at once by dragging over them. Position the mouse cursor on the first file you want, press and hold the right mouse button, press and hold the left mouse button, and drag the mouse to the last file in the series. Release both mouse buttons.

Subdirectory Inclusion

The Subdirectory Inclusion option is a toggle that you turn off and on (it's normally on). When on, selecting a subdirectory also selects any subdirectories contained within it. When off, selecting a subdirectory affects only the directory you choose.

To turn Subdirectory Inclusion on or off:

1. Pull down the Options menu and choose **S**election Options. A submenu appears, listing the four selection options.

2. Select **Su**bdirectory Inclusion. A check mark next to the option indicates it's on.

Include/Exclude Files

The Include/Exclude files command lets you indicate the subdirectories and file types you want to either include or exclude in the backup. To include or exclude a group of files, pull down the Options menu, choose **S**election Options, and then Include/Exclude Files. The Include/Exclude Files dialog box appears as in Figure 8.13. You can type up to 16 directories and wild-card entries to specify the directories and files you want included and excluded in the backup.

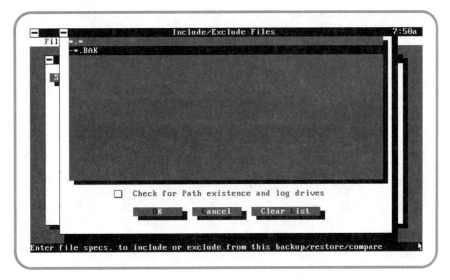

221

Figure 8.13   The Include/Exclude files dialog box with the default *.* entry.

To enter a directory, type the path name. To enter a file, type the file name (you may use the * and ? wild cards, as necessary). To exclude a directory or group of files, type a hyphen (-) before the entry. Here are some examples:

. includes the whole disk. (This is the default CP Backup starts with.)

. includes all files under the root directory.

\PCTOOLS*.* includes all files under the PCTOOLS subdirectory.

-\PCTOOLS*.* excludes all files under the PCTOOLS subdirectory.

*.COM includes files with the .COM extension (in all directories).

*.COM includes files with the .COM extension (in the root directory only).

-\WP50*.DOC excludes files with a .DOC extension in the WP50 subdirectory.

Attribute Exclusions

The Attribute Exclusions command lets you exclude those files on the entire hard disk that conform to any or all of the following attributes:

▶ Hidden
▶ System
▶ Read Only

222

> ▶ **Note:** With the Include Subdirectory option on, including or excluding a particular subdirectory will also affect any subdirectories contained within it. If the Include Subdirectory option is off, only the indicated subdirectory is affected. You should set the Include Subdirectory option before using the Include/Exclude Files command. If you change the Include Subdirectory option, rechoose the Include/Exclude Files command, and press the **OK** button. This resets the selection and prepares the program for the backup.

The following steps describe how to set the Attribute Exclusions option:

1. Pull down the Options menu and choose **S**election Options.
2. Select **A**ttribute Exclusions. The dialog box shown in Figure 8.14 appears.
3. Select the attribute type for the files you want to exclude from the backup. You can indicate any or all of the attribute options.
4. Press **O**K when you're done.

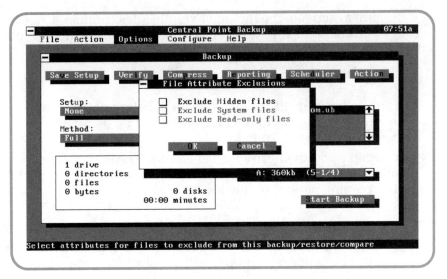

Figure 8.14   The File Attribute Exclusions dialog box.

223

Date Range Selection

The Date Range Selection command lets you set a time frame for files to include in the backup. Set a starting and ending range date, and CP Backup backs up only those files created or edited between the two dates.

To set the Date Range Selection:

1. Pull down the Options menu and choose **S**election Options.
2. Select **D**ate Range Selection.
3. Turn the Date Range Selection function on by choosing the **ON** option.
4. Enter a starting date into the Range From field.
5. Enter an ending date into the Range To field.
6. Press the **O**K button to activate your date selection.

Be sure to activate the Include/Exclude Files command, or the settings you make in the Date Range Selection box will have no effect.

Other suggestions:

▶ You can back up all files made after a certain date by entering the desired date in the From field and by using the current date in the To field.

▶ You can back up all files made before a certain date by entering 01/01/80 in the From field (the start of the PC clock timekeeping period) to the desired date.

▶ **Tip:** The Date Range Selection command is best used when your computer is equipped with a clock/calendar (with battery backup) function. If the files you create always say they were made on January 1, 1980, then your computer does not have a battery-supplied clock/calendar, and you should not use the Date Range Selection technique.

224

Saving Setup Selections

Setting the backup options and selected directories and files to include in a backup can be time-consuming. To save time, save your settings and selections in a *setup file*. For example, you can create one setup file for your weekly (full) backup and another setup file for your daily (incremental) backups. Once all your settings are entered, perform the following Quick Steps to create a setup file:

 Saving the Current Setup

1. Press the Save Setup button.	A dialog box appears, prompting you to type a name for the setup file.
2. Enter a name for the setup file. (Don't use an extension.)	Names the setup file.
3. Press the OK button.	Stores the setup file. □

The settings are now saved in a special file. These settings include the Backup From entry, specifications about the drive and backup media you're using, the Compress option you selected, the directories and files you want included and excluded, and any other options you may have chosen. The following Quick Steps tell how to use the setup files you create:

 Using a Setup File

1. Be sure that you don't need to save any options you've changed during the current session with CP Backup.	Prevents you from losing any important setting you've made in the current session.
2. Press Alt-U or click on the Setup box.	This pulls down the Setup list, displaying the setup files you created.
3. Select the setup file you want to use.	Identifies the setup you want to use. ☐

Saving Default Settings

225

If you don't care for the defaults CP Backup initially presents you, and you don't want to bother with creating a special setup file just for various types of backups, use the Save as **D**efault command from the File menu to record your own selections. The options stored when using the Save as Default command are the same as those saved in the setup file. The settings are recorded in the PCBACKUP.CFG file. If this file is ever damaged or erased, your new defaults will be lost.

Restoring a Hard Disk

Should anything ever happen to the data on your hard disk, you can recover it with the backup disks you made with CP Backup. You can restore the entire contents of the hard disk, or only the subdirectories and files you lost.

Should you experience a complete loss of data on your hard disk, you'll need to reformat your hard disk (using PC Format) and replace DOS before you can use CP Backup. The CP Backup files must reside on the hard disk before you can restore the lost data. However, before you reformat your hard disk, you should try to fix your disk using one of the PC Tools data recovery programs explained in Chapter 9.

> ▶ **Tip**: During the restore process, you'll be asked to insert a specific numbered disk into the drive. If you forgot to number the disks, use the CPBDIR program, included with PC Tools. CPBDIR reads the contents of the disk and displays its number, as provided by CP Backup (refer to the example in Figure 8.15). To use the program, change to the C:\PCTOOLS\SYSTEM directory, type `cpbdir`, and press Enter. Enter the letter of the drive that contains the backup floppy disk (for example `a:`). Remember to write the number on the disk.

```
C:\COLLAGE>cd\pctools\system

C:\PCTOOLS\SYSTEM>cpbdir
Central Point Backup Directory Report V7
Copyright (c) 1990,1991 by Central Point Software. All Rights Reserved.

What floppy drive contains the backup disk (default A:), Q to quit?a:

Disk is number 1 of a CP Backup set, backed up at 10:17a on 06/20/1991.
Disk was created with release 6.0 or 7.0 of CP Backup
The directory starts on track 70 (46h) of this disk.
This disk is recorded in DOS standard format.
Advanced Error Correction was ON for this backup.


What floppy drive contains the backup disk (default A:), Q to quit?q
```

Figure 8.15   *Disk information provided by the CP Backup program.*

Full Restore

A full restore completely rebuilds the files and subdirectories on your hard disk.

1. Start CP Backup, and select **R**estore from the opening menu. The Restore screen appears, shown in Figure 8.16.

2. Select the Restore From box. This opens a pull-down list, also shown in Figure 8.16.

3. Select the type of disks that contain the backup files you want to restore.

4. Select Retrieve Hist to use the history that's stored on the backup disks. A prompt appears, telling you to insert the last disk of the backup set in the drive.

5. Insert the last floppy disk of your backup set into the drive. The backup history is retrieved.

6. Replace the last disk of the backup set with the first disk of the set.

7. Select **S**tart Restore. CP Backup starts restoring the files from the floppy disk to the hard disk. The progress is displayed as in Figure 8.17. If Restore finds a file on the hard disk whose name matches one of the backup files, you'll see the Warning box offer the following options:

> **Overwrite** replaces the hard disk file with the backup file.
>
> **Overwrite with Newer File Only** replaces the hard disk file with the backup file only if the backup file is more recent.
>
> **Skip This File** does not replace the version on the hard disk.
>
> **Repeat for All Later Files** tells the program to perform the operation you selected on all subsequent files.

8. If the Warning box appears, enter your selection, and then select **O**K. The restoration continues.

9. Follow the on-screen prompts, and swap disks when told to do so.

227

As soon as possible, you should check the integrity of the program and data files to make sure the restoration was a success. If you make another backup of the hard disk, use a new set of diskettes and keep the original backup until you are sure that all files on your hard disk are intact.

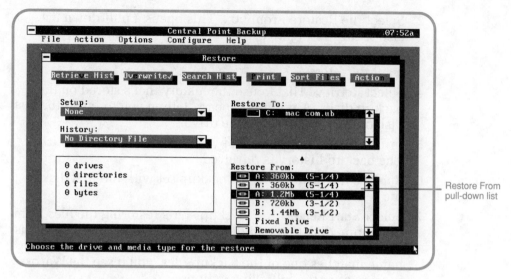

Figure 8.16 *The Restore screen with the Restore From pull-down list displayed.*

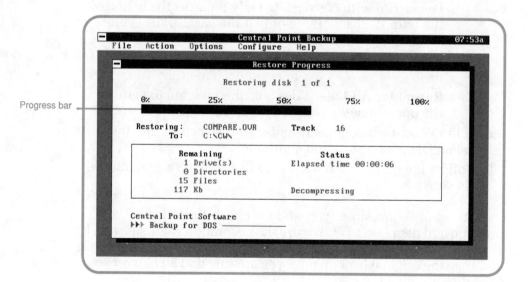

Figure 8.17 *CP Backup displays the progress of the restoration.*

> ▶ **Tip**: If your hard disk is partitioned into several drives (for example C, D, E, F), you can use the Restore **To** command on the Action menu to restore the backup files to a hard disk other than the original. You can also restore the files to a hard disk on another computer, assuming CP Backup is installed on the other computer. Just make sure you don't overwrite files of the same name on the other computer.

Partial Restoration

Partial restoration lets you restore only selected files or subdirectories. Use this procedure if only some of the files on your hard disk have become corrupted or erased. (Before using Restore, try to undelete files using the PC Tools Undelete command, as discussed in Chapter 9.)

229

For partial restoration of hard disk data:

1. Start CP Backup and select **R**estore from the opening menu.
2. In the Restore **T**o box, select the drive that contained the files you want to restore.
3. If you used the Save History option to save the backup history to your hard disk, select a history from the History box. A directory tree appears, as in Figure 8.18, showing the directories that will be restored.

   If you did not use Save History, insert the last disk in the backup set into the floppy drive and choose Retrieve History. Then, select Inserted Floppy from the History box.
4. To select or unselect a directory in the tree, highlight it and press Enter or click on it. Selected directories are highlighted; unselected directories are not.
5. Press the Tab key or click in the File List window to activate the file list. To select or unselect a file in the list, highlight it and press Enter.
6. Repeat Steps 4 and 5 until you've selected all the directories and files you want to restore. Press Esc when you're done.
7. Select **S**tart Restore. CP Backup starts restoring the files from the floppy disk to the hard disk. If Restore finds a file on the hard disk whose name matches one of the backup files, you'll see the Warning box.

8. If the Warning box appears, enter your selection, and then select **OK**. The restoration continues.

9. Follow the on-screen prompts, and swap disks when told to do so.

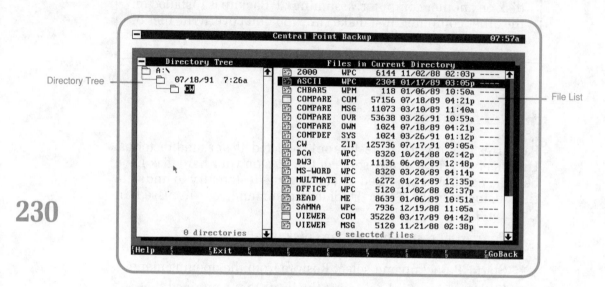

Figure 8.18   *Select only the directories and files you want to restore.*

As soon as possible, you should check the integrity of the program and data files to make sure the restoration was a success. If you make another backup of the hard disk, use a new set of diskettes and keep the original backup until you are sure that all files on your hard disk are intact.

Refer to the PC Tools Hard Disk Backup manual for additional information if you are attempting to restore hard disk data with damaged or lost disks.

Comparing Data on Disks

Making backups helps preserve your data. But things can go wrong. There's always a danger that you will lose perfectly good files by

230

restoring them with older versions. For example, you create a file on Monday, then back it up on Tuesday. On Wednesday, you edit the file making significant changes. Then, something happens to the hard disk on Thursday. Do you use Tuesday's backup to restore the data? If you do, you forfeit the alterations you made to the file.

You may not always be aware of the number and extent of changes between the data on your hard disk (if any of it is still good) and the data on your backup disks. You may want to be sure that the information on your backup disks is an exact duplicate of the data on your hard disk. CP Backup offers a Compare feature where you can compare the data on a hard disk against that on your backup diskettes (or tape). Differences are noted.

We'll assume you are checking the data on a new set of backup diskettes with the original on your hard disk.

1. Start CP Backup, and select **C**ompare from the opening menu. The Compare screen appears; it is very similar to the Restore screen.
2. Select the Compare **F**rom box.
3. Select the type of disks that contain the backup files you want to compare.
4. If you used the Save History option to save the backup history to your hard drive, select a history from the Histor**y** box. Otherwise, insert the last disk in the backup set into the floppy drive and choose Retrieve History.
5. Replace the last disk of the backup set with the first disk of the set.
6. Select **S**tart Compare.

At the end of the comparison, CP Backup summarizes its findings, indicating the number of files that were equal, and those that were missing, older, newer, mismatches, and/or had different times/dates. It marks each file with one of the characters shown in Table 8.2 to indicate the results. Select **O**K when you are done.

231

Table 8.2   *Symbols Used During Backup Comparison*

Symbol	Meaning
=	Backup file is identical to original.
s	Backup file date differs from date of original file, but otherwise files compare.
<	Backup file is older than original, and files do not compare.
>	Backup file is newer than original, and files do not compare.
-	Backup file missing from hard disk.
x	Backup file does not compare with original, but date/time matches.

Notice that file comparisons are not always accurate if:

▶ A terminate-and-stay-resident program is currently running.
▶ You have changed backup speeds.

Changing User Levels

As with PC Shell, CP Backup lets you adjust the user level. The default user level is Advanced, meaning all the commands are available to you and listed in the menus. If you desire, you can change the user level to Beginning or Intermediate. Doing so will remove some of the more advanced commands from the menus, making the program less intimidating.

To change the user level:

1. Pull down the Configure menu and select **U**ser Level.
2. Select one of the user level options: **B**eginner, **I**ntermediate, or **A**dvanced.
3. Choose the **E**xpress Mode option if you want the Directory Tree and File List window displayed at all times, as in Figure 8.19. Some users find this screen easier to work with, but it may slow you down.
4. Click **OK** to accept the change.

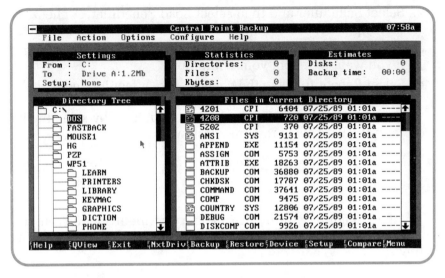

*Figure 8.19   With Express Mode off, the Directory Tree and File
List window are displayed at all times.*

233

Scheduling Backups

An interesting tool you can use along with CP Backup is the
Scheduler, which lets you schedule automatic backups. This is
useful if you back up to a tape drive or to your hard disk drive,
because it lets you perform backups while you're away from your
computer. If you back up to floppy diskettes, the Scheduler is useful
in reminding you to perform your backups.

Before you can use the Scheduler, you need to create your
backup setup files, as explained earlier. If you use both the DOS and
Windows versions of CP Backup, you must create setup files separately for each program. You can't access the setup files you create
for the DOS version in Windows or vice versa.

Also, your computer must be on and the Scheduler must be
loaded into your computer's memory in order for it to initiate the
backup process. If you plan on using the Scheduler daily, you should
have it loaded into memory automatically whenever you start your
computer. If you did not choose to do this while installing PC Tools,
do it now:

1. Change to the PC Tools directory, type `install`, and press
    Enter.

2. Select **Sc**heduler and then select **L**oad Scheduler. A check mark appears, indicating that the option is on.

3. Select **OK, Ex**it, and then **OK**. A prompt will appear, asking if you want to reboot your computer.

4. Select **R**eboot to make the changes take affect immediately.

You can load the CPS Scheduler in Windows by selecting its icon from the PC Tools program window.

Scheduling Backups in the DOS Version

With the Scheduler running in memory-resident mode, you can specify which setup files you want to use on each day of the week as follows:

1. Start CP Backup and choose **B**ackup.

2. Press the Scheduler button. The Schedule Backups dialog box appears (see Figure 8.20).

3. In the Name box, type the name of the setup file you created for performing this backup.

4. Select all the days of the week on which you want to perform this particular backup. For example, you may want to perform a full backup on Friday or perform incremental backups on Monday through Thursday.

5. In the Run Time box, type the time of day you want the backup performed.

6. Select **OK**.

7. Press the **S**ave button. This returns you to the Backup screen.

Remember, the Scheduler is running in the background. It will notify you 15 seconds before the backup is to begin. If you're backing up to floppy disks, you'll be told to insert a disk into the floppy drive, and then the CP Backup will automatically perform the specified backup. If you are backing up to a tape drive or to your hard drive, the Scheduler will automatically perform the necessary backup; you won't have to insert a disk.

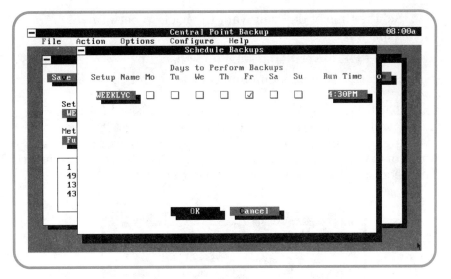

Figure 8.20   Specify the dates and times you want the specified backup to be run.

235

Scheduling Backups in Windows

Once the Scheduler is running in memory-resident mode, you can specify which setup files you want to use on each day of the week as follows:

1. Start CP Backup from Windows and select **B**ackup.
2. Press the Sche**d**uler button and then the **B**ackup button.
3. Select **A**dd to add a setup file. The Add New Backup Schedule Item dialog box appears (see Figure 8.21).
4. Select the Setup File box to see a list of setup files you created.
5. Select a setup file from the list.
6. Select all the days of the week on which you want to perform this particular backup. For example, you may want to perform a full backup on Friday and perform incremental backups on Monday through Thursday.

7. Set the time of day you want the backup performed.

8. Select **OK**.

9. Select **OK** to verify the scheduled backup.

10. Open the Control menu and select **Minimize**.

The CPS Scheduler is minimized, but it's still running. It will notify you when you need to insert a disk, and then it will automatically perform the specified backup. If you are backing up to a tape drive or to your hard drive, the Scheduler will automatically perform the necessary backup; you won't have to insert a disk.

Figure 8.21 *Specify the dates and times you want the specified backup to be run.*

236

What You Have Learned

In this chapter you learned the procedures for backing up and restoring hard disks using CP Backup. You also learned:

▶ Backups are only as good as the last backup you made. An old back up means you have old data.

▶ CP Backup recognizes the archive bit and can use it to decide which files on your hard disk need to be backed up.

▶ There are five types of backups: full, full copy, incremental, separate incremental, and differential.

▶ An ideal backup strategy is one full backup every week, plus an incremental backup at the end of each day.

▶ Before you can use CP Backup for the first time, you must tell it what drive types you have in your computer and the type of media you'll be using.

▶ Backups made with the High Speed option go faster, but your computer must be compatible.

▶ You can back up your entire hard disk or just selected portions of it.

▶ CP Backup allows you to restore the entire hard disk or just selected subdirectories and files.

237

Recovering Lost Files and Damaged Disks

In This Chapter

239

- ▶ *How DOS disks are structured*
- ▶ *Protecting your files*
- ▶ *Reclaiming accidentally erased files*
- ▶ *Recovering from accidental format*
- ▶ *Verifying files and disks*

Computer disks are not safe-deposit boxes where you can stockpile files and always expect to retrieve them unharmed. While you can be reasonably sure that the files you place on the disk will remain in good condition, not all fare so well. You may accidentally erase a file or reformat your hard disk. Or, maybe your computer experiences a glitch and accidentally records data on the disk where it's not supposed to.

PC Tools provides many features to help you restore lost files and disks. These include an Undelete command to assist you in reclaiming files you or an applications program deleted in error. PC Tools also offers the Mirror program for recording backups of the file allocation table (FAT), as well as Unformat to recover disks you may have accidently formatted.

Limitations and Caveats

As with all tools, your success in using PC Tools to restore lost files and disks relies heavily on your personal knowledge and expertise. While PC Tools provides many automatic measures for restoring lost files and damaged disks—and these measures will be used for the majority of file and disk recovery operations you supervise—certain situations may require manual intervention. The more you know about your computer and the way it operates, the better chance you have of recovering lost data.

Don't Panic

You may never need to use the file and disk recovery features of PC Tools, but it's nice to know they're there in case you do. If a problem arises, follow three simple rules:

1. Don't panic.
2. Don't turn off your computer.
3. Don't save or copy any files to disk.

Often, the error can be corrected with one or two minor steps. Working in a frenzy because you're afraid you've lost valuable data will cloud your reasoning. Slow down and analyze the situation before you proceed. As long as you don't do anything, the problem can't get any worse. If you're not sure about what you're doing, seek capable help.

Important Terms

Before you use PC Tools for automatic or manual file and disk recovery, you need to acquaint yourself with some basic terms. These terms relate to data files and how they are recorded on your disks.

Data on a computer disk is recorded in concentric tracks. If you could see the tracks, they would appear as rings starting at the center of the disk and spreading outward. Unlike the groove on a record, which is a continuous spiral from the outside to the inside, computer disk tracks are self-contained rings.

The number of tracks varies depending on media type and capacity. Standard double-sided, double-density (360K) diskettes contain a total of 80 tracks—40 on each side. A moderate size hard disk (about 40M) may contain 600 or more tracks, divided among 3 or 4 separate disks.

The data on the disk is further divided into sectors, as shown in Figure 9.1. A *sector* is a particular segment of the track. By dividing each track into individual sectors, the computer can more readily store and later retrieve data. As with tracks, the number of sectors differs from disk to disk. Regular IBM 360K floppy diskettes contain 9 sectors per track; many hard disk drives use 25 or 30 sectors per track. Some hard disk drives exceed 31 sectors per track, but these are considered nonstandard to many PC utility programs. Fortunately, PC Tools is not one of them.

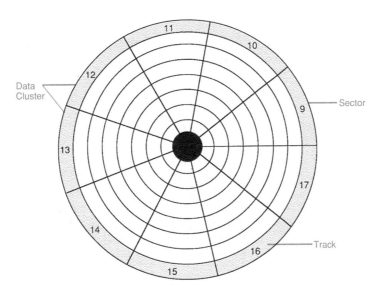

Figure 9.1   Sectors and clusters.

Sectors are grouped into clusters. A *cluster* is the smallest unit the computer can manipulate. Cluster size is expressed in kilobytes (K) and determines the smallest amount of space that a given file will take up. Even if a file is only 2 bytes long, it will still consume an entire cluster.

Each disk you format on your computer—whether it's a hard or floppy disk—is composed of four parts:

▶ Boot Record (or boot block)
▶ File Allocation Table (or FAT)
▶ Root Directory
▶ Data Area

These parts are located on the disk in a specific sequence, as shown in Figure 9.2. Depending on the type of media and its capacity, the physical size of the FAT, root directory, and data area may vary.

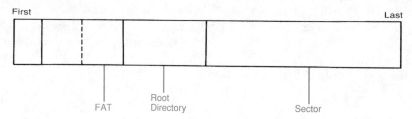

First   Last

              FAT   Root   Sector
                         Directory

Figure 9.2   Arrangement of vital data on your hard disk drive, starting with the boot record.

Boot Record

Every disk has a *boot record*, even if the disk isn't bootable; that is, even if you can't use it to start your computer. The boot record contains vital information that your computer uses to begin operation when it's first turned on. If the disk also contains the necessary system files (IBMBIO.COM, IBMDOS.COM, and COMMAND.COM), you can use it to start your computer. If the disk lacks system files, and you try to use it to boot your computer, you'll get a *nonsystem disk error*.

The data in the boot record is necessary if you want to start your computer with that disk. If something happens to the boot record data, it's likely that the disk will no longer start your computer.

File Allocation Table

The *file allocation table (FAT)* can be likened to a seating chart in a school room. On the sheet are check boxes that correspond to the seats in the room. When a student is present, the corresponding check box is marked. When the student is absent, the check box is empty.

The FAT records all the clusters on the disk that contain valid data. When you save a file to disk, it is stored in one or more clusters. The FAT keeps track of which clusters are occupied and which are empty. The FAT also keeps track of which clusters hold the information contained in each individual file. For example, if a single file is stored on several clusters in various areas on the disk, the FAT tells your computer where to look for the data. When you delete a file, you notify the FAT that certain clusters are no longer occupied and can be used to store a new file.

Damage to the FAT can be disastrous. Even if the files you stored on disk are in perfect condition, your computer will not be able to find them.

Root Directory

Every disk has a *root directory*, even if you don't use subdirectories. The root directory contains a list of all the files and subdirectories contained on the disk. (*Subdirectories* branch off from the root directory.) Damage to the root directory generally means that one or more of the files or subdirectories on your disk may be inaccessible.

The root directory plays an important role when formatting a hard disk using the DOS FORMAT command. Because reformatting the entire disk can consume a lot of time, DOS takes a shortcut and simply erases the file and subdirectory names in the root directory. The actual files and subdirectories remain. PC Tools uses this method to its advantage when reclaiming a hard disk you've accidentally reformatted.

Data Area

The actual files—whether they are contained in subdirectories or not—are placed in the *data area* of the disk. Each file consumes a specific amount of the data area, as dictated by the size of the file and the cluster size of the disk.

Files larger than one cluster are distributed among two or more clusters. As illustrated in Figure 9.3, these clusters may not always be together (contiguous) on the disk. In fact, depending on how often you erase and add data, files may be strewn all over the disk, reducing its efficiency. To read a file, the drive's read/write head will have to move back and forth over the disk.

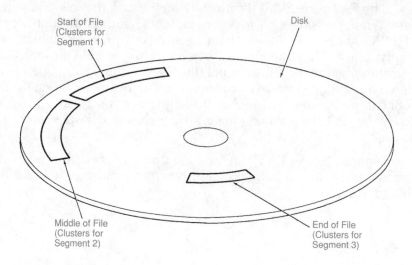

Start of File
(Clusters for
Segment 1)

Disk

Middle of File
(Clusters for
Segment 2)

End of File
(Clusters for
Segment 3)

Figure 9.3   A fragmented file is stored in noncontiguous clusters distributed over the disk.

Preparing for Disaster

While the PC Tools data recovery programs are often used successfully with little preparation, they're much more reliable if you take the proper steps before disaster strikes:

▶ *Back up your hard disk daily.* The best protection for your files is an up-to-date backup. If anything happens to the files on your hard disk, you can then restore the files without loss. (Refer to Chapter 8 for details on backing up your hard disk.)

▶ *Create a recovery disk.* The recovery disk contains the files required to boot your computer along with copies of the PC Tools data recovery programs. You may have created a recovery disk during the installation process. If you didn't, this chapter will lead you through the process.

▶ *Use PC Format instead of DOS Format to format disks.* PC
Format prevents you from accidentally formatting your hard
disk. It also offers a Safe Format option that lets you recover
data in the event of an accidental format. (See Chapter 6 for
information on using PC Format to format floppy diskettes.
See Chapter 10 for formatting hard disks.)

▶ *Install Mirror in your AUTOEXEC.BAT file.* This runs the
Mirror program every time you start your computer. Mirror
takes a picture of the FAT. If the FAT gets damaged, you can
use the Unformat program or DiskFix to rebuild the FAT
using Mirror's copy. (Mirror is discussed in the next section.)

▶ *Install the Delete Tracker or Delete Sentry in your
AUTOEXEC.BAT file.* The Delete Tracker keeps track of the
names of any files you delete. When you use the Undelete
program, you can then select the files you want to undelete
from a list of deleted files. Delete Sentry keeps a copy of
each file you delete in a separate, hidden directory called
\SENTRY. If you delete a file by mistake, you can get a copy
of it from the \SENTRY directory.

▶ *Run Compress regularly.* The Compress program reduces file
fragmentation, making sure each file is stored in contiguous
clusters. This makes it easier for the data recovery programs
to undelete files without losing parts of the file. (Refer to
Chapter 10 for more on Compress.)

▶ *Run DiskFix regularly.* DiskFix scans your disks and discovers any problems, such as bad clusters. DiskFix can often
correct problems with the disk or prevent problem areas
from being used. (Refer to Chapter 10 for more on DiskFix.)

245

Most of these preventive programs run in the background, once
you set them up; PC Format is automatic, Mirror runs when you start
your computer, and Delete Tracker or Delete Sentry are loaded into
memory on startup. You'll hardly know they're there, until you need
them.

Running Mirror

Each time the Mirror program is run, it samples the contents of the
FAT, root directory, and boot record of your hard disk. (You can also
use Mirror on floppy disk drives; the technique is the same.) Mirror
is not a memory-resident program. Once you run it, it creates the
backup file of the FAT, root directory, and boot record and returns
control of your computer to you.

You can run Mirror manually or you can have it run automatically each time your computer starts. To run it manually, type

```
MIRROR
```

at the DOS prompt. Mirror assumes you want to take a snapshot of the FAT, root directory, and boot record of the same disk that contains the Mirror program. If you want to take a snapshot of a different disk, type

```
MIRROR d:
```

where *d:* is another drive in your computer.

To run Mirror automatically when you start the computer, add the MIRROR command to your AUTOEXEC.BAT file. The PC Tools manual suggests you add the Mirror command *after* the commands that load your mouse drivers and print spooler (if any), but *before* you install any other memory-resident programs, including PC Shell and Desktop. You can edit your AUTOEXEC.BAT file if you know how, or you can have the INSTALL program add the Mirror command for you by following these steps:

1. Exit any programs that are currently running and display the DOS prompt.
2. Change to the drive and directory that contains the PC Tools program files. This is usually C:\PCTOOLS.
3. Type `install` and press Enter. The PC Tools Program Configuration screen appears.
4. Select Mirror. The Mirror dialog box appears.
5. Select **R**un Mirror. A check mark next to the option indicates it's on.
6. Select **O**K to return to the main Configuration screen.
7. Select E**x**it.
8. Select **S**ave Configuration to put a check mark in the box, and then select **O**K.
9. Select **R**eboot if you want to run Mirror now, or select **D**OS if you want Mirror to run the next time you boot your computer.

At the very least, you should run Mirror once a day. If you've done a lot of work during a particular day, you may want to quit whatever you're doing and run Mirror again to update Mirror's copy of the FAT. Like backups, a copy of the FAT is best if it's up-to-date.

Using the Delete Tracker or Delete Sentry

When you delete a file, DOS doesn't actually remove the contents of the file from disk. DOS deletes the first character of the file name from the listing in the disk directory. This tells your computer that the space which the file occupied is available to store another file. As long as you don't save another file to disk, you can get back the file(s) you deleted. All you have to do is run the PC Tools Undelete program and supply the first letter of each deleted file's name.

PC Tools includes a Data Monitor that offers additional protection for deleted files. Whenever you delete a file, the Data Monitor keeps a record of it, allowing you to undelete it. The Data Monitor offers two programs from which you can choose: Delete Tracker and Delete Sentry.

Delete Tracker is a small memory-resident program that creates a copy of the disk directory (in a file called PCTRACKER.DEL). This file contains the full names of all deleted files. If you run the Undelete program to undelete files protected with the Delete Tracker, you don't have to supply the first character of the deleted file's name. You simply select the file(s) you want to undelete from a list. The Delete Tracking file is updated every time you erase or delete a file.

247

Delete Sentry offers more protection than Delete Tracker, but requires more disk space. This memory-resident program stores a copy of each deleted file in a separate, hidden directory (\SENTRY) on each disk that it protects. Because you have a copy of the file, you can undelete a file even if you've saved another file on the clusters which the deleted file once occupied.

Unless you've already installed Delete Tracker or Delete Sentry during the installation process, you should install one of them now by using the PC Tools Program Configuration menu:

1. Exit any programs that are currently running and display the DOS prompt.
2. Change to the drive and directory that contains the PC Tools program files. This is usually C:\PCTOOLS.
3. Type `install` and press Enter. The PC Tools Program Configuration screen appears.
4. Select Data Monitor. The Data Monitor dialog box appears.
5. Select Delete **S**entry or Delete **T**racker. A dot next to the option indicates it's active.
6. Select **O**K to return to the main Configuration screen.
7. Select E**x**it.

248

8. Select **S**ave Configuration to put a check mark in the box, and then select **O**K.

9. Select **D**OS.

Before you load either program, you should check its configuration settings to make sure the program will protect the files you want protected. At the DOS prompt, type `datamon` and press Enter. Thisbrings up the Data Monitor configuration screen as in Figure 9.4. Select **D**elete Protection. Select Delete **T**racker or Delete **S**entry and then press **O**K to configure the program you just installed.

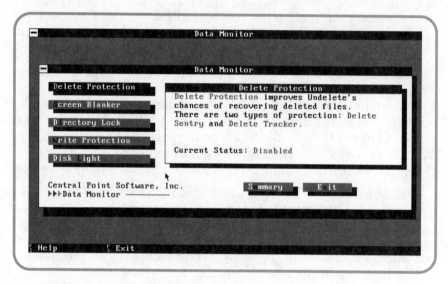

Figure 9.4   The Data Monitor configuration screen.

If you choose Delete **T**racker, a dialog box appears, prompting you to specify the drives you want Delete Tracker to protect. Choose one or more drives and then select **O**K.

If you choose Delete **S**entry, you'll see the dialog box shown in Figure 9.5. Select the options as follows:

1. To protect all files on all selected disks, select All **F**iles.

2. To protect selected groups of files, select Only **S**pecified Files, and then type entries in the Include and Exclude lists to indicate files you want included (protected) or excluded (unprotected). Most word processing, spreadsheet, and graphic packages use standard file extentions such as .DOC (Microsoft Word), .WPF (WordPerfect), .PCX (PC Paint), and .WK1 (Lotus 1-2-3). By entering these extensions in the

Include list, you will protect your work from accidental deletion.

To exclude backup files with the extensions .BAK or .BK, you would type `*.bak` and `*.bk` in the Exclude list.

3. Select Do **N**ot Save Archived Files to prevent Sentry from saving any files that are marked as backed up.

4. Type a number in the Purge Files After *<blank>* Days box to have Sentry automatically delete the files in the \SENTRY directory after every specified number of days. This prevents the directory from getting packed with useless files.

5. Type a percentage in the Reserve box to specify the amount of space you want reserved on the hard disk for the \SENTRY directory. When the directory reaches the specified size, Sentry will begin to purge files, starting with the oldest one.

6. Select **D**rives and specify the drives you want Sentry to protect. Select **O**K when you're done.

7. Select E**x**it and then select **O**K to accept the changes you entered or **C**ancel to return to the default settings.

249

Once the Data Monitor program is configured, you must reboot your computer in order to install the program with its new settings in effect.

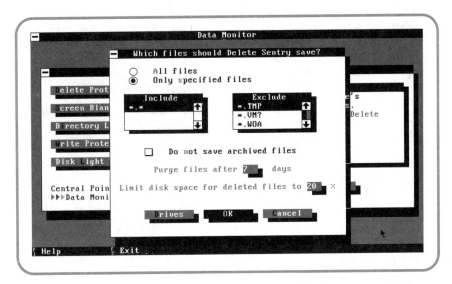

Figure 9.5   Use the Configure Sentry dialog box to specify how you want Sentry to run.

> ▶ **Note:** Because Delete Tracker and Delete Sentry are memory-resident programs, they may interfere with the operation of other memory-resident programs, or even your main applications. If you're receiving Out of Memory error messages, enter `datamon /unload` at the DOS prompt to remove Data Monitor from memory. Be sure to run the INSTALL program later, to remove the program from your AUTOEXEC.BAT file; otherwise, the program will load the next time you start your computer. You'll still be able to run the Undelete program, although it's success may be limited.

Making A Recovery Disk

250

If you did not create a recovery disk during the Installation process, create one now. First, use PC Format to format a blank diskette for use in drive A (see Chapter 6); use the Install system files option to make the disk bootable. (The INSTALL program won't allow you to create a recovery disk for use in drive B, because your system won't initially look to drive B for a bootable disk). Now, you can run the INSTALL program to turn the disk into a recovery disk:

 Making a Recovery Disk

1. Insert the PC Tools Installation Disk (Disk 1) into floppy drive A or B.

   You can't create a recovery disk by running INSTALL from your hard disk.

2. Type `install /rd` and press Enter.

   This starts the recovery disk section of the INSTALL program.

3. Select **OK**, specify the drive and directory in which PC Tools is installed, and select OK again.

   A dialog box appears, telling you to insert a disk formatted with the /S option into the drive. (The /S option is the same as the Install system files option.)

4. Insert the floppy disk into drive A and select **OK**.

   The INSTALL program creates the recovery disk and tells when the process is complete.

5. Select **OK** to exit the INSTALL program.

   □

You should test the recovery disk to make sure it can boot your computer. Insert the recovery disk into drive A and press Ctrl-Alt-Del. Because the disk does not include your system's AUTOEXEC.BAT file, you'll be prompted to enter a date and time, your DOS prompt will not include a directory, and without a path statement, you won't be able to run PC Tools from any DOS prompt. This is known as a *clean boot*. It's useful to clean boot if you can't boot from your hard disk or if you've modified your AUTOEXEC.BAT or CONFIG.SYS file and find that your changes have created all sorts of problems. You can clean boot and then edit the files to change them back to the way they were.

When Disaster Strikes

251

Most data is lost due to user error. You might format a disk by mistake or delete a group of files you thought you no longer needed. But even if you're a very careful user, your system is not infallible. The magnetic media on your hard disk can go bad, your FAT can get damaged, your boot sector can get wiped out, and other problems can arise for no apparent reason.

But now you're prepared. You should have a complete, up-to-date backup of all files on your hard disk, a recovery disk that you can use to clean boot your system and run many of the PC Tools recovery programs, a copy of your FAT (compliments of Mirror), and some protection for any files you recently deleted. So, what do you do when something goes wrong? That depends on the problem, but here are a few things you shouldn't do:

▶ Don't turn your computer off or reboot it. If your hard disk is capable of booting your computer, it may run Mirror every time you boot. If your FAT is damaged, Mirror will replace its good copy of the FAT with a copy of the damaged FAT, which will do you little good.

▶ If you turned your computer off, reboot it using the recovery disk you created. That way, you bypass the hard disk and won't inadvertently run any programs that could do more damage.

▶ Don't save any files to your hard disk or move any files. By saving or moving files, you risk writing information over the clusters that contain valuable information. This caution includes PC Tools files; don't install PC Tools on a drive that contains files you accidentally deleted.

Now that you know what *not* to do, here's a list of what you should do based on some of the more common problems you'll run into:

Problem	Approach
Deleted file by accident	Use the Undelete program. You can run Undelete from your hard disk or from the recovery disk. If Undelete cannot recover the file, use the Restore program, discussed in Chapter 8, to restore the lost files from your backup disks.
Accidentally formatted a disk	Use Unformat. You can run Unformat from your hard disk or from the recovery disk.
Missing files for no apparent reason	Try locating the files with FileFind, discussed in Chapter 5. You may not have saved the files where you think you saved them. Run DiskFix; it will perform a series of tests to help you determine the next step.
`Invalid Drive Specification` message; you can't access one of your drives	Run Rebuild to rebuild the partition table. (See the later section entitled, "Running Rebuild" for information about the partition tables.)
Computer won't boot from hard disk or unable to access disk	Run Rebuild to rebuild boot sector or CMOS. (See the later section entitled, "Running Rebuild" for information about CMOS.)
DiskFix or Compress marks many sectors on disk as bad	Run Rebuild to rebuild CMOS.
Other disk error or file error messages	Run DiskFix.

Reclaiming Deleted Files

PC Tools offers several methods for reclaiming deleted files either automatically or manually. If you use Delete Tracker or Delete Sentry, you can usually undelete recently deleted files simply by selecting them from a list, and the recovered files will be in good shape. If you don't use one of the data monitors, or if you want to recover files you deleted several days ago, you may be able to recover the files using one of the manual recovery techniques which you can access through the Undelete program.

Undeleting Files Automatically

253

Undelete is a stand-alone program run from Shell or from the DOS prompt. PC Tools also contains a Windows Undelete program, which is fully compatible with Windows. The Windows version functions in a similar fashion, but under a graphical interface. You can run Undelete in a variety of ways:

> ***From the DOS prompt***, change to the PC Tools directory, type `undel`, and press Enter. The Undelete screen appears as in Figure 9.6. If you're running Undelete from the recovery disk, change to the A drive before typing `undel`
>
> ***From PC Shell***, pull down the File menu and select Undelete.
>
> ***From Windows***, using a mouse, double-click on the Undelete icon (it's the icon showing an arrow coming out of a trash can). The Windows Undelete screen appears as in Figure 9.7. Using the keyboard, highlight the Undelete icon and press Enter.

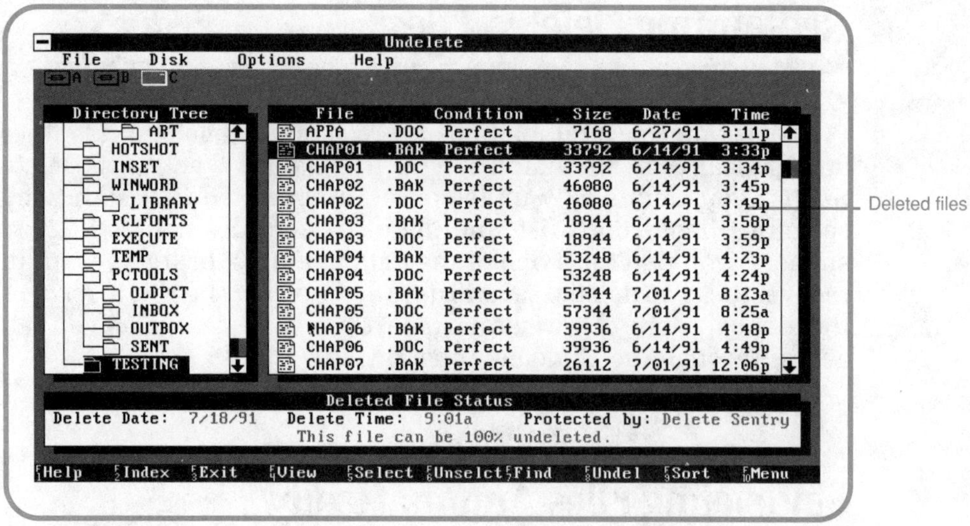

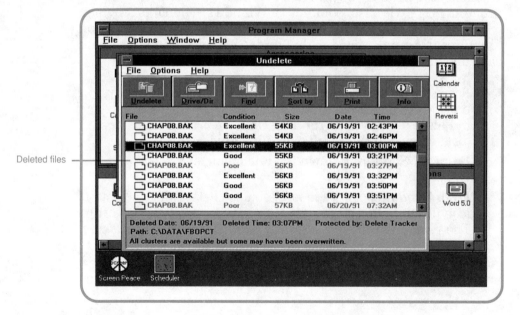

Figure 9.6   The Undelete screen running under DOS.

Figure 9.7   The Undelete screen running under Windows.

For best results, you should recover accidentally deleted files immediately after erasing them. That way, there's no chance that DOS will refill the space on the disk with new data.

The Undelete program works a little differently depending on whether the deleted files were protected (with Delete Tracker or Delete Sentry) or unprotected. With unprotected files, you need to supply the first letter of the file's name. The following sets of Quick Steps describe the undelete procedure for both protected and unprotected files:

 Undeleting Protected Files

1. Start the Undelete program as explained earlier.

   The Undelete screen appears as shown in Figure 9.8.

2. Change to the drive and directory that contains the files you deleted. (To change drives in Windows Undelete, press the **Drive/Dir** button.)

   A list of recently deleted files appears in the File List window, along with information about each file's condition. (Refer to Table 9.1.)

3. Select the files you want to undelete.

4. Press F8 or (in Windows) press the **Undelete** button.

   The selected files are undeleted. The file's condition is updated to show that the file has been recovered. □

If the file was not successfully undeleted, you'll have to try the manual recovery method. (See the section entitled "Manual File Recovery" below for more details.)

> ► **Tip:** If the names of the files you just recovered are not listed in the File List window in Shell, pull down the View menu and select **R**efresh. PC Shell rereads the disk and displays an updated file list, including the files that were recovered.

255

Table 9.1   Deleted file's condition

Condition	Chances of Recovery
Perfect	Delete Sentry has a perfect copy of the file. You won't lose any data.
Excellent	Delete Tracker or DOS has an excellent record of all clusters on which the file is stored. You'll probably recover the file unharmed.
Good	DOS has a good record of the clusters on which the file is stored, but the clusters may be scattered. You can probably get the file back unharmed.
Poor	There's no record of the first cluster on which the file is stored. You'll have to use an advanced method to restore the file.
Destroyed	Another file has been written over the clusters that stored the deleted file. You can't restore the file.
Recovered	File was successfully recovered.

 Undeleting Unprotected Files

1. Start the Undelete program.

2. Change to the drive and directory that contains the files you deleted.

   A list of recently deleted files appears in the File List window, as shown in Figure 9.8. Note that the first character in each file name is a question mark.

3. Select the files you want to undelete.

4. Press F8 or (in Windows) press the Undelete button.

   The Enter First Character dialog box appears as in Figure 9.9.

5. Type a character and press Enter or select **OK**.

   Undelete recovers the file and updates the file's condition to "Recovered."

6. Repeat Step 5 for all the selected files.

□

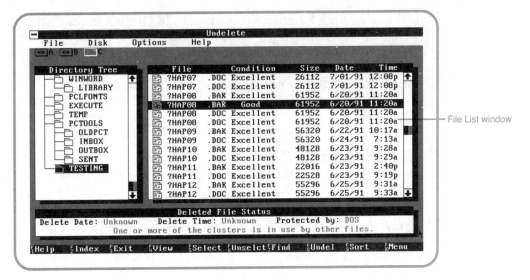

Figure 9.8   *File names for unprotected files appear with the first character missing.*

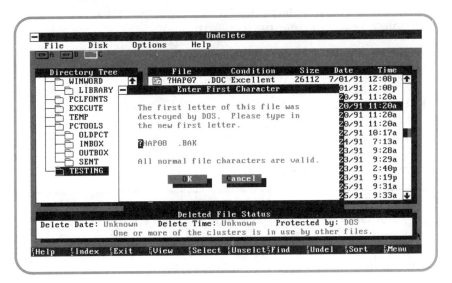

Figure 9.9   *To undelete an unprotected file, you must supply the first letter of the file's name.*

Undelete may not allow you to type the correct first character of the file's name if a file with the same name is in the current directory. If that happens, press F7 to view the directory tree and file list. Choose Show **E**xisting Files to include all files in the list, and then highlight the file you want to rename. Pull down the File menu and select **A**dvanced Undelete and the **R**ename Existing File. Type a new name for the file and select **OK**. You can now undelete the deleted file using the correct first letter of its name.

Manual File Recovery

If a deleted file is in perfect, excellent, or good condition, Undelete can reliably restore the file. However, if the file is in poor condition or has been destroyed, you won't be able to undelete the file by simply selecting it from a list. The easiest way to get the file back is to restore it from your backup disks. But if an up-to-date copy of the file is not stored on your backups, you can try to recover the file using one of Undelete's advanced manual recovery options. Manual File Recovery is most often used when a file has been erased and partially overwritten by new data. It can also recover a file that's been corrupted by a computer or disk error.

> ▶ **Tip:** If you are recovering a file from a floppy diskette, make a backup of the original diskette first. Use the DOS DISKCOPY command or the Disk menu's Copy command in PC Shell. (Don't use the DOS COPY command, as this copies only valid files and not the entire contents of the disk.) Work with the copy and not the original. If you're manually recovering a file from a hard disk, back up the drive first.

Manual File Recovery is intended primarily for straight ASCII documents and binary text documents, and not binary-only files. Recall from Chapter 5, "Managing Files with Shell," the differences between these three:

▶ ASCII documents contain just text and no special control characters. A text-only file (created by a word processor or communications program) is an ASCII document.

▶ Binary text documents contain mostly text, but can also include special control characters. Most word processing programs, including WordStar and WordPerfect, and some electronic spreadsheet programs produce binary text files as their main document type.

▶ Binary-only files contain little, if any, text. All you see when looking at a binary-only file is a collection of weird control characters. Applications programs are examples of binary-only files.

Manual File Recovery requires you to look for clusters on your disk and indicate the data you think goes with the file you're trying to restore. You need to identify the data to piece the file back together. You can easily recognize portions of an ASCII and binary text document because you can read along with it. Binary-only files provide no coherent or recognizable pattern.

To reclaim a file using the Manual Recovery method, select the file you want to undelete as explained earlier. Then,

1. Pull down the File menu and select **A**dvanced Undelete. A submenu appears showing the advanced options.
2. Select **M**anual Undelete. If the file you selected is missing its first character, supply the character.

259

The Manual Undelete window appears as in Figure 9.10. This window contains several options and information panels that you can use to piece together a file:

File Information Panel—displays information about the selected file, including its size and date of creation. The file size is useful in determining if the file you piece together matches the original (at least in terms of size).

List of Added Clusters—displays a list of the clusters you added to the file. Look to the Clusters Needed and Clusters Added lines to make sure you added the correct number of clusters to make up the file. You can use the **M**ove and **D**elete buttons in this window to delete and rearrange the clusters as needed.

Add Cluster—lets you add the currently selected cluster to the file. Pressing this button opens a dialog box that lets you choose from the following:

Add All Clusters—adds the first cluster and the required number of following clusters to match the Clusters Needed number displayed in the List of Added Clusters window. If the file was not stored on contiguous clusters, the clusters added may not be the correct ones.

Add This Cluster—adds only the next available cluster to the list of added clusters.

View This Cluster—lets you view the contents of the part of the file that is stored on the current cluster. Use this option to decide whether you want a cluster added.

Scan for Contents—searches all clusters not assigned to a file to find a specified text string. For example, you can search clusters to find a unique word or phrase that was contained in the lost file.

Enter Cluster #—lets you specify a particular cluster (by number) to add to the list.

Skip Cluster—bypasses the selected cluster, without adding it to the file.

View File—lets you view the file you've pieced together at any point in the process. Page through the file to see if any sections do not belong, are missing, or are out of place. You can then move, delete, or add clusters to make corrections.

Update—lets you assign the clusters to the designated file, saving your changes to disk.

Cancel—lets you quit without saving changes.

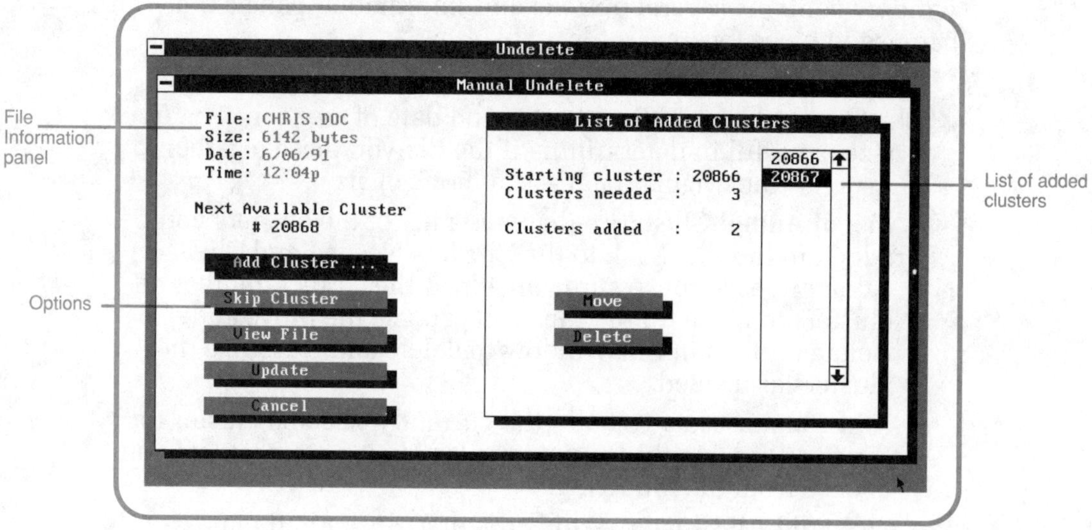

260

Figure 9.10   The Manual Undelete window.

After you've recovered the file, you should test it to make sure everything fits properly. If the file contained only ASCII text, make sure there are no breaks or obvious defects in the progression of the data. If the document is a binary text file, pay particular attention to the words as well as the formatting and layout.

Recovering Binary Text Files

Binary text files (created with a program like WordStar or WordPerfect) often include special header and trailer sections that provide information about the file. Without the header and trailer, the applications program will likely reject the file, even if the remainder of data from the file is intact. When recovering files, pay special attention to the very beginning and end of the file, as these play a pivotal role in your success in reconstructing the file.

Note that in some documents, the header contains a code for the length of the file. This code helps the program determine the amount of RAM it should provide to load the complete document. Further data corruption could occur if the code and actual length of the file don't match.

Recreating a Lost File

261

The name of the erased file must be in the directory before you can undelete it. But there are times when the directory entry for a file is replaced by a new file, but the data for the old file still remains on the disk. In other words, there's no record of the file's name, but you're sure you didn't overwrite its contents. As a last-ditch effort, you can scour the disk in search of the lost data; using the Undelete Create command to piece the file back together. This is a tedious process, so if you have a backup of the file, you'll probably save time by restoring from the backup instead.

To recreate a file:

1. Change to the drive and directory where you want the recreated file stored.
2. Pull down the File menu and select **A**dvanced Undelete.
3. Select **C**reate a File. A dialog box appears, prompting you to type a name for the recreated file.
4. Type a name and select **OK**. The Manual Undelete window appears.
5. Use the Manual Undelete window, as described earlier, to add clusters to the new file.
6. When you're done, select **U**pdate to save your created file.

As with Manual File Recovery, the Create File method is best suited for ASCII text and binary text documents only. You cannot reliably recreate a binary-only file.

Unformatting a Disk

Central to PC Tool's disk recovery features are the Mirror and Unformat programs, included in PC Tools. Mirror is intended to make an extra copy of the FAT, root directory, and boot record of the disk and store them safely out of the way of most of the other data on the disk. The Unformat program literally unformats the FAT and root directoryusing the data stored in the Mirror file or (if you didn't run Mirror) using data it finds on the hard disk.

The main purpose of the Mirror and Unformat duo is to undo an accidental ERASE *.*, RECOVER, or FORMAT command. Suppose you or someone else in your office intended to format a new floppy diskette, but reformatted the hard disk instead. Normally, it would mean most or all of the data on the hard disk is lost. But with Unformat, the original FAT and root directory (the parts erased during a hard disk format) are replaced with backup copies.

262

> **Caution:** Do not use the Unformat program until you absolutely need it. Using it when it's not required may cause data loss, depending on the last time the Mirror program was run. Because Unformat depends on the contents of the Mirror backup file to reconstruct the contents of the hard disk, if you use Unformat with an old Mirror file, you'll lose any changes made since the last time Mirror was run.

Running Unformat

Remember to use Unformat only when you need it. Otherwise, you could lose important data. If your computer is off, first boot clean with the recovery disk. Your computer may not boot from the hard disk, but you should boot clean just to make sure you don't damage the Mirror file. To run Unformat, perform the following steps:

1. With the recovery disk still in drive A, change to drive A.
2. Type `unformat` and press Enter. A dialog box appears prompting you to select the disk you want to unformat.
3. Specify which disk you want unformatted and then select **OK**. A dialog box appears, asking if you've run Mirror.

4. Select **Y**es if you've run Mirror on the disk, or select **N**o if you haven't run Mirror or if you haven't run Mirror recently. Unformat searches the root directory for data files you may have added to it since the accidental format.

If Unformat displays a list of files it found, cancel Unformat, copy the files to another disk, and then start Unformat again.

5. Select **C**ontinue.

If you're unformatting using a Mirror file, Unformat searches for the Mirror files and displays a dialog box showing any Mirror files it found, as in Figure 9.11. Select **L**ast to use the most recent Mirror file or **P**rior to use the older Mirror file. If you ran Mirror since your hard disk crashed, answer **N**o to use the previous Mirror file (the latest Mirror file will contain a copy of the damaged FAT, and you don't want to use that). If you did not run Mirror after the crash, select **Y**es to use the most recent Mirror backup file. By using the most recent version of the backup file, you have more chance of recovering up-to-date files.

263

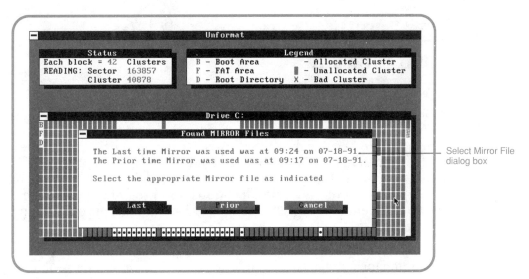

Figure 9.11   *Select the Mirror file which you think contains the most up-to-date information.*

If you're unformatting without a Mirror file or if Unformat cannot find a Mirror file on the disk, Unformat starts to unformat the disk using the information it finds on disk. You are then asked if you want to proceed with the second part of the unformat operation that writes data to disk. Select **OK** to continue. Unformat restores any of the files it finds to the disk.

Don't run Mirror yet or reboot your computer. As long as you don't run Mirror again, you still have the original two copies of the Mirror backup file: the recent version and the previous version. If one Mirror file doesn't generate the results you expected, you can run Unformat again using the other file. If neither Mirror file provides up-to-date files, try running Unformat and selecting **No** when asked if you ran Mirror. The information on your disk may be more up-to-date than the information in the Mirror file.

⊘ **Caution:** Never assume that once you use PC Tools to recover a file or disk the data is returned to its original form. If you've undeleted an erased file, inspect it with Shell's View command or—if the file is a program file—use the application that the program belongs to in order to make sure it operates correctly.

264

Using DiskFix to Recover Lost Files and Directories

DiskFix is a stand-alone program that automatically tests for, and optionally corrects, problems on hard and floppy disks. DiskFix can repair a number of disk failures, like lost clusters, missing data, even problems in the FAT and root directories. The benefit of DiskFix is that it does not require intimate knowledge of disks, DOS, or computers. With very few exceptions, the program is completely menu-driven, with English-language instructions, prompts, and warnings.

As you'll see in Chapter 10, DiskFix is invaluable as a disk-maintenance program. It can catch and repair minor problems before they become major problems. In this section, however, we focus on DiskFix's ability to help you recover lost files due to disk errors or accidental formatting.

You can start DiskFix several ways:

From Shell, use the Program menu.

From Windows, select the DiskFix icon.

From the DOS prompt, type `diskfix` and press Enter.

It's best, however, to run DiskFix from the DOS prompt after unloading all memory-resident programs from memory. The reason for this is that DiskFix uses your system's memory while fixing disks. If information gets jumbled in your system's memory, you may lose data.

> ⊘ **Caution:** If you can't run DiskFix from your damaged hard disk, boot your computer using your recovery disk. Then, insert your backup copy of the System Utilities disk—PC Tools disk 3 (3-1/2") or disk 5 (5-1/4")—and start DiskFix from that disk. If you copy the files to your hard disk, you may wipe out the files you want to recover.

When you run DiskFix it first checks that the critical data on your hard drive is not corrupt. It also checks that your computer and hard drive mechanism are running properly. These initial checks are necessary so that your disks are not damaged further. Assuming that your hard drive is capable of limping along, DiskFix asks if you want to repair a disk now. Answer **OK** to continue. Note that you can test any disk in your computer with DiskFix without actually repairing it. DiskFix always asks if you want to repair any damage it finds.

The DiskFix Main menu appears as shown in Figure 9.12. Select **R**epair a Disk. The Drive Selection dialog box appears. The drives shown are all those that DiskFix could find in your computer. (If a drive is missing it means that DiskFix is unaware of it; thus, cannot repair it. If that's the case, run Rebuild as explained at the end of this chapter and then run DiskFix again.) Highlight a drive, and select **OK**.

DiskFix now analyzes the drive (see Figure 9.13) and checks the following areas:

- ▶ DOS Boot Sector
- ▶ File Allocation Tables
- ▶ Media Descriptors (identify the type of disk)
- ▶ Directory Structure
- ▶ Cross Linked Files (portions of data that appear to belong to more than one file)
- ▶ Lost Clusters (portions of data that don't appear to belong to a file)

265

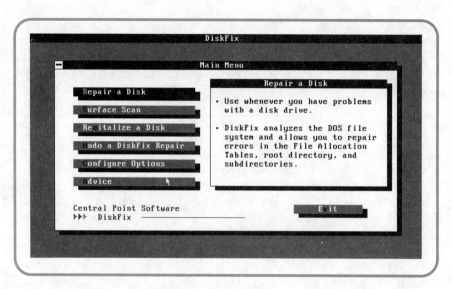

Figure 9.12   The DiskFix Main menu.

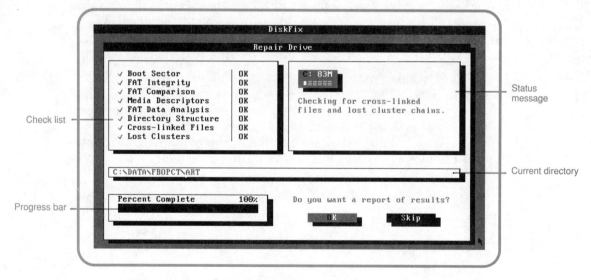

Figure 9.13   Analysis Report dialog box.

Note that a surface scan can take a long time, depending on the size of your hard drive. A 100M drive may take several hours to scan. All clusters of your hard drive are analyzed, not just those parts that have data. So even if your 120M hard disk drive only has 10M of data in it, DiskFix will still check all 120M of real estate.

▶ **Note:** Answering **N**o to certain repair questions will terminate the remainder of the analysis, as the repair tasks must be conducted in a specific sequence.

An error during media analysis means that DiskFix has sensed a problem, and that you'll probably want to have it corrected. DiskFix will ask if you want to correct the problem now; answer **Y**es or **N**o accordingly.

DiskFix attempts to do what it can for a damaged disk, especially for clusters that are cross-linked or lost. Occasionally, lost clusters cannot be reunited with the rest of the file, so DiskFix saves the data in a lost cluster file, in much the same way that the DOS CHKDSK program corrals lost data into error files. The DiskFix lost cluster files are named PCTxxxx.FIX, where the *xxxx* begins at 0000 and increments by one for every separate file you have. If the data in the lost cluster file is recognizable text, you may be able to piece it back into a usable form.

Similarly, if DiskFix locates lost subdirectories, they are placed under the root directory and given new names, using the format LOSTxxxx, such as

```
LOST0000
LOST0001
LOST0002
```

and so forth. Now that the subdirectories are reclaimed, you can look inside and retrieve important data.

If DiskFix identified a number of errors, it may be a good idea to make a special backup of your hard drive, and use the Compare feature of PC Tools Backup to make sure that the archive and hard disk data are identical. You can then revitalize your hard drive as explained in Chapter 10.

267

Running Rebuild

Catastrophe strikes! You turn on your computer one day and find that an unexplained glitch has ruined your hard disk. Files that were there yesterday seem permanently lost. Your directories, your files, everything is gone.

Regular backups are your best protection against calamities such as this. But we're humans after all, and despite the importance of hard disk backups, we occasionally forget to do them. Luckily, you made a recovery disk. The recovery disk contains a stand-alone program called Rebuild. In addition, the disk contains a file called PARTNSAV.FIL which contains information that is essential to your system:

268

Partition Table. Although your computer may have several hard disks (C, D, E, etc.), it probably has a single hard drive, which is divided or *partitioned* into several hard disks. The partition table tells your system how the disk is divided. If this table gets damaged, your computer may not be able to find one of the disks.

Boot Sector. The boot sector contains information your computer needs to start up. If the boot sector gets damaged, you may not be able to boot from your hard drive.

CMOS. This is an electronic device used by many computers to store information such as the number and types of disk drives your computer has, and the time and date. If this gets damaged, your computer may not be able to access the hard drive, and information may mysteriously disappear from your disk.

If you run into problems (such as those just described), run DiskFix to see if it can correct the problem. If DiskFix doesn't work, run Rebuild from the recovery disk to rebuild one of the elements listed above. Rebuild one element at a time, and then test your system after each correction. That way, when the problem is corrected, you'll have a better idea of what caused it. For example, if your CMOS is damaged, you can rebuild the CMOS information with Rebuild, but you may want to replace the CMOS battery or have your computer serviced to prevent the problem from recurring.

To run Rebuild:

1. Insert the recovery disk in drive A, and change to drive A.
2. Type `rebuild` and press Enter. The Rebuild program starts and prompts you to insert the disk with the PARTNSAV.FIL into the drive.
3. Because the requested file is on the recovery disk, which is already in the drive, press Enter.

A prompt appears, asking if you want to Quit (Q), rebuild CMOS (C), or rebuild the boot sector and partition table (A or 1-8). Take one of the following actions:

▶ To rebuild the CMOS, press C and then Enter. Type `yes` and press Enter to confirm. Rebuild rebuilds the CMOS information, tells you to remove the disk from drive A, and then reboots your computer.

▶ To rebuild the boot sector and partition table, press A to rebuild the partition table for all hard drives in your computer or type a number between 1 and 8 to specify a single drive. Type `yes` and press Enter to confirm. Rebuild restores the boot sector and partition table, tells you to remove the disk from drive A, and then reboots your computer.

▶ To cancel Rebuild without effecting any changes, press Q and then Enter.

269

What You Have Learned

This chapter detailed ways to use PC Tools to recover files and disks that have been accidentally erased or damaged. You also learned:

▶ Every disk has a boot record, even if the disk can't be used to start the computer.

▶ The FAT records the locations of files on the disk.

▶ The root directory contains a list of all the files and subdirectories contained within the disk.

▶ The PC Tools Undelete command can unerase files that have been recently deleted.

▶ For best results, you should recover accidentally lost files immediately after erasing them.

▶ The Delete Tracker stores a record of files deleted from the disk and aids in recovering erased files.

▶ The Delete Sentry stores an exact duplicate of each file you delete in a hidden directory called \SENTRY.

▶ The Mirror and Unformat programs are designed to help you reconstruct a hard or floppy disk after it has been accidently formatted.

▶ The Unformat program should be used only when needed. Otherwise, important data could be lost.

▶ The DiskFix program can be used to reclaim damaged disks automatically.

▶ Rebuild uses the information on your recovery disk to re-build the boot sector and partition table and to restore the CMOS information to your system.

Maintaining Your Disks

In This Chapter

▶ *Increasing hard disk efficiency*
▶ *Testing your disks for errors*
▶ *Formatting your hard disk safely*
▶ *Revitalizing your hard disk*
▶ *Parking your hard disk drive for safety*

Keeping your hard disk in shape is the best way to protect your valuable data. PC Tools provides numerous facilities for maintaining your hard disk and hard disk drive (the mechanism that runs the disk). Most maintenance procedures take only a few moments but go a long way to extend the life of your data. This chapter explains the following PC Tools programs, which are designed to keep your hard disk and hard disk drive in top working order.

Compress—rearranges the data stored on a disk so that each file is stored in a contiguous series of clusters.

DiskFix—scans the disk for defective sectors, corrects fixable sectors, and locks out unfixable sectors. This refreshes the disk, making it a more reliable storage facility.

PC Format—formats your hard disk safely, allowing you to recover from an accidental format.

PC-Cache—stores often used information in computer's memory so your computer accesses the hard disk less often. This reduces the wear and tear on your hard disk.

Park Disk—parks the hard disk heads over a part of the disk that does not store a file. This prevents the hard disk heads from crashing down on (or touching) the disk and wiping out data when you turn off your computer.

Note that many of the functions and procedures also apply to floppy disks as well.

Hard Disk Fragmentation

Hard disk fragmentation is not dropping the drive and watching it shatter into thousands of tiny pieces. Rather, fragmentation refers to the order and continuity of the individual files on your hard disk.

Recall from Chapter 9, "Recovering Lost Files and Damaged Disks," that a disk (hard or floppy) is divided into many tracks. These tracks are further divided into sectors, which are grouped into clusters, the smallest chunk of data that your hard disk can deal with. Cluster size varies between drives (considering media type and capacity) but is generally 1K to 4K in size. That is, your files are composed of many 1K to 4K chunks, all placed strategically on the disk.

When files are fragmented, their component parts are located on two or more noncontiguous clusters on the disk. The first half of a file may occupy Cluster 1000, for instance, but the second part may be located in Cluster 2050. To retrieve the entire file, your hard disk must first move to Cluster 1000, read the data stored there, then jump to Cluster 2050 to continue reading the file.

Depending on the size of the file, it may be stored in several dozen clusters. A large database file may even be stored in several hundreds of clusters. Imagine each cluster of a large file located in some distant part of the disk. Your drive must work overtime to retrieve all the parts.

At a minimum, file fragmentation slows down your hard disk. The actual degree of speed-decrease depends on the hard disk, the data, and the amount of fragmentation, but you can expect some loss of performance. What is worse is that fragmented files are harder to recover after they have been accidentally erased. Files contained in contiguous clusters are undeleted more reliably than those scattered over many noncontiguous clusters.

Fortunately, PC Tools provides a handy and easy-to-use program that eliminates file fragmentation. The Compress program is designed to detect and purge file fragmentation on both hard and floppy disks. You can access Compress from within Shell (as long as you've loaded Shell as a stand-alone program, and not as a memory-resident program) or directly from the DOS prompt.

Note that Compress is a *disk defragmentor*. It's not a compression utility that condenses data into a smaller packet. PC Tools provides this utility with the PC Secure program, discussed in Chapter 5.

Starting Compress

Compress uses the same menu and window interface shared by all the PC Tools programs. The program includes on-line help in case you need assistance in using any of the commands. You can also start Compress with one or more command-line parameters. These parameters assist you in automating disk defragmenting, especially if you develop the habit of regularly compressing your hard disk.

273

You have the option of starting the Compress program from within Shell or at the DOS prompt. Before you run Compress,

▶ Unload any memory-resident programs (except PC Tools programs) from memory. Memory-resident programs could interfere with the proper operation of Compress and cause considerable data damage. If you run Compress and receive an Out of Memory message, you may also need to unload PC Tools programs.

▶ Make sure no disk-caching program (other than PC-Cache) is running. Disk-caching programs can also interfere with the operation of Compress.

▶ If you want to undelete accidently deleted files, do it now. Running Compress will probably overwrite any deleted files.

▶ To really play it safe, back up your hard disk before running Compress. If anything should happen to the data, you can restore it using the backed up version.

You can start Compress from PC Shell or from the DOS prompt, as explained in the following Quick Steps:

Starting Compress from PC Shell

1. Start Shell in the usual manner.

2. Select F10 (Menu) and select PC Tools.

   Opens the PC Tools program menu.

3. Choose System Tools and then select Compress.

   In a few moments, Compress loads and analyzes the current disk. □

⊘ **Caution:** Do not run Compress from Windows or from any other multitasking system. It may confuse Compress and cause loss of data.

If you did not specify a disk to compress when loading Compress, the program assumes you want to compress the disk that contains your PC Tools program files. Compress analyzes the disk and displays the screen shown in Figure 10.1, indicating whether or not compression is necessary.

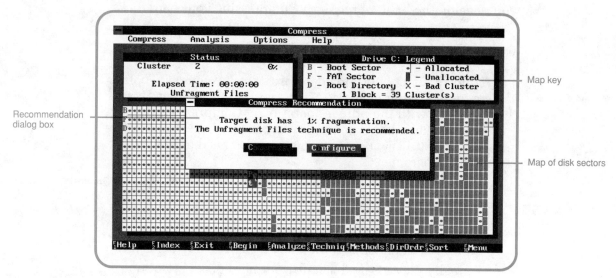

Figure 10.1   Compress analyzes your disk to determine if compression is required.

To compress a different disk, press Esc, pull down the Compress menu, and select **C**hoose Drive. Select the disk you want to compress and then select **OK**. You can also use Compress from the DOS prompt, as the following Quick Steps describe:

 Starting Compress from the DOS Prompt

1. Change to the drive and directory that contains the PC Tools program files. | If you installed PC Tools to run from any directory, this step is unnecessary.
2. Type **compress** and press Enter. | The Compress opening screen appears. □

Table 10.1 shows the command-line parameters you can use when starting Compress. The options invoked by these parameters are detailed later in this chapter. To use one or more of these parameters, add them after the COMPRESS command at the DOS prompt. For example,

```
compress /sf
```

275

starts the Compress program and automatically selects the Sort by File Name option. If you want to defragment a disk other than your hard disk, add the drive letter immediately after the COMPRESS command, as in

```
compress a:
```

Table 10.1   Compress Command-Line Parameters

Parameter	Function
Compression Technique (choose one only)	
/CF	Unfragments files and moves free space to end of disk. This prevents any new files you save to disk from getting fragmented.
/CU	Unfragments files without moving free space to end of disk.
/CC	Full compression; clears data from any unused sectors.
/CS	Moves all data clusters to the beginning of the disk, leaving empty clusters at the end of the disk. Does not unfragment existing files.
/CD	Moves all directories to the beginning of the disk

(continued)

Table 10.1   (continued)

Parameter	Function
/OD	Moves each directory just before the files it contains.
/OO	Moves directories to beginning of disk; files follow in groups that correspond to each directory.
/OF	Moves specified files to beginning of disk.

Sorting Options (choose one only)

/SF	Sorts files by file name.
/ST	Sorts files by time.
/SE	Sorts files by extension.
/SS	Sorts files by size.

Sort Order Options (choose one only)

/SA	Sorts files in ascending order.
/SD	Sorts files in descending order.

Additional Options

/NM	Suppresses running Mirror after Compress is done.

> ▶ **Tip:** You can also include these command-line parameters in the program menu of Shell. To do so, open the Program Item Information dialog box for the Compress program, and add those parameters you want to include. (Refer to Chapter 7.) Whenever you run Compress, your command-line parameters will automatically be included.

Note that with the exception of the /NM parameter, you can select any option from a menu within the Compress program.

Setting the Compression Technique

The compression technique tells Compress the depth of defragmentation you wish. To select the compression technique, pull down the Options menu and select **C**ompression Technique.

The Choose Compression Technique dialog box appears, as in Figure 10.2 offering the following options:

▶ Optimize **D**irectories. If you added or deleted subdirectories since the last Compress session, choose this option to reorganize the directories.

▶ O**p**timize Free Space. This moves all data to the beginning of the disk, leaving empty clusters at the end of the disk. If you save files after running Compress, the files will then be saved in contiguous clusters, preventing fragmentation. (See Figure 10.3.)

▶ **U**nfragment Files. Defragments the files, but doesn't attempt to consolidate the empty clusters toward the end of the disk. Use this option when you're short on time. The problem with this option is that it promotes fragmentation of the files you subsequently save to disk.

▶ **F**ull Optimization. Unfragments files and moves the unallocated clusters toward the end of the disk.

▶ Full Opt. w/**C**lear. Same as Full Optimization but also erases all data in the unused sectors. Use this option if you work with restricted or classified data and want to prevent prying eyes from looking at what you've been up to. (Note: You can achieve an even higher degree of privacy by using the PC Secure program, discussed in Chapter 5.)

▶ File **S**ort. Sorts the files but does not defragment them.

277

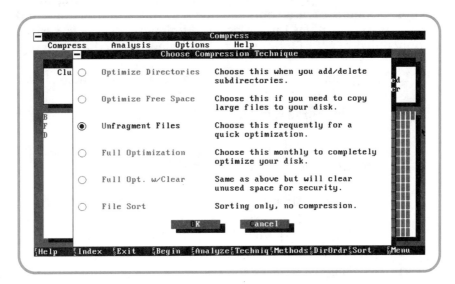

Figure 10.2   The Choose Compression Technique dialog box specifies a compression technique.

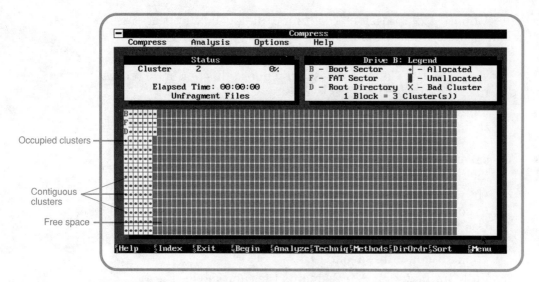

Figure 10.3   *A disk with all unallocated clusters placed at the end of the disk.*

278

Sorting and Ordering Options

For added efficiency, the PC Tools Compress program can optionally sort the files on your hard disk while it is defragmenting them. Compress offers several options that let you sort the files and directories on your disk to increase its efficiency. To select a sorting option, pull down the Options menu and select one of the following:

▶ **O**rdering Methods displays the Ordering Method dialog box, which offers the following options:

Standard moves the directories to the beginning of the disk, followed by the files.

File Placement puts the directories first, followed by any files you specify (with the Files to Place First command).

Directories First puts the directories first, followed by the files grouped according to directories.

Directories with Files moves the directories near the files that each directory contains.

▶ **D**irectory Order displays the Directory Ordering dialog box as in Figure 10.4. On the left is a directory tree. On the right are any directories included in the path statement of your AUTOEXEC.BAT file. The directory order tells Compress the order in which to place the specified directories at the beginning of the disk. To add a directory to the path, highlight it in the tree and press the **A**dd button. You can then move or delete directories listed in the Path window.

▶ **F**iles to Place First displays the Files to Place First dialog box. Usually you'll want any files that initiate programs (files with the .EXE, .COM, or .BAT extension) placed first on a drive, so DOS can find a program quickly when you enter the command to run the program. You can use this dialog box to specify which files you want placed first on the drive.

▶ **U**nmovable Files prevents Compress from moving files. You may want to use this option for copy-protected programs.

▶ File **S**ort Options tells Compress how you want files sorted on disk. You can sort files by the name, extension, size, or by the date and time they were created. You can also select to sort in ascending or descending order, or choose not to sort the files. Sorting slows down the compression process.

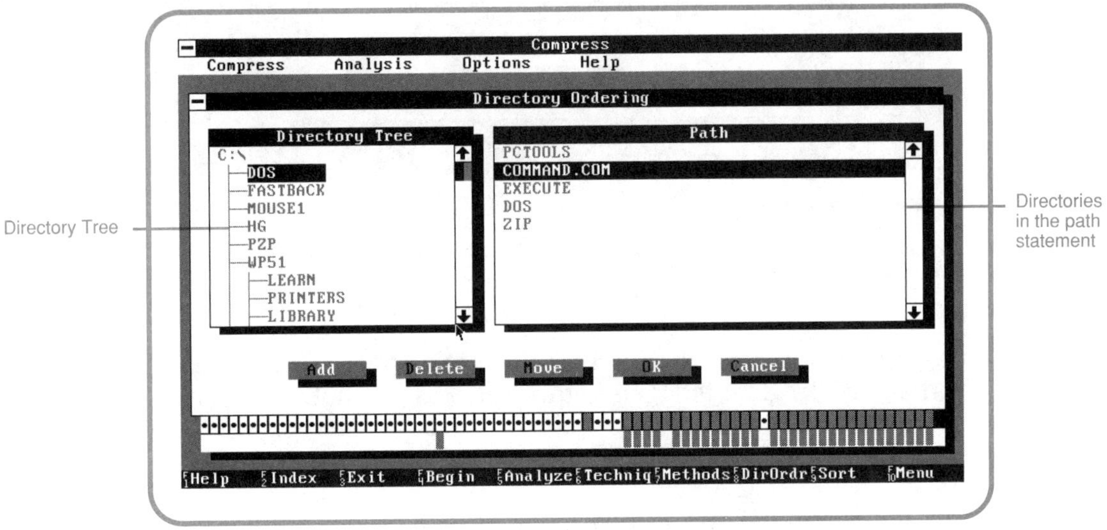

279

Directory Tree

Directories in the path statement

Figure 10.4   The Directory Ordering dialog box specifies the order in which you want the directories stored on disk.

Testing for Fragmentation

PC Tools Compress runs a quick test to see if defragmenting is advisable. If you think that the files in your disk are fragmented, choose the **D**isk Statistics command from the Analysis menu. As shown in Figure 10.5, Compress will report the number of allocated and unallocated clusters, the number of bad clusters (as marked in the disk's FAT), and other technical data. In almost every case, Compress will detect at least some fragmentation and encourage you to complete the Compress operation.

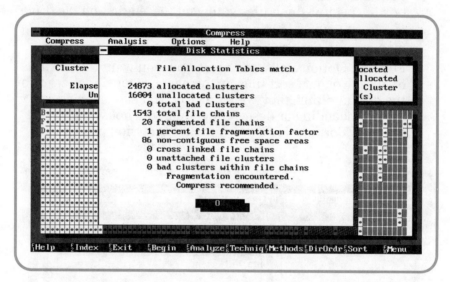

Figure 10.5   *Select the Disk Statistics command to determine if compression is required.*

You can obtain more concrete information about which files on the disk are fragmented using the **F**ile Fragmentation Analysis command, also found in the Analysis menu. As shown in Figure 10.6, the File Analysis command displays:

▶ The files in the currently selected directory (as well as any subdirectories located within the directory).

▶ The number of clusters occupied by each file.

▶ The number of pieces each file is broken into (areas).

▶ The percent of fragmentation of each file.

If any file is shown to be located in more than one area, it's fragmented. You can view a different subdirectory by highlighting it with the cursor keys or clicking on it with the mouse.

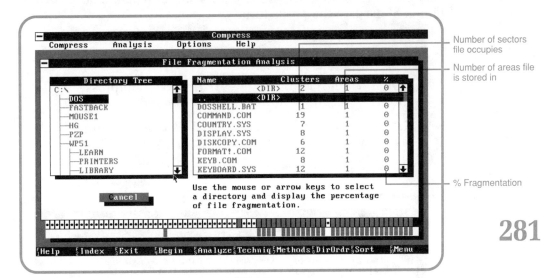

Figure 10.6   The File Fragmentation Analysis test provides more details about fragmented files.

Problems in the File Allocation Table

PC Tools Compress checks the integrity of the file allocation table (FAT) while analyzing the disk. If the program detects a mismatch in the FAT (one or more files allocated to the same clusters or one or more previously allocated clusters mysteriously detached from a file, for example), it will warn you to use the DiskFix program before running Compress.

Printing a Compression Report

If you'd like a report of the defragmenting process and what it did to your files, choose the **P**rint Report command from the Options menu before starting Compress. Select the destination of the report: **P**rinter (connected to LPT1:) or **D**isk file. When choosing a disk file, Compress automatically names it COMPRESS.PRT.

Running Compress

Once you've selected the options you want to use, you're ready to run Compress and defragment the files on your hard disk. The following Quick Steps give the procedure:

 Running Compress

1. Pull down the Compress menu and select **B**egin Compress.

   Invokes Compress command.

2. Read the warning that appears (as shown in Figure 10.7) and press **O**K or Cancel.

   OK starts Compress; **C**ancel takes you back to Shell or DOS. □

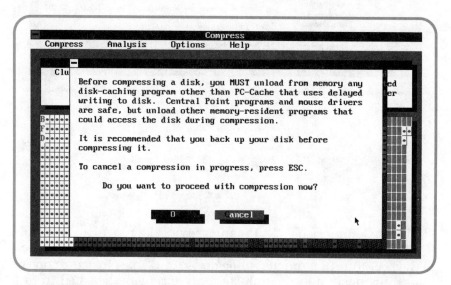

Figure 10.7   This Warning dialog box appears each time you compress a disk.

Compress now proceeds to examine your hard disk and defragment its files. You can safely interrupt the Compress operation at any time by pressing the Escape key. PC Tools Compress will finish shuffling the cluster it's currently working on, then ask if you want to cancel. Answer accordingly.

When the defragmenting process is complete, Compress asks if you want to exit or run the Mirror program. Since you've moved the files on the disk, your old Mirror backup file is no longer valid and should not be used. You are advised to run Mirror at this time, then restart your computer.

Analyzing and Verifying Your Disks

It's a good idea to check your hard disk regularly to make sure the disk is in good shape. Disk analysis pinpoints clusters on a hard disk that have gone bad since you originally formatted the disk. By finding these bad clusters and then blocking them from being used, you can prevent your computer from trying to store files in unreliable clusters.

The PC Tools DiskFix program performs a variety of tests that can locate and mark bad clusters automatically. If a file is stored on a bad cluster, DiskFix will attempt to retrieve the entire file and move it to a safer place on the disk, then mark the cluster as bad in the FAT. If the cluster is unallocated, DiskFix will lock it out against future use.

If you're running DiskFix to repair an existing problem or recover lost files, refer to the discussion in Chapter 9 on using DiskFix to repair a disk. The following sections focus mainly on using DiskFix as a preventive tool to optimize the performance of your disks.

283

Starting DiskFix

You have the option of starting DiskFix from within Shell or at the DOS prompt. You can also run DiskFix from Windows to analyze a disk, but the program will not allow you to take any corrective measures. Before you run DiskFix,

▶ Unload any memory-resident programs (except PC Tools programs) from memory. Memory-resident programs could interfere with DiskFix's corrective measures and actually cause data corruption.

▶ Make sure no disk-caching program (other than PC-Cache) is running. Disk-caching programs can cause problems as well.

▶ To really play it safe, back up your hard disk before running DiskFix. If anything should happen to the data, you can restore it using the previously backed up version.

The following Quick Steps explain how to use DiskFix from PC Shell, then from the DOS prompt:

 Starting DiskFix from PC Shell

1. Start Shell in the usual manner.

2. Select F10 (Menu) and select PC Tools. — Opens the PC Tools program menu.

3. Choose **R**ecovery Tools and then select **D**iskFix. — A warning box appears, reminding you to remove memory-resident programs from memory.

4. Select **O**K to continue or select **C**ancel to exit DiskFix if you need to unload memory-resident programs. — If you select **O**K, the DiskFix Main menu appears as inFigure 10.8

□

284

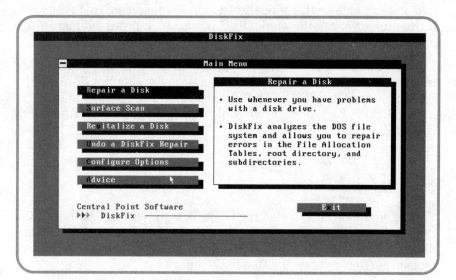

Figure 10.8   The DiskFix Main menu.

 Starting DiskFix from the DOS Prompt

1. Change to the drive and directory that contains the PC Tools program files. — If you installed PC Tools to run from any directory, this is unnecessary.

2. Type `diskfix` and press Enter. | A warning box appears, reminding you to remove memory-resident programs from memory. □

3. Select **OK** to continue or select Cancel to exit DiskFix if you need to unload memory-resident programs. | If you select **OK**, the DiskFix Main menu appears as in Figure 10.8.

Performing a Surface Scan

One of the options listed on the DiskFix Main menu is **S**urface Scan. DiskFix will read information off each sector of the disk and write information back onto the sector to determine if the sector is defective. If DiskFix finds a bad sector, it marks the sector as bad (preventing its future use) and then writes the information it read from that sector onto another (good) sector. To start the scanning process, perform the following steps:

1. Select **S**urface Scan from the DiskFix Main menu. A Disk Selection dialog box appears, asking you to specify which disk you want to scan.
2. Select a disk to scan and then select **OK**.

Whenever you select an option from the Main menu and specify a drive, DiskFix automatically performs several tests to find any serious problems that can cause loss of data. These tests include an in-depth analysis of the hard disk partition tables and the boot sector, a comparison of the FATs, and a scan for viruses. If DiskFix finds a problem, it displays a dialog box telling you what to do next.

If you select **S**urface Scan and none of these problems exists, DiskFix displays the Pattern Testing Options dialog box shown in Figure 10.9. The Read/Write Only option tells DiskFix to perform a standard scanning operation; DiskFix will read and write information on each sector. The remaining three options—Minimum, Average, and Maximum Pattern Testing—tell DiskFix to analyze each sector more thoroughly. If you select any of these three options, the scanning operation will take more time, but it will do a better job of revealing damaged or weak sectors. Select an option and then select **OK**.

285

> ▶ **Tip:** A surface analysis of an average 40M hard disk attached to an 80286 computer can take several hours (faster drives on faster computers with smaller hard disks take less time). After the scan, you can view the disk map that's displayed to see which sectors, if any, are marked as bad. You'll also be given the option of sending a report of the results to disk or to your printer for future reference.

286

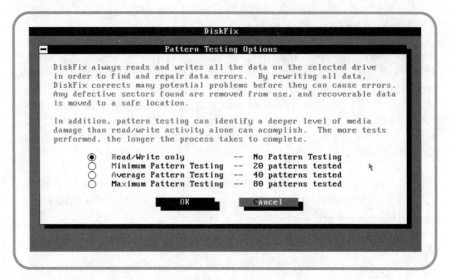

Figure 10.9   Select a pattern testing option to provide a more thorough analysis of the disk.

During the surface analysis, DiskFix uses the following codes to indicate the status of the clusters on the disk:

B	Boot sector.
F	FAT sector.
D	Root directory.
X	Bad cluster; cluster is locked out.
Dotted square	Allocated cluster with no errors.
Shaded square	Unallocated cluster with no errors.
1-9	Media defects in sector that contains no data. The number indicates the number of defects found.
C	Corrected error on sector containing data. Data was moved to good sector, if necessary.

c	Corrected error on sector not containing data.
U	Uncorrectable error on sector containing data. Print a log report when the scan is completed to see if you need to take corrective measures.
u	Uncorrectable error on sector not containing data.

Disks that reveal a number of bad clusters (see Figure 10.10) indicate a catastrophic disk crash or partial erasure. If you're testing a hard disk, you should make a backup of the files that remain and reformat it completely. If you're testing a floppy diskette, copy those files that are still intact and throw the disk in the trash.

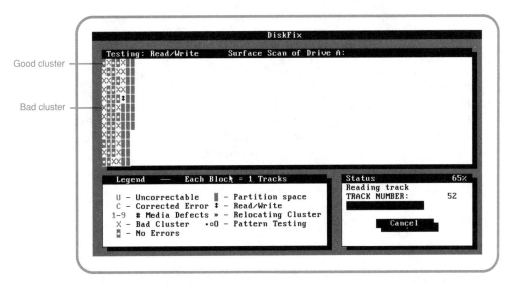

Figure 10.10   Analysis report of a severely damaged disk.

Revitalizing a Disk

Although the surface scan can reveal and correct most disk problems, your disk may need more help. If you begin to get an increasing number of DOS error messages indicating that DOS cannot read or write information to a disk, you may need to reformat the disk. But if the disk already contains information that you don't want to lose, the last thing you want to do is format it.

What's the solution? DiskFix includes a program that can revitalize a disk by performing a low-level formatting operation. This program reads information off the disk (one sector at a time), reformats the sector, and then writes the information back onto it. You get the benefits of formatting without losing files. You can also revitalize any disk—hard or floppy.

To revitalize a disk, perform the following steps:

1. Select Revitalize a Disk from the DiskFix Main menu. A Disk Selection dialog box appears, asking you to specify which disk you want to revitalize.
2. Select a disk and then select **OK**.

DiskFix automatically performs several tests to find any serious problems that can cause loss of data. These tests include an in-depth analysis of the hard disk partition tables and the boot sector, a comparison of the FATs, and a scan for viruses. If DiskFix finds a problem, it displays a dialog box telling you what to do next.

If DiskFix finds no problems, select **OK** to continue. DiskFix begins revitalizing the disk. You may see many of the same codes mentioned earlier to mark bad sectors and errors. You'll see an additional code that looks like an asterisk (*). This code indicates that DiskFix is formatting the sector. DiskFix will display a dialog box, telling you when the process is complete.

Formatting a Hard Disk with PC Format

Once your hard drive is formatted, either by you or your computer dealer, you probably will never format it again, because that could destroy any information stored on the disk. If you need to format a disk after it's already been formatted, use a low-level formatting program, such as DiskFix's Revitalize option.

If your disk goes completely bad and you need to format it more thoroughly, use PC Format. Although this program is not strictly required when formatting a hard disk, it does provide a safe alternative to the DOS FORMAT command. If you accidently format a hard disk using PC Format, you'll have a better chance of recovering it by using Unformat.

Before you start PC Format to reformat your hard disk, take the following precautions:

▶ If your hard disk contains any files you want to undelete, undelete them now. You won't be able to undelete deleted files after formatting the disk.

▶ Make sure you have a reliable backup of any files that may be stored on your hard disk.

▶ If your computer is off, insert your recovery disk into drive A and turn on your computer. This boots the computer clean, preventing damage to the Mirror file. (The Mirror file can help you unformat the disk if you format it by accident.)

You'll also have to copy the two PC Format program files (PCFORMAT.EXE and PCFORM.EXE) from the PC Tools disks to your recovery disk. PCFORM.EXE is on Disk 2 of the 3-1/2" disks and Disk 3 of the 5-1/4" disks. PCFORMAT.EXE is on Disk 4 of the 3-1/2" disks and Disk 8 of the 5-1/4" disks. Once these files are copied to the recovery disk, you can run PC Format from this disk. To run PC Format from the recovery disk, follow these steps:

289

1. Insert the recovery disk into drive A.
2. Type `a:` and press Enter to change to drive A.
3. Type `pcformat` and press Enter. A dialog box appears, prompting you to select a disk.
4. Select the disk you want to format, and then select **OK**. A dialog box appears (see Figure 10.11) prompting you to enter format instructions.
5. Select the type of format you want to perform. The following two options leave the on-disk data intact. (The Full and Destructive Format options are not available for hard disk formatting.)

    Safe Format. This is the default option, and it's the safest option. If you perform a safe format on a disk that contains data, you can usually get the data back, as long as you don't store any other files on the disk.

    Quick Format. To quickly format a previously formatted disk so it can be unformatted.

6. To make the disk bootable, select **I**nstall system files.
7. If you ran the Mirror program on the disk previously, select Save **M**irror Info to save that information, giving you a better chance of recovering files.

8. To label the disk, select **L**abel and type a label (up to 11 characters). A label indicates what's on the disk. If you access the disk in PC Shell, the label appears at the top of the Directory Tree window.

9. Select **OK** to start the process. The Validating Drive message box appears for a moment. Then,

   If the disk you're trying to format has files on it, PC Shell displays a warning box. Select **OK** to go ahead with the format or **C**ancel to quit.

   If the disk does not have files on it, the format process begins.

10. Wait until the formatting is complete, and then select **OK**.

> ▶ **Tip:** You can stop PC Format at any time during the format process by pressing the Escape key. If you realize that you've formatted the disk by mistake, run Unformat from your recovery disk as soon as possible.

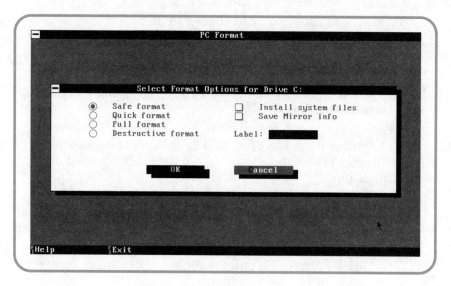

Figure 10.11   The Select Format Option dialog box prompts you to enter formatting instructions.

Shell provides a status report during formatting. Sectors formatted correctly are shown as a dot (·); uncorrectable errors are shown as an E. Shell will attempt to format and verify troublesome sectors several times before it assigns an error. Unlike the DOS FORMAT command, PC Format continues with the formatting process even when errors occur.

After formatting is complete, Shell provides you with some important information about your disk, including total bytes of disk space and bytes in bad sectors. Press the **C**ancel and **E**xit buttons to quit.

Disk Caching

The dictionary defines the word *cache* as "a hiding place for storing provisions and other necessities." In computer terms, a cache is a portion of *random access memory (RAM)* set aside for storing bits of data.

291

The most common form of cache is *disk caching*, where commonly used data from the disk is temporarily stored in memory. By keeping the information in fast RAM instead of fetching it from the disk every time it's needed, many operations go much faster. Depending on the amount of memory set aside for the cache, you can practically store entire programs in memory. Your work will go faster because your computer won't have to access the disk so much.

If you have a late model 80286, or a 386- or 486-class PC or clone, it probably already has a caching program. The caching program included with PC Tools is compatible with almost every PC compatible, and it is designed to be used safely with the rest of PC Tools (including Compress, DiskFix, PC Format, Shell, and Desktop). The PC Tools caching program, called PC-Cache, also provides additional features that you may not find in similar caching utilities, including the ability to use regular, expanded, or extended memory.

⊘ **Caution:** If you're already using a caching program with your computer, you must disable it before installing PC-Cache. Under no circumstances should you run two caching programs at the same time. It may cause serious data loss.

Using PC-Cache

PC-Cache is straightforward. Because it's a memory-resident program, you'll probably want to load it when your computer is first started, so you should include the PC-Cache command in your AUTOEXEC.BAT file. Simply add the following line in the AUTOEXEC.BAT file, and PC-Cache will be activated the next time you start or reset your computer:

```
pc-cache
```

If you don't want to add the command manually, you can have the PC Tools Program Configuration program do it for you. Type `install` at the DOS prompt and press Enter. Select **P**C-Cache and then select **L**oad PC-Cache. A check mark next to the option indicates it's on. Select **O**K and **E**xit. Select **S**ave Configuration and then **O**K. Select **R**eboot to load PC-Cache.

Entering the name of the PC-Cache program alone installs PC-Cache with its defaults. This enables caching on all available drives and assigns 64K of base RAM to caching, 256K of extended memory (if your system has it), and 256K of expanded memory. PC-Cache adjusts automatically as necessary, so you shouldn't need to make any manual adjustments. However, if this arrangement is not satisfactory to you, you can include command-line parameters by editing the PC-Cache command in your AUTOEXEC.BAT file (you can use Shell's File Editor as explained in Chapter 5). The most common parameters are shown in Table 10.2.

Table 10.2   PC-Cache Optional Command-Line Parameters

Parameter	Function
/Ix	Ignores (does not enable) the indicated drive. Substitute the x for a valid drive letter, such as /IA or /IB. You can use the /I parameter as many times as you need to ignore multiple drives.
/SIZE=nnnn	Sets the amount of base memory for use by PC-Cache. The default is 64K; the maximum is 512K.
/SIZEXP=nnnn	Sets the amount of expanded memory for use by PC-Cache.
/SIZEXT=nnnn	Sets the amount of extended memory for use by PC-Cache.

Parameter	Function
/EXTSTART=nnnn	Specifies the starting address of the cache in extended memory. The EXTSTART number must be greater than 1024. Use this option with care.
/PAUSE	Pauses at the PC-Cache status window, so you can read it. This is useful if you load PC-Cache from AUTOEXEC.BAT.
/QUIET	Disables the PC-Cache status window when PC-Cache first starts.
/WIN	Automatically resizes the cache when running in Windows.
/WRITE=ON /WRITE=OFF	Controls the time delay before write operations are sent to the disk. With write delay off, write operations are sent to disk immediately. Use this option with care.
/?	Displays help on PC-Cache parameters.
/FLUSH	Use after PC-Cache is loaded to clear the Cache. This command is usually not required because the cache clears itself regularly.
/UNLOAD	Use after PC Cache is loaded. Clears the cache, and unloads PC-Cache from memory.
/STATUS	Displays the relative performance and speed improvements provided by PC-Cache.

293

Here are some examples of using PC-Cache with some of the more common command-line parameters:

PC-CACHE /IA /IB—Starts PC-Cache and ignores (disables from cache) both drives A and B.

PC-CACHE /SIZE=128K—Starts PC-Cache and allocates 128K of base memory for caching.

PC-CACHE /IA /IB /SIZEXP=512K—Starts PC-Cache, ignores (disables from cache) both drives A and B, and allocates 512K of expanded memory for caching.

Testing the Performance of PC-Cache

PC-Cache provides a handy indicator for testing its performance. For a cache utility, performance is rated in the number of transfers saved between disk and computer. By reducing the number of transfers, overall performance of the computer is increased.

After you've loaded PC-Cache, you can view the transfer savings by entering

```
pc-cache/status
```

at the DOS prompt. PC-Cache displays the following tidbits of information, as shown in Figure 10.12.

Cache Accesses. The total number of data transfers that have occurred between the cache and the current application since loading PC-Cache.

Disk Accesses. The total number of data transfers that have occurred between the disk and the current application since loading PC-Cache.

Savings. The percentage of transfers saved by PC-Cache.

The Status report also shows the amount of RAM occupied by PC-Cache and the amount of free RAM.

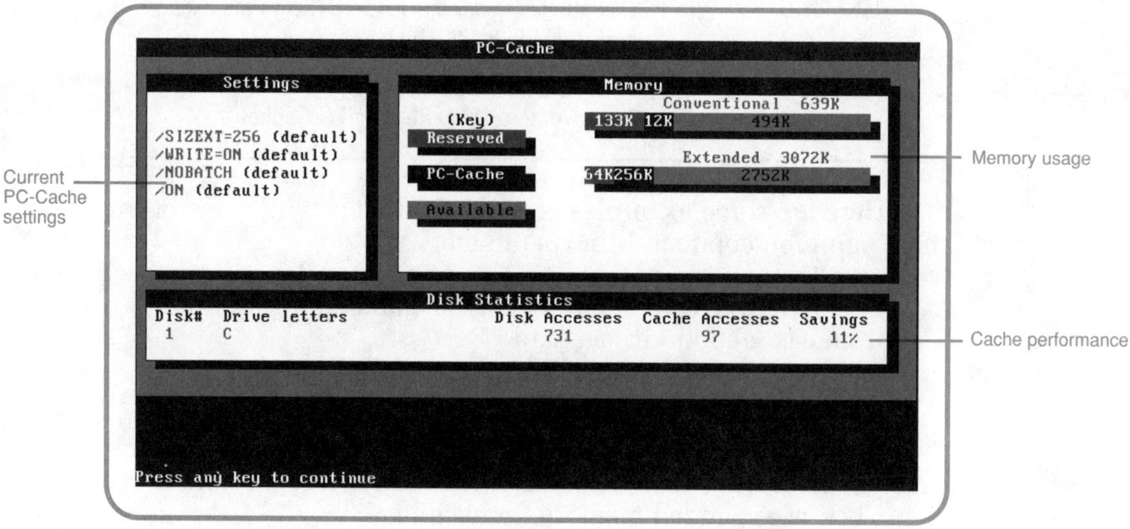

Figure 10.12   A sample efficiency report provided with the /STATUS PC-Cache parameter.

Use the /STATUS parameter to test various installations of PC-Cache. Try loading PC-Cache with just 32K of memory and perform a strict set of commands on your computer. (For example, start PC Tools Shell, access a couple of commands, and quit.) Note the performance as displayed with the STATUS parameter and then reset the cache using an extra 32K of RAM. (Note: Use the /UNLOAD parameter to unload PC-Cache, then manually reload it using more memory.)

Repeat these steps several times until PC-Cache displays no extra performance even when adding more RAM. At a certain point—which differs among computers—the performance of PC-Cache will "top out," no matter how much memory you give it.

Differences in Memory Types

PC-Cache can allocate memory for caching in regular, extended, or expanded RAM. If your computer is equipped with just 512K or 640K of base RAM (the minimum suggested for running PC Tools), you'll be using a portion of base RAM as a cache reservoir. But if your computer is equipped with additional RAM—either extended or expanded—you should use it instead. This frees the base 512K or 640K of memory to your applications programs.

295

The terms "extended" and "expanded" can be confusing, and they are often used interchangeably. However, they indicate two different forms of memory which can be installed in your computer. Typically *expanded memory* is installed in a computer in the form of a board or card. This memory board or card swaps information into and out of conventional memory (640K RAM) at high speeds, giving the user the impression that the computer has direct access to much more random-access memory (RAM) than the conventional 640K. Some programs are written to use expanded memory, allowing larger programs to run under DOS. The amount of expanded memory varies from as little as 64K to as much as 32M; many computers today come with 1M or 2M of expanded memory.

Extended memory is a special memory scheme used in computers with at least an 80286 processor. The computer contains additional RAM chips, which may be installed on a card or board. Special software memory drivers can tell your computer how to use the additional memory. Although DOS cannot address this additional RAM directly, multitasking programs, such as DESQview and Microsoft Windows 3.0, can access the memory indirectly, allowing the user to work with two or more programs simultaneously.

Note what kind of extra memory, if any, your computer has. Once again, PC Tools comes to the rescue. To determine the type and amount of memory in your computer, enter mi at the DOS prompt. This displays the Memory Information screen shown in Figure 10.13.

```
C:\TEMP>mi
Memory Info V7
(c)1991 Central Point Software, Inc.

Addr.   Total bytes   Program or device driver
-----   -----------   -------------------------
0BB3h     4,512        Device=ANSI        Attr=C053h   Name=CON
0CCEh     2,896        Device=HIMEM       Attr=A000h   Name=XMSXXXX0
0D84h    12,624        Device=MOUSE       Attr=8000h   Name=MS$MOUSE
149Ch     6,672        SHARE         /F:2048  /L:40
163Eh     5,952        COMMAND
17C0h    13,024        PC-CACHE C:\PCTOOLS\PC-CACHE.COM/WRITE=OFF
1AF0h    15,152        DATAMON       /SENTRY+
1EA4h    80,752        SAVE          C:\COLLAGE\SAVE.EXE /cg /h
325Dh   448,048        <largest free area>

654,336 bytes (639k) total DOS 4.00 conventional memory.
448,048 bytes (438k) largest executable program.

      0 bytes Extended (AT/286/386) memory, reported by BIOS.
  2,752k bytes free, reported by XMS driver version 2.0 (2.60).   HMA exists.

C:\TEMP>
```

Figure 10.13   The Memory Information screen shows total and available memory.

If there are no entries for expanded or extended memory, it means your computer doesn't have any. You may want to consider adding some. You can add expanded memory by installing an expanded memory board inside your computer. Along with the board you'll receive a diskette containing driver software that activates the memory.

Parking Your Hard Disk Drive

One of the most dangerous moments for your hard disk drive is when you turn your computer off at the end of the day. When the power is switched off, the spinning metal platters inside the drive coast to a stop. The air pressure that has been built up inside the drive subsides as the platters slow. This air has been keeping the delicate magnetic heads floating a safe distance from the disk media, but now that it's beginning to diminish, the heads begin to float toward the metal. (See Figure 10.14.)

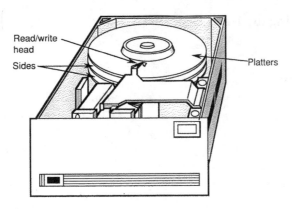

Figure 10.14   Sides and platters.

297

If the heads happen to strike against the metal disks while they are still turning, damage to the hard disk could result. While the heads themselves probably won't be hurt, whatever data was recorded at the point of impact could be gone.

You can eliminate almost all hard disk crashes caused by the heads striking the disk by using the Park Disk program. This program moves the read/write heads in the hard disk drive over an area on the disk that contains no data. While the Park Disk program won't prevent the heads from striking the disk surface accidentally (if it happens), at least no valuable data will be lost.

You'll especially want to park the heads of your hard disk if you plan on moving the computer. Even with the computer off and the hard disk drive inactive, moving the mechanism could cause the heads to drop against the disk surface.

Note that many late-model hard disks include their own automatic head-parking mechanism. This mechanism retracts the heads after a short period of inactivity, or the moment the computer's power is turned off (enough power remains in the circuitry of the hard disk drive to move the heads to a *safe zone*, anywhere that doesn't contain a file).

Although it's rare, double-parking could damage your hard disk drive. That is, damage could result if the heads are parked first with PC Tools Shell, then by the drive's own internal autoparking mechanism. Check the instructions that came with your computer or hard disk drive to be sure.

Follow these simple Quick Steps to park the heads in your hard disk:

Parking the Hard Disk Drive

1. If you haven't done so already, load the PC Tools Shell program.

2. Change to the drive you want to park.   Park the disk that contains the PC Tools program files last.

3. Pull down the Disk menu and select **P**ark Disk Heads.   Parks the hard disk drive.

4. Repeat Steps 2 and 3 for each disk you want to park.

5. Turn off the computer.   □

298

> ▶ **Tip:** You can also run the Park Disk program from the DOS prompt. Change to the drive and directory that contains the PC Tools program files. Type `park x` (where x is the letter of the drive you want to park) and press Enter. Remember to park the disk that contains the PC Tools program files last.

Unlike some disk-parking programs, Shell doesn't disable the computer when the hard disk is parked. If you choose another command or press the **O**K button, as shown in Figure 10.15, the heads will *unpark*. You'll have to repeat the steps outlined above to repark the heads before you turn the computer off.

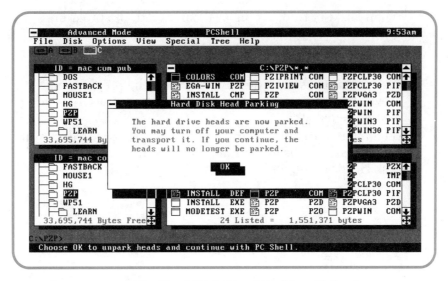

Figure 10.15   The Hard Disk Head Parking dialog box.

299

What You Have Learned

In this chapter you learned how to maintain your hard disk and hard drive and keep it in good working order. You also learned:

▶ A file is said to be fragmented when it is stored on two or more noncontiguous clusters on a disk.

▶ The main task of the PC Tools Compress program is to eliminate fragmentation.

▶ Compress can optionally provide a printed report of the defragmentation operation.

▶ DiskFix's Surface Scan command can be used to test for formatting and data errors.

▶ DiskFix's Revitalize a Disk command reads information from each cluster, one at a time, formats the cluster, and then writes the information back onto it.

▶ When DiskFix finds a cluster it can't read, the program marks it as bad so it can't be used by DOS again, and DiskFix writes any information it found on the cluster to another (reliable) cluster.

▶ Disk caching, as provided by the PC-Cache program, improves hard disk performance by storing commonly used data in memory.

▶ When you're finished using your computer for the day, you should park the heads in the hard disk drive using the Park Disk Heads command.

300

System Information and Virus Protection

In This Chapter

- ▶ *Knowing your system*
- ▶ *How your system compares to others*
- ▶ *Understanding viruses and how they work*
- ▶ *Protecting your system against viruses*
- ▶ *Recovering from a virus*

New to PC Tools 7 are two programs specially designed to help you learn about and protect your system: the System Information program and VDefend. The System Information program acts as a computer consultant, pointing out important details about your computer system, including the size and speed of your hard disk, the types and amount of memory installed on your system, and a measure of how your computer compares to other similar models on the market.

VDefend is an antivirus program that notifies you whenever a virus tries to infect your system. A *virus* is a program, unleashed by a computer vandal, that is designed to destroy data. Although the program cannot eradicate a virus from files that are already infected, it defends your system against initial infection.

Getting Information About Your System

Whenever you purchase or use a program, many questions arise concerning your computer and its configuration. A program may specify a list of system requirements: a hard disk, a high-density floppy disk drive, 640K base memory and 2M extended or expanded memory, and a VGA adapter. Does your system meet these requirements? To find out, you could turn to the documentation that came with your computer, but where do you look? And even if you find a section explaining what your computer does and does not have, the documentation will usually tell you that your system may vary.

With the PC Tools System Information program, you'll no longer need to search vague documentation for answers or call your computer dealer to find out about your system. Simply start the program, and you'll see a screenful of information about your system. If that information doesn't answer your question, you can get more information by selecting topics from convenient pull-down menus. The program will even test your system and compare it against similar systems.

You can start the System Information program from Shell, from the DOS prompt, or from Windows:

From the DOS prompt, change to the drive and directory that contains the PC Tools program files (for example, C:\PCTOOLS), type `si` and press Enter.

From Shell, pull down the Special menu and select System Info.

From Windows, double-click on the System Info icon or highlight the icon and press Enter.

No matter how you start the program, you'll see the System Information screen, shown in Figure 11.1. This screen displays three windows, which provide the following information:

Computer

▶ System Type indicates the type of processor installed in your system (for example, 80286 or 80386). Multitasking programs, including Windows, may require a 386 processor for optimum performance.

▶ Operating System indicates the version of DOS your system is using. Most programs require that you use a specific version of DOS. For example, PC Tools requires version 3.0 or higher.

302

► Video Adapter shows the type of video driver your system has (for example, EGA or VGA). Some programs, graphics programs especially, require a certain type of adapter in order to display high-resolution graphics.

► I/O Ports indicates the type of ports installed in your computer. You'll often need to know which ports are available when installing a printer or mouse.

► Keyboard/Mouse lets you find out more about the mouse or keyboard connected to your computer.

► CMOS allows you to view the CMOS information stored in your system. This includes the number of logical hard drives, the number and type of floppy drives, and the system date and time.

► Network provides information about the various users connected to the network and the amount of space available on the network server. (For more information about this feature, see Chapter 13.)

► Drive Summary defines the number and types of drives your computer has.

Relative Performance

► Displays a graph which shows how your computer stacks up against a comparable model.

Memory

► Conventional indicates the base memory installed in your system. This memory, broken down into Allocated and Free, is memory that DOS can access directly.

► Extended shows the extended memory in your system. This is broken down into Allocated and Free memory.

► Expanded shows the expanded memory in your system. This is broken down into Allocated and Free memory.

The screen shown in Figure 11.1 answers many questions. The computer uses a 386 processor with DOS version 4.0 and has a VGA adapter installed. It has an 82M hard drive and 2 floppy drives (1.2M and 1.44M). 640K base RAM is installed, and about 3M of extended RAM is available.

303

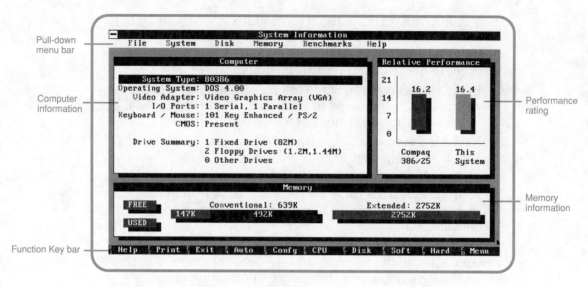

Figure 11.1   The main System Information screen.

To get more information about any of these topics, type the highlighted letter in the topic's name, or highlight the topic and press Enter, or click on the topic with your mouse. An information dialog box will appear, as in Figure 11.2, providing additional details.

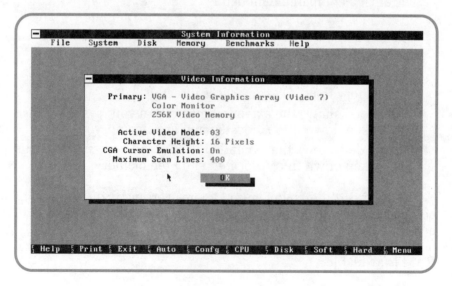

Figure 11.2   Select a topic to view additional information.

Viewing Your AUTOEXEC.BAT and CONFIG.SYS Files

If you enter a change in your AUTOEXEC.BAT or CONFIG.SYS file (or you run an installation program that changes the file for you), your computer and programs may not run the way you want them to run. Either of these files can contain commands that load incompatible programs when you start your computer, causing all sorts of havoc.

If you change one of these files, and you start to run into problems, you should view these files to see if any command looks strange. For example, if you're getting error messages concerning memory usage, two disk-caching programs may be loaded. If you look at your AUTOEXEC.BAT file and it contains the PC-CACHE command and then you look at your CONFIG.SYS file and it contains the DEVICE= SMARTDRV.SYS command, you know that you have to get rid of one of these commands and then reboot your computer to correct the problem.

305

The System Information screen allows you to view either of these files. Simply pull down the File menu and select the appropriate command or select F4 (Auto) or F5 (Confg) from the Function Key bar at the bottom of the screen. A dialog box appears, as in Figure 11.3, showing the contents of the selected file. If you find a command that you want to edit, you'll have to quit System Information, return to PC Shell, and then use the Shell File Editor to modify the file, as explained in Chapter 5.

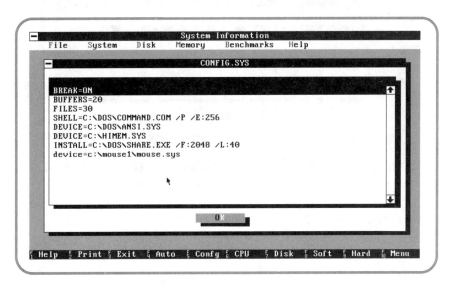

Figure 11.3   You can view the contents of AUTOEXEC.BAT or CONFIG.SYS to troubleshoot common problems.

More Disk Information

To obtain more information about your disk drives, pull down the Disk menu and select one of the following options:

Drive Summary—displays the Logical Drive Information window, shown in Figure 11.4. This window displays the number of drives installed, the type or size of each drive, the capacity of each drive, and the default or root directory on each disk.

Disk Details—displays the Logical Drive Detailed Information screen, shown in Figure 11.5, which provides additional information about the structure of each hard disk. To view information about a disk, select it from the list (if you're checking a floppy disk, make sure it's in the drive).

What's a *logical drive*? Most PCs that have a single drive. This is called the *physical drive*. Because a hard drive can store so much information, some computer dealers and users divide the drive into logical units (C, D, E, F, etc.) to make it more manageable.

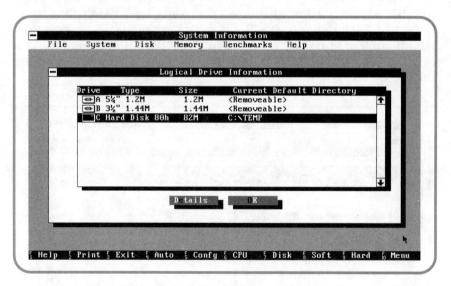

Figure 11.4   The Logical Drive Information window provides a rundown of all installed drives.

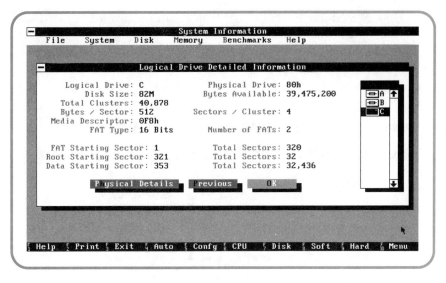

Figure 11.5   The Logical Drive Detailed Information screen provides information about the structure of the drive.

307

More Information About Memory

Although the main System Information screen can answer most of your questions about your computer's memory, you may need to know more. For example, you may need to know what programs reside in your computer's memory right now. To get this information, pull down the Memory menu and select the type of memory about which you want more information. A memory map appears, as in Figure 11.6, providing a list of all programs currently using your system's memory.

Performing Benchmark Tests

Ever wonder how your computer compares to others on the market? With the System Information Benchmark tests, you can test your computer's disk speed, CPU (Central Processing Unit) speed, and overall performance to find out how your computer stacks up.

To perform a benchmark test, pull down the Benchmark menu and select one of the following options:

CPU Speed Test—measures the speed of your computer's central processing unit and compares it to the speed of other computers.

Disk Speed Test—tests how fast your computer can read and write information to disk.

Overall Performance—compares your computer's overall speed to other computers, as in Figure 11.7.

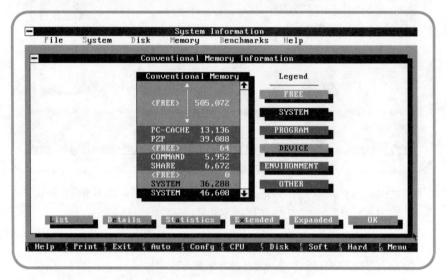

Figure 11.6   Select an option from the Memory menu to view a memory map.

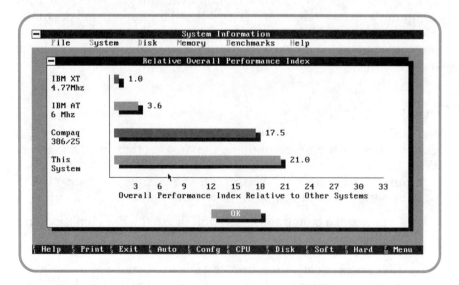

Figure 11.7   The Benchmark Overall Performance test shows the overall speed of your computer.

> ▶ **Tip:** If you're shopping for a computer, copy the SI.EXE file from your PCTOOLS directory to a floppy disk, and take the disk along. (Be sure to write-protect the disk, to prevent it from picking up any viruses from the dealer's computer). If you have questions about a particular computer that's on display, insert the disk and run the System Information program.

Printing a Report of the Results

It's a good idea to print a System Information report at least the first time you run System Information. Many times, when you call technical support for help about a particular program, the technical support person will ask questions about your system. With a printed report, you should be able to answer all questions.

309

> ▶ **Tip:** It's also helpful to have a printout of your original AUTOEXEC.BAT and CONFIG.SYS files. If anything happens to these files, the printout will help you re-create them or help you find out how the file has changed.

To print a report, pull down the File menu and select **P**rint Report. The Reporting Options dialog box appears, as shown in Figure 11.8. By default, all the options are selected to provide a full report. To turn any of these options off, press the highlighted letter in the option's name or click on the option box with your mouse. Once the options are set, select **P**rint to print the report.

Protecting Your System Against Viruses

A virus is a program specially designed to destroy files and lock up computer systems. A virus can enter your system through its modem, through network lines, or from an infected floppy disk. The virus then spreads to infect your hard disk and any floppy disks you happen to use after contracting the virus. The virus infects program files and then works in the background to destroy files on disk, sometimes wiping out an entire disk.

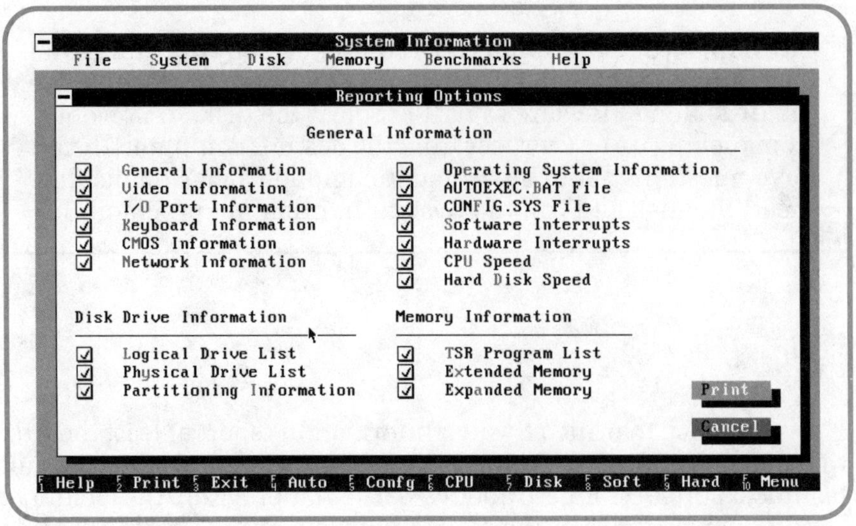

```
┌─────────────────────────────────────────────────────────────┐
│ ─              System Information                            │
│  File   System   Disk   Memory   Benchmarks   Help          │
│ ┌───────────────────────────────────────────────────────┐   │
│ │ ─                Reporting Options                     │   │
│ │                 General Information                    │   │
│ │                                                        │   │
│ │  ☑ General Information    ☑ Operating System Information│  │
│ │  ☑ Video Information      ☑ AUTOEXEC.BAT File          │   │
│ │  ☑ I/O Port Information   ☑ CONFIG.SYS File            │   │
│ │  ☑ Keyboard Information   ☑ Software Interrupts        │   │
│ │  ☑ CMOS Information       ☑ Hardware Interrupts        │   │
│ │  ☑ Network Information    ☑ CPU Speed                  │   │
│ │                           ☑ Hard Disk Speed           │   │
│ │                                                        │   │
│ │  Disk Drive Information    Memory Information          │   │
│ │                                                        │   │
│ │  ☑ Logical Drive List     ☑ TSR Program List          │   │
│ │  ☑ Physical Drive List    ☑ Extended Memory           │   │
│ │  ☑ Partitioning Information ☑ Expanded Memory    Print │   │
│ │                                                 Cancel │   │
│ └───────────────────────────────────────────────────────┘   │
│  Help  Print  Exit  Auto  Confg  CPU  Disk  Soft  Hard  Menu│
└─────────────────────────────────────────────────────────────┘
```

Figure 11.8   The Reporting Options dialog box lets you include any information you want in the report.

310

Fortunately, PC Tools includes the VDefend program to help defend against viruses. Once installed, VDefend starts every time you boot your computer and works in the background, keeping watch for incoming viruses. If your computer gets infected, VDefend provides an early warning that can help you stop the virus in its tracks.

How Susceptible Is Your System?

Computer viruses are not airborne diseases that your computer can mysteriously contract. To contract a virus, your computer must be on, and the virus must be introduced to your system through one of its ports or drives. Your computer may be at risk if:

▶ You are connected to other computers via modem. Your computer is more at risk if you obtain programs from BBS (Bulletin Board System) services.

▶ You are connected to other computers on a network. You can't do much to protect your individual computer in this case. Protection is up to the Network Manager.

▶ Somebody else uses your computer.

▶ You obtain program or data disks from outside sources.

Preventing Viruses from Infecting Your System

The best way to stop viruses from destroying files is to prevent them from infecting your system. Take the following precautions:

▶ Before you use a program obtained from a friend or BBS, back up your hard disk and install VDefend. If, after running the program, VDefend discovers a virus, you can reformat your hard disk and restore your program and data files using your backups.

▶ Before you install a commercial program, write-protect the disks you purchased. If your hard disk is infected with a virus, the write-protection will at least protect the disks you purchased. You can then use the disks to reinstall the program after you eradicate the virus.

▶ Back up your data files separately. Although viruses can wipe out data files, viruses rarely infect data files.

▶ When you back up files using CP Backup, run Backup with the Scan for Viruses Only option turned on. Backup checks the files you selected to back up and notifies you of any infected files. You can then rename the infected file to prevent it from being backed up.

▶ Don't let anyone else use your computer without permission. If your system does contract a virus, you can then track down the source.

▶ Write-protect your program files. You can change the write-protect attribute for files with the .EXE, .COM, and .BAT extensions; these are your program files. These files are common targets for viruses. By changing the attribute to Read Only, you can prevent many viruses from infecting these files. To change a file's write-protect attribute, use the Change File command from PC Shell's File menu, as explained in Chapter 5.

311

Installing VDefend for Early Warning

Preventive measures help, but most users can't afford to isolate their computers from the rest of the computer world. The next best protection you can hope for is to detect the virus soon after it has infected your system. You can then destroy the files that the virus has infected and restore them virus-free from your backup copies to purge the virus.

VDefend offers an early-detection system that warns you when your system is infected and can often stop a virus before it destroys any files. It does this by offering two forms of protection:

▶ Checks program files (files with the .COM and .EXE extensions) for infection by known viruses. If VDefend detects a virus, it displays a warning box. You can then use a separate virus-eradicating program, such as Central Point's Anti-Virus program (sold separately) to destroy the virus.

▶ Warns of low-level formatting attempts. Some viruses destroy files by performing a low-level formatting operation. If such an operation is attempted, even by you, VDefend will warn you. You can then proceed with the operation or stop it immediately.

It's best to run VDefend whenever you use your computer. To have VDefend run automatically, add the VDEFEND command to your AUTOEXEC.BAT file, or have the INSTALL program add it for you.

You'll be given the following two options for loading VDefend:

Load VDefend in AUTOEXEC.BAT—loads VDefend as a memory-resident program from your AUTOEXEC.BAT file. If you want to unload VDefend temporarily later, you can unload it by typing `vdefend/u` and pressing Enter at the DOS prompt. However, this loads VDefend after COMMAND.COM is loaded, so VDefend does not check this important file for viruses. (Viruses commonly infect COMMAND.COM.)

Load VDefend in CONFIG.SYS—loads VDefend as a driver from your CONFIG.SYS file. This loads VDefend before COMMAND.COM, so VDefend checks COMMAND.COM for viruses. With VDefend loaded in this way, however, you cannot temporarily unload it from memory. To remove VDefend from memory, you must delete its command from the CONFIG.SYS file and then reboot your computer.

To add VDefend to your AUTOEXEC.BAT or CONFIG.SYS file, perform the following steps:

1. Exit any programs that are currently running and display the DOS prompt.

2. Change to the drive and directory that contains the PC Tools program files. This is usually C:\PCTOOLS.

3. Type `install` and press Enter. The PC Tools Program Configuration screen appears.

4. Select **V**Defend. The Configure VDefend dialog box appears, as in Figure 11.9.

5. Select Load VDefend in **AUTOEXEC.BAT** or Load VDefend in CONFIG.**S**YS. A check mark next to the option indicates it's on.

6. Select **O**K to return to the main Configuration screen.

7. Select E**x**it.

8. Select **S**ave Configuration to put a check mark in the box, and then select **O**K.

9. Select **R**eboot if you want to run VDefend now, or select **D**OS if you want VDefend to run the next time you boot your computer.

When you reboot, you'll see the VDefend information box shown in Figure 11.10, indicating VDefend was successfully loaded.

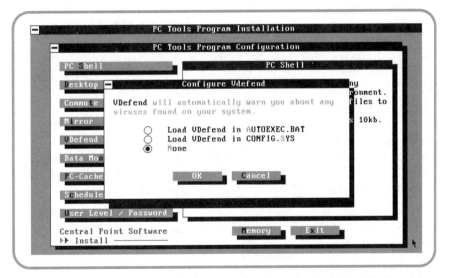

Figure 11.9   The Configure VDefend screen lets you load VDefend from your CONFIG.SYS or AUTOEXEC.BAT file.

> ▶ **Tip:** Although VDefend takes up very little of your computer's memory it may take up enough memory to interfere with other memory-resident programs. You can unload VDefend permanently by running INSTALL again and turning VDefend off. To unload VDefend temporarily, unload all other memory-resident programs, and then enter `vdefend /u` at the DOS prompt. This option is available only if you load VDefend from AUTOEXEC.BAT.

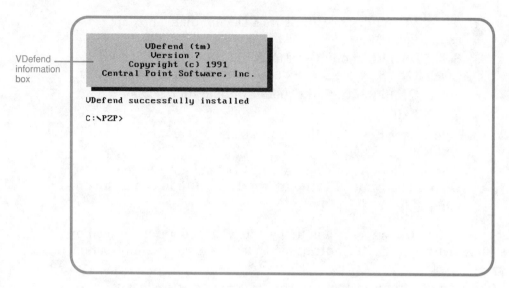

VDefend
information
box

```
                  UDefend (tm)
                   Uersion 7
                Copyright (c) 1991
          Central Point Software, Inc.

UDefend successfully installed

C:\PZP>
```

*Figure 11.10   When VDefend is successfully loaded, it displays
an information box to let you know.*

Poor Man's Way of Destroying Viruses

Although it's useful to have a program such as Anti-Virus that can
destroy existing viruses, such a program is not essential for recovering from a virus. The trick is to keep uninfected backups and to
prevent your original program disks from getting infected.

If VDefend displays the warning box, indicating a virus has
infected your system, you can then take the necessary steps to
eradicate the virus:

1. Save your work and quit whatever you're doing.
2. Back up any files that have been added or changed since the
   last backup. (Use CP Backup and turn on the Scan For
   Viruses Only option before performing the backup.)
3. Write-protect your backup disks to prevent them from
   getting infected.
4. If you know which files were infected, delete only those files
   and then restore them from your backups.

   If you don't know which files were infected, reformat your
   hard disk and restore all files using your backups.

5. If a program is not included in your full backup, reinstall the program from the write-protected disks.

After performing these steps, your system should be clean, but load VDefend immediately, in case the virus attacks again.

What You Have Learned

In this chapter, you learned how to use the System Information program to get important details about your computer. You learned how to load VDefend to protect your system against viruses. You also learned:

▶ You can use the System Information screen to find out about your computer's central processing unit, the size and speed of your hard disk, and the types and amount of memory installed on your system.

▶ The System Information program runs several benchmark tests that compare your computer to similar models.

▶ You can print a full report containing all the details about your system.

▶ Viruses are destructive programs that can invade your system from various sources.

▶ The best way to protect your system against viruses is to prevent them from being introduced into your system.

▶ The next best way to protect against viruses is to install a program which provides an early warning. You can then destroy any infected files before the virus spreads.

▶ Keeping virus-free backups will help you recover after a virus has infected your system and destroyed your files.

315

Using PC Tools Desktop

In This Chapter

- ▶ *Loading PC Tools Desktop*
- ▶ *Using the Desktop word processor*
- ▶ *Checking the spelling in your documents*
- ▶ *Maintaining data using the data manager*
- ▶ *Keeping an appointment schedule*
- ▶ *Using the Desktop calculators*

PC Tools offers a collection of handy miniapplications that you can use by themselves or within one of your applications. You can use these desk accessories, which are all contained within the PC Tools Desktop program, to augment your regular applications or in place of a more complex stand-alone program.

The following is a list of the miniprograms included with PC Tools Desktop:

- ▶ A word processor
- ▶ A data manager
- ▶ A communications terminal
- ▶ An appointment scheduler
- ▶ A selection of multifunction calculators

This chapter covers only the basics of the PC Tools Desktop applications, providing quick-start introductions to get you going. You should refer to the Desktop Manager manual that accompanies the PC Tools 7 package for in-depth coverage of the desk accessories.

In Review: Running Desktop

In Chapter 2, "Getting Started with PC Tools," you learned how to start Desktop as either a stand-alone or memory-resident program. For your convenience, we'll quickly review the methods of starting Desktop here. Recall there are four ways to run Desktop:

▶ As a stand-alone program at the DOS prompt.

▶ As a memory-resident program (loaded manually by you).

▶ As a memory-resident program (loaded automatically by the AUTOEXEC.BAT batch file when the computer is first turned on).

▶ As a stand-alone program from Windows.

The following steps assume you are currently logged on to the drive and directory that contains the PC Tools programs—usually C:\PCTOOLS. Note that if you installed PC Tools to run from any directory, you don't have to change to the PC Tools directory before entering the command. To run Desktop,

From the DOS prompt, type `desktop` and press Enter.

Manually in memory-resident mode, type `desktop /r` and press Enter. Press Ctrl-Spacebar to activate Desktop.

As a memory-resident already loaded with AUTOEXEC.BAT, press Ctrl-Spacebar to activate Desktop.

From Windows, double-click on the Desktop icon, or high-light the Desktop icon and press Enter.

The Control and Spacebar keys are hot-keys that activate Desktop from memory. Under most circumstances, you can activate Desktop from within DOS or any application. Some PC programs may require all the memory in your computer, however, and Desktop may not load.

You press these same keys to deactivate Desktop and return to the DOS prompt or to your application. Remember that even though Desktop is deactivated, it still resides in your computer's memory, so you can call it back up any time. It also continues to consume a portion of your computer's RAM, so if you need to reclaim that memory for use by another application, enter `kill` at the DOS prompt. This removes Desktop (as well as Shell, if it has also been loaded as memory-resident) from the computer's RAM. Note that KILL.EXE is a PC Tools program and must be on the currently selected drive, or DOS won't be able to find it.

After Desktop is loaded (and activated if you're using it in memory-resident mode), your computer screen should look like the one in Figure 12.1. If you loaded Desktop in memory-resident mode without the /CS option, you won't see the calendars; instead, you'll see the program you were using before running Desktop.

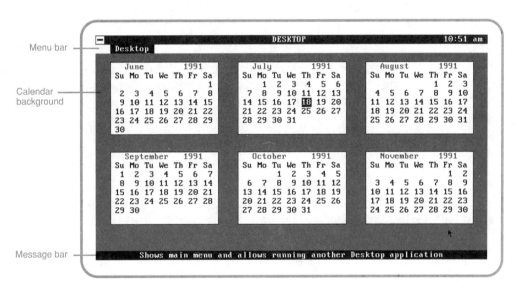

319

Menu bar

Calendar background

Message bar

Figure 12.1   The opening Desktop display with component parts.

Special Desktop Parameters

Parameters are switches or options you select when you load a program into your computer. Desktop supports about 10 parameters that control the way the program works and interacts with your computer. To use a parameter, type the parameter after the command you type to load Desktop; that is, type `desktop`, press the Spacebar, type a forward slash (`/`), and then type the parameter (for example, `desktop /bw`). You've already learned about one of Desktop's parameters, the /R switch that loads Desktop as a memory-resident instead of a stand-alone program. In most cases, you can combine switches to activate many options.

/BW

Starts Desktop in black-and-white mode.

/CS

Clears the screen and displays calendars in the background when Desktop is running in memory-resident mode. The Calendar background is automatically included when Desktop runs in stand-alone mode.

/C3 or /C4 = IRQ,xxx

Assigns a serial port to the Desktop autodialer. Refer to your modem manual for the Interrupt Request Level (IRQ) and port address (xxx).

/DQ

Disables the Quick-load feature when activating Desktop from the DOS prompt. (Quick-load helps load Desktop faster when you activate it; it's used only when Desktop is loaded as a memory-resident program.) Use the /DQ switch if you are experiencing problems running Desktop as memory-resident when activating the program from the DOS prompt.

/IM

Disables the mouse. It is helpful if you are using an older mouse driver that is not supported by PC Tools.

/IN

Runs Desktop in color with a Hercules InColor graphics card (memory-resident mode only).

/LE

Exchanges right and left mouse buttons to accommodate left-handed persons.

/LCD

For use with laptop computers equipped with liquid crystal displays.

/MM

Allows you to start Desktop without invoking a Desktop application that may have been running during the last session.

/Od

Selects a different drive to contain the Desktop overlay files (these include DESKTOP.OVL, DESKTOP.IMG, and DESKTOP.THM). Ordinarily, Desktop places these overlay files in the drive and directory containing the PC Tools files; you can change it if your drive (or RAM disk) gets too full. Replace the d with a drive letter, such as /Oa.

/50

Displays Desktop in 50 line resolution; used only with VGA monitors.

/R

Loads Desktop memory-resident.

/RA

Loads Desktop memory-resident and automatically starts the Appointment Scheduler.

Table 12.1 offers a quick reference guide to using the parameter switches with Desktop running as a stand-alone program from the DOS prompt, or as a memory-resident program.

Table 12.1   Parameter Switches for Desktop Operating Modes

Parameter	From DOS Prompt	As a Memory-Resident Program
/BW	X	X
/CS		X
/C3 & /C4	X	X
/DQ		X
/IM	X	X
/IN		X
/LE	X	X
/LCD	X	X
/MM		X
/Od	X	X
/50	X	X
/R		X

In the remainder of this chapter, we'll assume you've already loaded Desktop.

The Desktop Menu

When you start Desktop, you'll see the menu shown in Figure 12.2. This menu lets you access the miniapplications included in Desktop:

322

Notepads. Lets you create, edit, and print documents containing up to 60,000 characters. Advanced features let you copy and move blocks of text and check spelling.

Outlines. Lets you type text under outline headings, collapse the text to see only the headings, and expand the text to work with it again.

Databases. Lets you store and manage information, such as address lists and parts lists.

Appointment Scheduler. Helps you keep track of your daily appointments and things to do.

Telecommunications. Lets you connect your computer to other computers (via modem) and send FAX messages. (Refer to Chapter 13 for more information.)

Macro Editor. Lets you assign several keystrokes to a single keystroke so you can play back the keystrokes by pressing a single key.

Clipboard. A temporary storage area that lets you cut a section of text from one document and paste it into another document.

Calculators. Four calculators are available for your use: algebraic, scientific, financial, and programmer's.

Utilities. This group of utilities lets you modify the appearance and operation of Desktop.

323

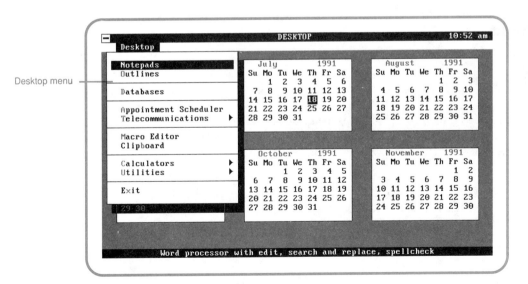

Figure 12.2   The Desktop menu shows a list of the Desktop applications you can run.

Working with Desktop's Windows

Whenever you run one of the applications on the menu, Desktop opens a window that lets you work in the application. You can open up to 15 separate windows stacked one on top of the other. A sample setup is shown in Figure 12.3.

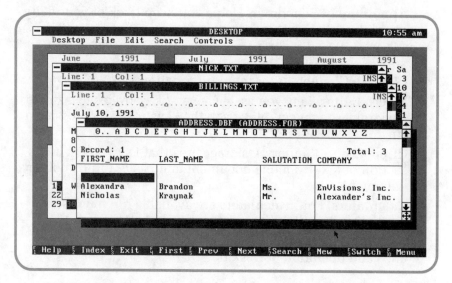

Figure 12.3   Desktop lets you work with several windows.

Switching Windows

To move from one window to another with the keyboard, select F9 Switch. A menu appears, like the one in Figure 12.4, listing the windows on screen. To activate a window, select it from the menu.

If you have a mouse, selection is even easier, as long as part of the window you want to switch to is visible. Click anywhere inside the window you want to activate. The window is moved to the front, and the cursor appears in it.

324

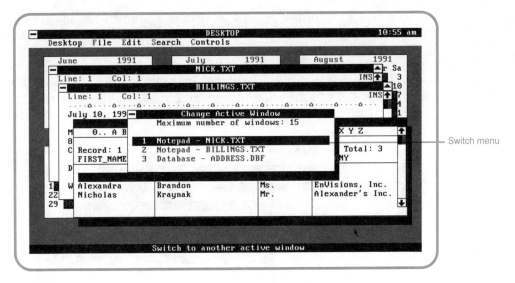

Figure 12.4   *The Switch menu lets you switch to another window.*

Moving, Sizing, and Closing Windows

You can move and resize windows at any time to reorganize the Desktop work surface. To move and resize a window, perform the following steps:

1. Press Alt-Spacebar or click on the close button in the upper left corner of the screen. The System Control menu appears as in Figure 12.5.

2. Select **M**ove. A message box appears, telling you to use the arrow keys.

3. Use the arrow keys to move the window in the direction desired. Press Enter when you're done.

4. Pull down the System Control menu again.

5. Select **S**ize.

6. Press Up Arrow to move the bottom of the window up or press Down Arrow to move it down. Press Left Arrow to move the right side of the window to the left or Right Arrow to move it to the right. Press Enter when you're done.

To move a window using a mouse, position the mouse cursor inside the top border of the window and hold down the left mouse button. Drag the window where you want it to appear and release the mouse button. To resize a window, point to the resize box in the lower right corner of the window (see Figure 12.5) and hold down the mouse button. Drag the cursor down and to the right to enlarge the window or up and to the left to shrink it.

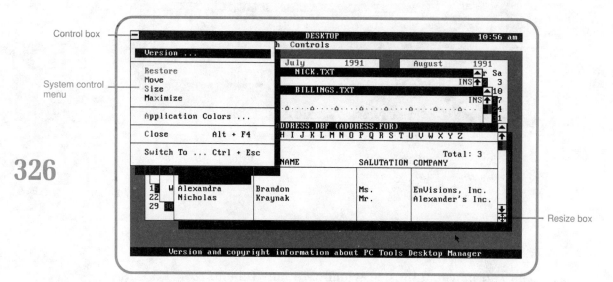

Figure 12.5   *Use the System Control menu to manage your desktop.*

> **Tip:** The quickest way to enlarge a window is to select Maximize from the System Control menu. The window then takes up the entire screen. To shrink the window back to its original size, select **R**estore.

To close a window you've been working with, press the Esc key or click on the close box in the upper left corner of the window. The window is closed and any changes are saved to disk.

Word Processing

PC Tools calls its Desktop word processor *Notepads*. With a name like that you'd think the word processor would be a simple note keeper, offering just rudimentary text writing and editing capabilities. Surprisingly, Notepads is a full-function word processor that boasts many powerful features, including a built-in spelling checker, search and replace, and headers and footers. If you're a WordStar user, you'll be pleased to learn that Notepads is compatible with WordStar files. Notepads can read and write documents in WordStar format. The following Quick Steps give the procedure for starting Notepads:

Starting Notepads

1. Pull down the Desktop menu and select Notepads.

   Starts Notepads. The dialog box in Figure 12.6 appears.

2. Press the New button if you want to create a new document, or select a file from the list and press the Load button.

   Creates a new document (named WORK.TXT), or opens an existing document.

327

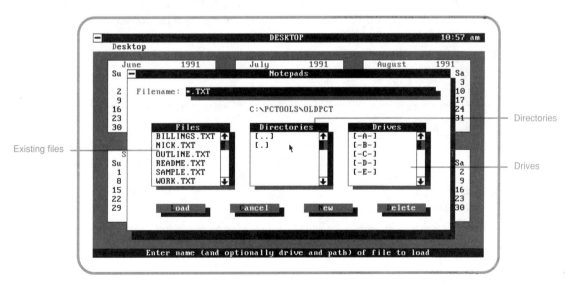

Figure 12.6   The Notepads Open/New Document dialog box.

When started, Notepads displays its own editing window and menu bar. As Figure 12.7 illustrates, the Notepads display contains the following basic parts:

Menu bar. Located at the top of the screen.

Window border. Shows the current active window (highlighted).

Title bar. Displays the name of the file.

Status line. Shows where the cursor is located in the document, as well as the current edit mode. In Insert mode (INS), whatever you type is inserted at the cursor; characters to the right of the cursor move to accommodate the new text. In overstrike mode, the text you type replaces existing text. To switch modes, press the Ins key.

Selection bar. The blank space at the far left of the window between the window border and text. It allows you to select entire rows at a time with the mouse.

Ruler line. Indicates current tabs or margins for document.

Vertical scroll bar. Scrolls through the length of the text.

Message bar. Located at the bottom of the screen, displays function keys you can use for common tasks, such as Load, Find/Replace, and Spell check.

Resize box. Used for resizing the window.

Close box. Used for closing the window. When you close a window, any changes you made to the file are saved to disk.

Maximize/Minimize box. Lets you zoom a window to take up the entire screen, or minimize a zoomed window to its original size.

▶ **Tip:** To enlarge a window quickly, use the Maximize command in the Windows Control menu. The window expands to full size. Choose **R**estore and the window returns to its smaller state. If you have a mouse, you can zoom and unzoom windows simply by clicking inside the Maximize/Minimize box.

Figure 12.7   *The component parts of the Notepads display.*

329

Writing and Editing Text

The most common task you do with any word processor is write and edit text. Follow these easy steps to begin a new document:

1. Pull down the Desktop menu and select **N**otepads.
2. Press the **N**ew button to start a blank document. All new documents use the blank template document WORK.TXT. Notepads will warn you that a file with that name already exists (unless you've erased it). At the dialog box that appears, press the **O**K button to continue.
3. Start writing when the empty window appears.

If you're familiar with computer word processors, you'll find Notepads intuitive and easy to learn. Words that are too long to fit on the current line are automatically wrapped to the next line. When you want to start a new paragraph or line, press Enter. If you make a mistake, press the Backspace key to erase characters to the left of the cursor. You can also use the Delete key to erase characters to the right of the cursor.

Press the cursor keys to move the cursor without editing or writing text. Table 12.2 shows the functions of the cursor keys within the Notepads editing window. Note that the cursor cannot be moved to an area in the window that does not contain text.

Table 12.2 Cursor Key Functions Within Notepads Editing Window

Key	Function
Right	Moves the cursor one character to the right
Left	Moves the cursor one character to the left
Up	Moves the cursor up one line
Down	Moves the cursor down one line
Ctrl-Right	Moves the cursor right one word
Ctrl-Left	Moves the cursor left one word
Home	Moves the cursor to the beginning of the current line
End	Moves the cursor to the end of the current line
Ctrl-Home	Moves the cursor to the top of the document
Ctrl-End	Moves the cursor to the end of the document
Home, Home	Moves the cursor to the top line of the window
End, End	Moves the cursor to the bottom line of the window
Page Up	Scrolls up one window
Page Down	Scrolls down one window
Ctrl-Page Up	Scrolls up one line (cursor remains stationary)
Ctrl-Page Down	Scrolls down one line (cursor remains stationary)

Selecting Text

Sometimes you may wish to work on a group of text rather than deal with each individual character. Let's say, for example, that you don't want the middle paragraph shown in Figure 12.8. Instead of deleting each character one at a time, you can select the whole paragraph and delete all the text in one step. With the keyboard,

1. Position the cursor at the beginning of the paragraph.
2. Pull down the Edit menu and choose **M**ark Block.
3. Move the cursor to the end of the paragraph. As you move the cursor, the text in between is highlighted.
4. Pull down the Edit menu and select Cu**t** to Clipboard. The text disappears from the screen.

The task of selecting or marking text is made easier if you have a mouse. Simply position the mouse pointer over the start of the paragraph, press and hold the left button, then drag the mouse button to the end of the paragraph. Press the Delete key and the paragraph vanishes.

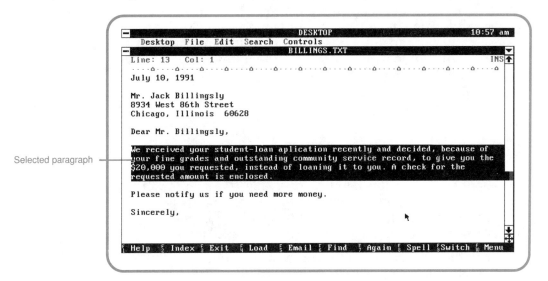

Selected paragraph

Figure 12.8   Notepads window with center paragraph selected, ready for deletion.

331

Cutting, Copying, and Pasting

A powerful feature of the Notepads word processor is its temporary clipboard. This clipboard stores a block of text that you previously selected and cut or copied using the appropriate commands from the Edit menu. You can then paste this text anywhere within the document, or even in another Notepads document.

To cut or copy a block of text to the clipboard, select it following the steps previously outlined. Then choose the Cut to Clipboard or Copy to Clipboard command from the Edit menu.

▶   Cut to Clipboard removes the selected text from the document and stores it in the clipboard.

▶   Copy to Clipboard takes a snapshot of the selected text and stores the copy in the clipboard. The original selection remains intact.

To paste the contents of the clipboard, move the cursor to where you want the text moved, then choose the **P**aste from Clipboard command from the Edit menu.

> ▶ **Tip:** The text stored in the clipboard remains until you quit Desktop or cut or copy other text. You can use this feature to paste the same block of text within one or more documents repeatedly. You can use this technique, for instance, as a quick means to fill in your return name and address in a series of letters you're writing.

Spell-Checking

You should get into the habit of checking the spelling of your documents before printing and distributing them. Spell-checking not only keeps a watchful eye over your spelling, but also helps nab the occasional typographical error. To spell-check a document:

1. With the cursor anywhere within the document, pull down the Edit menu and select Spellcheck **F**ile.
2. When Notepads catches a word it thinks is misspelled, it highlights the word and displays the dialog box shown in Figure 12.9. Press the appropriate key according to the action you want to take: **I**gnore (skip the word), **C**orrect (provide a new spelling), **A**dd (add the word to the spelling dictionary), or **Q**uit (finished with spell-checking).

If you press the **C**orrect button, Notepads scans its dictionary and displays a list of words close to the one that's misspelled. Scroll through the list with the mouse or keyboard, select the correct spelling, and press the **A**ccept button to confirm.

You can also spell-check just the current word or the text in the current window. Choose the Spellcheck **W**ord or Spellcheck **S**creen commands as desired.

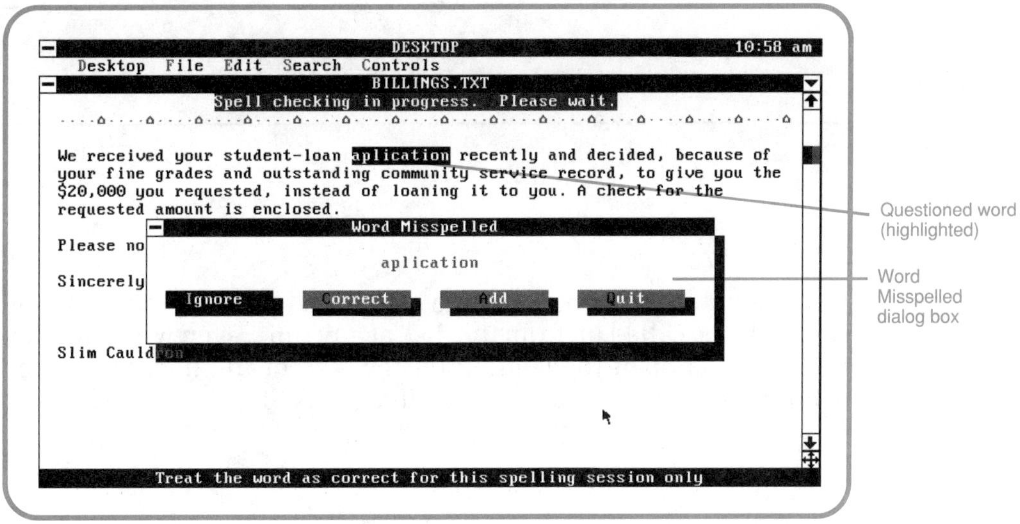

```
 ─                        DESKTOP                      10:58 am
   Desktop  File  Edit  Search  Controls
 ─                       BILLINGS.TXT                        ▼
              Spell checking in progress.  Please wait.       ▲
 ···∆··∆··∆····∆····∆····∆···∆····∆····∆····∆····∆····∆···∆···

 We received your student-loan application recently and decided, because of
 your fine grades and outstanding community service record, to give you the
 $20,000 you requested, instead of loaning it to you. A check for the
 requested amount is enclosed.
                          Word Misspelled
 Please no
                            aplication
 Sincerely
           Ignore      Correct       Add        Quit

 Slim Cauldron

                                              ▶

              Treat the word as correct for this spelling session only
```

Questioned word (highlighted)

Word Misspelled dialog box

Figure 12.9   *The Word Mispelled dialog box, asking you to ignore, correct, or add the highlighted word.*

333

Saving a File

Notepads automatically saves the document for you when you close its window, but you'll want to save the document periodically while you work. To do so manually (at approximately 10 to 15 minute intervals) choose the **S**ave command from the File menu. If you want to change the name of the file, edit the entry in the Filename field. The File Format selectors let you save the file in PC Tools Desktop (WordStar) format or straight ASCII text.

If you select the Make Backup File option, Notepads will keep the previously saved version of the document and name it *<FILENAME>*.BAK, where *<FILENAME>* is the unique name of your document.

You can also tell Notepads to automatically save the document for you. Choose the **A**utosave command from the File menu. Select ON and indicate a time delay between savings (a 5- to 10-minute delay should be satisfactory). Press **O**K.

> ▶ **Tip:** To exit without saving your changes, pull down the File menu and select Exit Without Saving.

Loading a File

Documents that you or someone else have previously written and saved can be called up from the disk at any time, even when another document is open (depending on the size of the documents and available memory). Use the following Quick Steps to load a file into Notepads.

 Loading a File

1. Pull down the Desktop menu and select Notepads.

2. Highlight the file you want from the list.   Selects the file to open.

3. Press the Load button.   Loads the file into Notepads.   □

> ▶ **Tip:** If the file is on another disk, select one of the drive letters (A, B, C, etc.) in the Drives list. You can change directories by selecting a directory from the Directories list; to move up the directory tree, select [..]. You may need to navigate around the directory tree to find the file you want. When you find the file, highlight it in the Files list.

Changing the Format

Notepads lets you specify the unique formatting of your document. You can add a header or footer to every page, control the margins, indicate line spacing, and more.

▶ To set a header or footer (text that appears on the top or bottom of every page), choose the **H**eader/Footer command from the Controls menu. As shown in Figure 12.10, enter one line of text in the Header or Footer fields.

▶ To set the margins, choose the **P**age Layout command from the Controls menu. Indicate the left, right, top, and/or bottom margins. The left and right margin settings are in characters, assuming 10 characters per inch. Both numbers are relative to the left side of the page. The top and bottom margin settings are in lines, assuming 6 lines per inch.

▶ To set a new paper size, choose the **P**age Layout command from the Control menu. Type a new number in the Paper Size field. Sixty-six lines is the default for 11-inch paper.

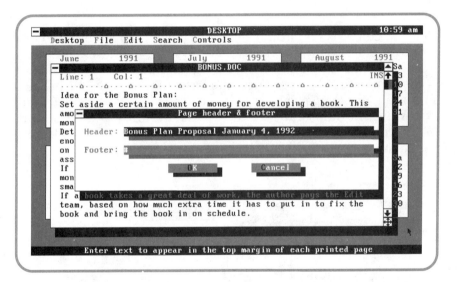

Figure 12.10   Sample header entry.

Printing a File

After you write, edit, spell-check, and format the document to your liking, you're ready to print it out. To print the file, choose the **P**rint command from the File menu. Select the port your printer is connected to (LPT1, COM1, etc.). Select any of the other options as desired:

▶ If you wish to print more than one copy of your document at a time, enter a new number in the Number of Copies field.

▶ To set line spacing, type a number in the Line Spacing field.

▶ To set a new starting point for page numbering, type the page you want to start with in the Starting Page Number field.

When you're done entering your choices, press the **P**rint button to start printing.

Writing Outlines

Desktop contains an outline generator (sometimes referred to as a "thought organizer") that easily lets you write and format outlines. You start and use the Outlines feature much the same way as Notepads. In fact, Outlines uses the basic text writing, editing, and formatting functions as Notepads, but adds special commands for controlling the appearance of the outline headings and formatting. When you use Outlines, an additional menu (Headlines) appears in the Menu bar, as shown in Figure 12.11.

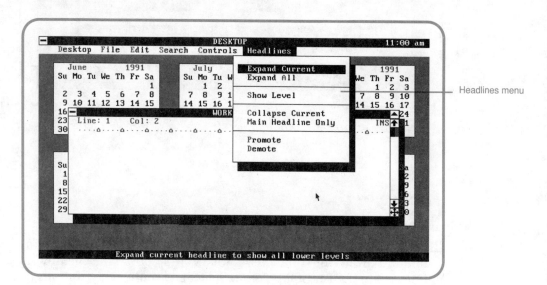

Headlines menu

Figure 12.11   The Headlines menu.

To best understand the commands in the Headlines menu, you need to know a little about the way Outlines works with text. Outlines has headlines such as:

A. Introduction

B. Chapter 1

C. Chapter 2

and so forth. Each headline occupies a certain level. The levels start at Level 1 for a headline that starts at or near the left margin. Subsequent levels (Level 2, Level 3, etc.) are indented from the main headline using the Tab key. Each level is indented 5 spaces over from the one preceding it to create an outline format as depicted in Figure 12.12.

Outlines gives you the ability to manipulate the display of levels and headlines, which allows you to work with only certain parts of the outline at one time. For example, you may wish to view only the most important topics of an outline, so you display just the Level 1 headlines. Figure 12.13 shows the previous outline with all levels under Level 1 "collapsed." At any time, you can expand the collapsed headlines to reveal additional levels.

337

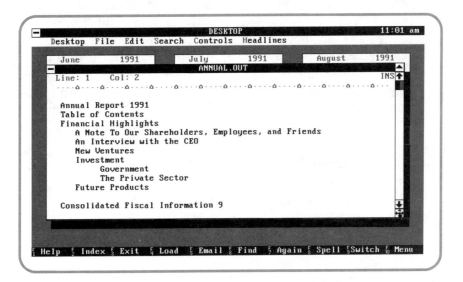

Figure 12.12   A basic outline showing all levels.

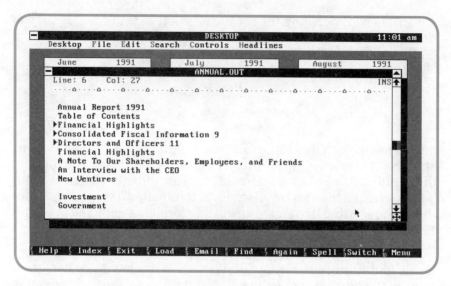

Figure 12.13   *An outline with all headlines but Level 1 collapsed.*

The following is a list of the commands in the Headlines menu:

▶ **E**xpand Current. Expands all the headlines below the current headline. Works only when headlines under the current one have been collapsed.

▶ Expand **A**ll. Expands all collapsed headings in the outline. Works only when headlines have been collapsed.

▶ **S**how Level. Displays the headlines to the level you indicate. For example, if you select to Level 3, you'll see Levels 1, 2, and 3.

▶ **C**ollapse Current. Collapses all levels following the one that's current.

▶ **M**ain Headline Only. Collapses all levels except for the main headline.

▶ **P**romote. Moves a headline to the next higher level.

▶ **D**emote. Moves a headline to the next lower level.

Keeping Track of Data

The Desktop database manager (Databases) lets you organize, store, and manage information. For example, you can create a form that lets you enter the names and addresses of everyone on your Season's

Greetings list. Databases will automatically organize the list according to the options you select. You can display only those people who live in a certain city, for example, or list only those people who sent you a card last year.

Of Fields and Records

A *database* is a complete document or file that is divided into individual records, as shown in Figure 12.14. Each record is further divided into fields. The *field* is the smallest chunk of data that the database can manipulate. One field may be the last name of a client; another field may be the zip code where the client resides. Each *record* contains the fields of a separate person or thing. One record may list the name and address of Uncle Joe, and another may list the name and address of Grandpa Fred.

339

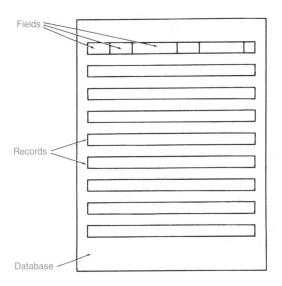

Figure 12.14   The component parts of a database file.

Like most data managers, Databases has certain limitations regarding the number of fields and records it can contain.

- ▶ You can store up to 10,000 records per database file.
- ▶ Each record can contain up to 4,000 characters.
- ▶ Each record can be divided into as many as 128 fields.
- ▶ Each field can contain up to 70 characters.

Creating a New Database

The best way to learn how to use Databases is to create a new database. The process involves three discrete steps: defining the structure of the new database, customizing a new form file, and entering record data.

To define the structure of a new database, you must create a special .DBF document file. This document file (compatible with dBASE III and IV) specifies how the database fields are named and classified. Follow these steps to make and define the structure of a new database:

1. Pull down the Desktop menu and select **D**atabases.

2. Press the **N**ew button in the dialog box that appears. Another dialog box pops onto the screen as shown in Figure 12.15.

3. Enter your choices and specifications for each field you want to create. Specifically, give the field a unique name, indicate its type (whether character, numeric, logical or date) and length (in number of characters), then save the field structure by pressing the **A**dd button.

4. At any time, you can examine the fields you've created by pressing the **N**ext and **P**rev buttons.

5. Delete a field you don't want by pressing the **D**elete button.

6. When you're done defining the structure, press the **S**ave button.

340

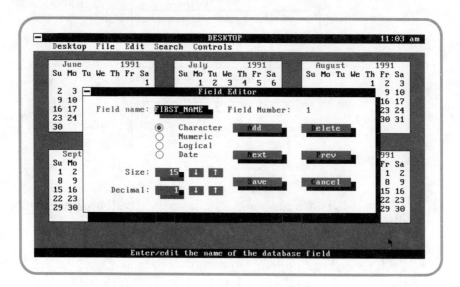

Figure 12.15   The Field Editor dialog box lets you create and add fields to your new database.

The following four field types indicate the type of information that will be stored in each field:

Character field—contains letters, numbers, and special characters that you want treated as text. Examples: name, address, and telephone number.

Numeric field—contains numbers you might want to use in a math calculation. (PC Tools Desktop lacks a math calculation feature in Databases; the Numeric field is intended for use when sharing Databases files with dBASE.) Examples: balance due and age.

Logical field—contains a single character that represents true or false. Enter Y or N, T or F, as desired. Use the Logical field to provide additional field entries if a certain condition is met. Example: If a customer has not paid, enter N or n.

Date field—contains eight characters for storing numeric data codes. The format follows the MM/DD/YY standard.

341

For each field you create you need to indicate its length. The maximum is 70 characters. Plan ahead to give each field enough space to contain the required information. You should provide a minimum of 30 characters for names, 40 characters for street addresses, 20 characters for cities. If you plan on entering only local phone numbers, leave room for just 7 characters. Long distance numbers must have at least 10 characters to store the area code.

When dealing with dollars and cents (in numeric fields), you may want to indicate the number of digits to the right of the decimal point. Select the Decimal field and enter a number.

When you press the **S**ave button, Databases automatically stores the new structure and displays the fields in a database window, as shown in Figure 12.16. Each column on this screen represents a field you created. When Databases first displays your database, the display is shown in Browse mode, so you can see columns of entries in each field. For entering data for each record, you may find it more convenient to turn Browse mode off to view all the fields for a single record, as shown in Figure 12.17. To toggle Browse mode on and off, pull down the File menu and select **B**rowse.

To type data in a field, first press Enter to activate the cursor. In either screen you can move the cursor from field to field by pressing the following keys:

Press	To Move
Tab	To the next field
Shift-Tab	To the previous field
F5	To the previous record
F6	To the next record
F4	To the first or last record

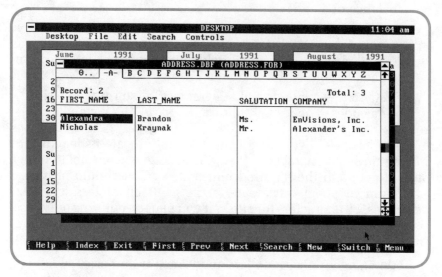

Figure 12.16   Completed database showing entry fields.

If you have a mouse, you can move to a field by clicking anywhere inside the field. If the field is not displayed, hold down the mouse button and drag the cursor to the right or bottom of the screen to scroll through the database.

When you're done entering all the data for the first record, select F8 New to add the record to the database. Enter the data for the next record, select F8 New, and so forth, until your database is complete. Bear in mind that at any time you can reopen this database file and add new records. You don't need to provide all the records for the database in one sitting. When you're done entering all the records for the current session, close the window.

Databases lets you display the fields in just about any way you want. When you create a new database file (with the extension .DBF), the program creates a special document file (with the extension .FOR) that you can edit with Notepads. As shown in Figures

342

12.18 and 12.19, you can use Notepads to manipulate the file names and placeholders (where the actual data from the .DBF file will be placed) within the window. Load the document file (with the .FOR extension) into Notepads and edit it as you would edit any document.

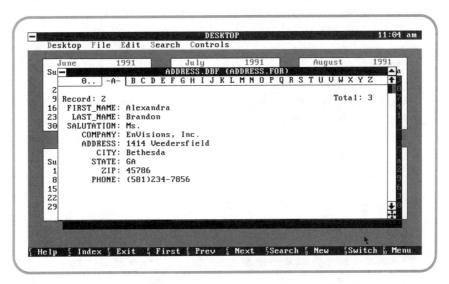

Figure 12.17   With Browse mode off you can see all fields for a single record.

343

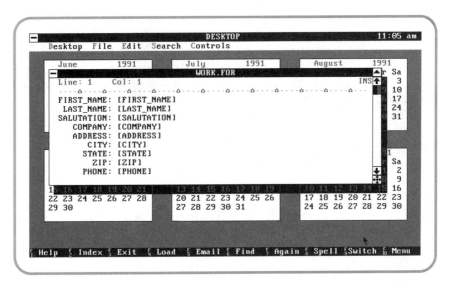

Figure 12.18   A sample unformatted database form.

> ▶ **Tip:** If you're preparing a form letter (for use with a name and address database file, for example) write the standard text that will appear in the letter and indicate where the data is to be placed by entering the placeholders at the appropriate spot. Figure 12.20 shows the form letter that prints the name, company, address, city, state, and zip code of the entries in a correspondence database.

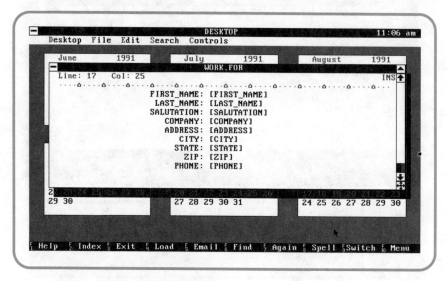

Figure 12.19   A sample database form formatted with all fields centered in the window.

After the form has been edited, save it (as explained in the section on Notepads) and return to Databases. If you haven't done so already, open the .DBF file you've been working with. You can now view the data merged into the rest of the form by choosing the Load Form command from the File menu and then selecting a form from the Files list. To print the filled-in form, choose the Print command, also located in the File menu.

Sorting Records

To make Databases more efficient and to help you find records you've previously added, you'll want to sort the records within the database file. The following Quick Steps give the sort procedure.

Sorting the Database

1. Pull down the Edit menu and select **S**ort Database.

   Activates the Sort Database command.

2. Press the **N**ext and **P**rev buttons as required to select a field to sort on.

3. When the field you want to sort on is displayed, press the Sort button.

   Sorts the database.

   □

```
┌─────────────────────────────────────────────────────────────┐
│ ▬                        DESKTOP                    11:07 am  │
│   Desktop  File  Edit  Search  Controls                      │
│  ┌──────────────┐ ┌──────────────┐ ┌──────────────┐          │
│  │ June    1991 │ │ July    1991 │ │ August  1991 │          │
│  ▬─────────────────────LETTER.FOR──────────────────────▲     │
│   Line: 10   Col: 17                              INS  ▲      │
│   ···△···△···△···△···△···△···△···△···△···△···△···△···        │
│   July 10, 1992                                              │
│                                                              │
│   [FIRST_NAME] [LAST_NAME]                                   │
│   [COMPANY]                                                  │
│   [ADDRESS1]                                                 │
│   [CITY], [STATE]  [ZIP]                                     │
│                                                              │
│   Dear [SALUTATION] [LAST_NAME]:                             │
│                                                              │
│   We would like to introduce you to the Compumate line of travel │
│   computers from Laser Computer.  Measuring only 10 inches wide by │
│   7.5 inches deep by 1.5 inches high, it is the smallest full ▼  │
│  ─────────────────────────────────────────────────────────  │
│  Help  Index  Exit  Load  Email  Find  Again  Spell  Switch  Menu │
└─────────────────────────────────────────────────────────────┘
```

Field placeholders

345

Figure 12.20   A database form containing data inserted from the database into locations specified by placeholders.

Searching and Selecting Records

While you could hunt through hundreds or even thousands of records to find the one you want, an easier way is to use Databases' built-in record searching and selecting tools.

To search for a particular record, choose the **F**ind Text in All Fields command from the Search menu. In the dialog box that appears, as illustrated in Figure 12.21, type the text you want to search for in the Search Data box, select the Search Selected Records option, and press the **S**earch button.

To review an example of how the search feature might work, let's suppose you want to find a client named Smith. Choose the **F**ind Text in All Fields command, type `Smith` in the Search Data text box, select the **S**earch Selected Records option, and press the **S**earch button. Databases finds the first entry with Smith and displays its records. If you have more than one Smith in the database, you can use the Search command again.

346

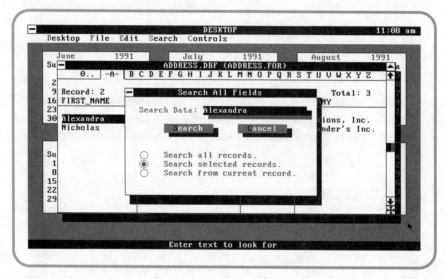

Figure 12.21   The Search All Fields dialog box.

Selecting records provides a way to display only those that meet certain criteria (for example, city or state). Normally, Databases selects all records in a database; the changes you make in the selection criteria narrows the number of records that are displayed.

To select records that meet a certain criteria:

1. Pull down the Edit menu and choose Select **R**ecords.
2. In the dialog box that appears (as illustrated in Figure 12.22), enter the field names you want to select from and the criteria you want to use for the selection.
3. Press the **S**elect button when you're done.

The selection criteria can be explicit—a certain name or state, for example—or it can be a range of entries. To display all records where the Age field is from 18 to 24, for instance, enter `18..24` beside the Age field. The range can be open-ended, for either the start or finish: `18..` starts the Age criteria at 18, with no stop range; `..24` starts the Age criteria at the lowest number contained in the database and stops it at 24. You also can use letters to display a range of text entries: A..C entered in the Name field displays those records where the name begins with A, B, or C.

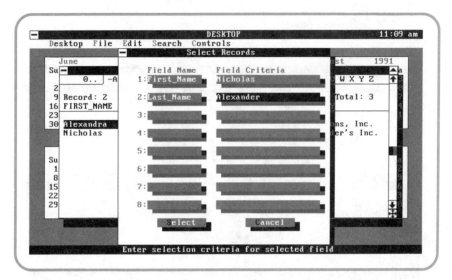

Figure 12.22   Sample Select Records dialog box with field names and criteria entered.

347

Appointment Scheduler

The Appointment Scheduler, shown in Figure 12.23, is an electronic cross between an appointment book and a to-do list. For each day of the month (for any month of the year), you can enter a list of tasks you need to get done. Desktop automatically numbers the tasks you must do in the To-Do List. If you have more than about six tasks for any particular time frame, you can scroll the To-Do List display to see the rest.

Before you can use the Scheduler, you must create an appointment file, which lays out your overall schedule:

1. Pull down the Desktop menu.

2. Select Appointment Scheduler. The Appointment Scheduler dialog box appears, asking you to enter the name of your appointment file.

3. Type a path to the directory where you want your appointment file stored followed by the name of the file, and press
Enter. For example, type `c:\pctools\data\myappt`. Desktop
will attach the extension .TM to the file name.

4. Select **N**ew to create the file. The Appointment Scheduler
appears.

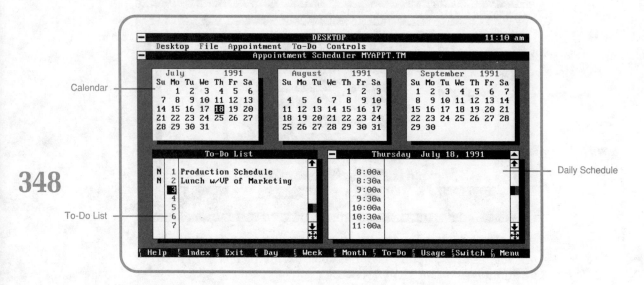

Figure 12.23   Basic Appointment Scheduler window.

The Appointment Scheduler consists of the three following
sections. You can move from section to section by pressing the Tab
key or using your mouse.

▶ The *Calendar* shows the days of the current month. Press the
Left or Right Arrow key to move from day to day. Press
Home to move to the current day. Move before the first day
to go to the previous month or move past the last day to go to
the next month. Press Ctrl-PgDn to go to the next year or
Ctrl-PgUp to go to the previous year.

▶ The *Daily Schedule* lets you set appointments at fifteen- or
thirty-minute intervals.

▶ The *To-Do List* lets you enter a list of things to do in the
order of priority.

Defining Your Work Days

Before you begin, define the days and hours you work and the holidays you have. To set your work hours, pull down the Controls menu and select **A**ppointment Settings. The Appointment Settings screen appears (see Figure 12.24). To move from one setting to another, press the Tab key. When you're done, press the **O**K button.

To set your holidays, pull down the Controls menu and select **N**ational Holiday Settings. A list of the national holidays appears. If you don't have one of these holidays off, tab down to the holiday and press Enter. You can also choose the **U**ser Holiday Settings option to schedule additional days off.

349

Figure 12.24   Change the Appointment Settings to reflect your weekly schedule.

Entering Appointments

Once your weekly schedule is set, you can start entering your appointments.

1. Move to the Monthly Calendar and highlight the day on which you want to set an appointment.
2. Move to the Daily Schedule.

3. Highlight the time of the appointment, and press Enter. The Make Appointment screen appears as in Figure 12.25.

4. Type a brief entry and press Enter. This entry will appear on the Daily Schedule.

5. To define a time block of more than one day, enter a start date and end date in the corresponding boxes.

6. Set the duration of the meeting in days, hours, and minutes. This will help prevent you from scheduling two meetings at the same time.

7. Select **S**ettings to see the Special Appointment Settings screen. Use this screen to schedule the meeting on a regular basis and to notify you in advance of the meeting. Select **OK** or **S**ave.

8. Select **M**ake to enter the appointment.

The appointment appears in the Daily Schedule, as shown in Figure 12.26. The N indicates a note is attached. The musical note indicates that an alarm will sound to notify you of the appointment.

350

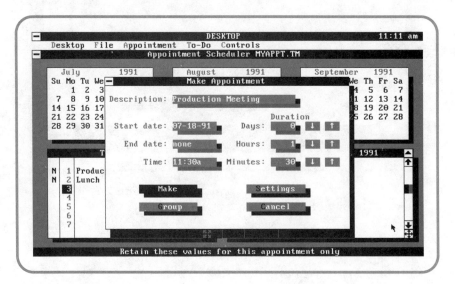

Figure 12.25   Use the Make Appointment dialog box to schedule meetings.

You can delete an appointment by highlighting it and selecting **D**elete from the Appointment menu. You can then enter a different appointment in that time slot.

> **Caution:** If you want Desktop to notify you of upcoming meetings, you must run Desktop in memory-resident mode. If it's not loaded, it can't notify you.

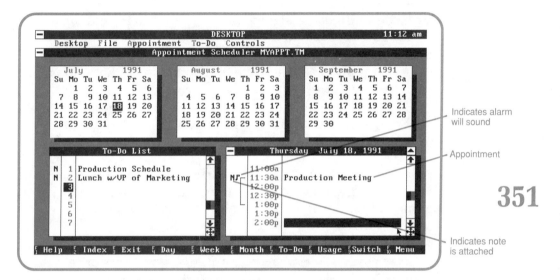

Figure 12.26   The appointment appears on the Daily Schedule.

Saving an Appointment File

When you're done entering your appointments, pull down the File menu and select **S**ave. You can also save a file simply by pressing the Esc key to exit the Scheduler.

Creating a To-Do List

Although the Monthly and Daily Schedules are linked together, the To-Do List stands on its own, providing a general list of what you must do and when you must do it.

1. Move to the To-Do window and press Enter. The New To-Do Entry window appears as in Figure 12.27.

2. Type the item you want to appear in the list (up to 24 characters) and press Enter.

3. Type the date on which you intend to start the task in the form MM-DD-YY and press Enter.

4. Type the date when the task must be completed and press Enter.

5. Type a number, assigning priority to the item, and press Enter. For example, if you type 5 (and you have five or more items in the list), the item will appear fifth.

6. If you want to attach a note to the item, press Enter to put an X next to this option, and then press Tab.

7. If you want to have this item on each year's To-Do List, press Enter to put an X next to this option.

8. Select **M**ake to add the item to the list.

If you choose to attach a note, a Notebook screen appears, prompting you to type additional information. Type the information and press Esc. The item now appears in the To-Do List.

352

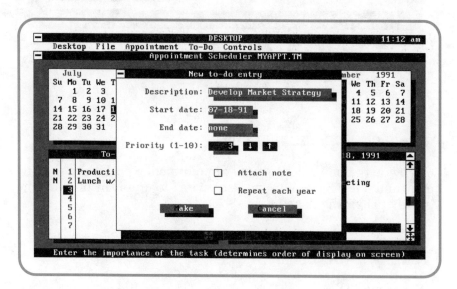

Figure 12.27   Use the New To-Do Entry dialog box to create an entry.

To delete or edit an item in the To-Do List, highlight the item and press Enter. A dialog box will appear asking if you want to delete or edit the item.

Desktop Companions

PC Tools Desktop contains several additional miniapplications, including several desktop calculators, keyboard macros, and a data clipboard for sharing text.

Desktop Calculators

PC Tools Desktop comes with the following four types of electronic calculators:

> **Algebraic Calculator**—for routine arithmetic. (See Figure 12.28.)
>
> **Financial Calculator**—for figuring out financial matters such as computing present value, future value, and bonds. (See Figure 12.29.)
>
> **Programmer's Calculator**—for converting between hexadecimal, octal, binary, and decimal notation. (See Figure 12.30.)
>
> **Scientific Calculator**—for solving trigonometric and other scientific equations. (See Figure 12.31.)

To call up any calculator, choose the **C**alculators command from the Desktop menu, then select the calculator type you want to use.

353

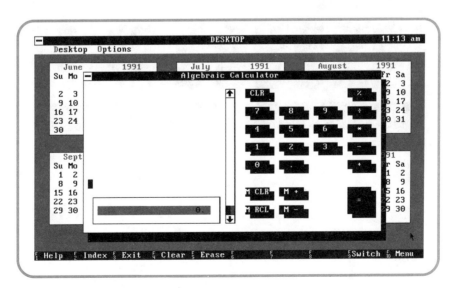

Figure 12.28   The Algebraic Calculator.

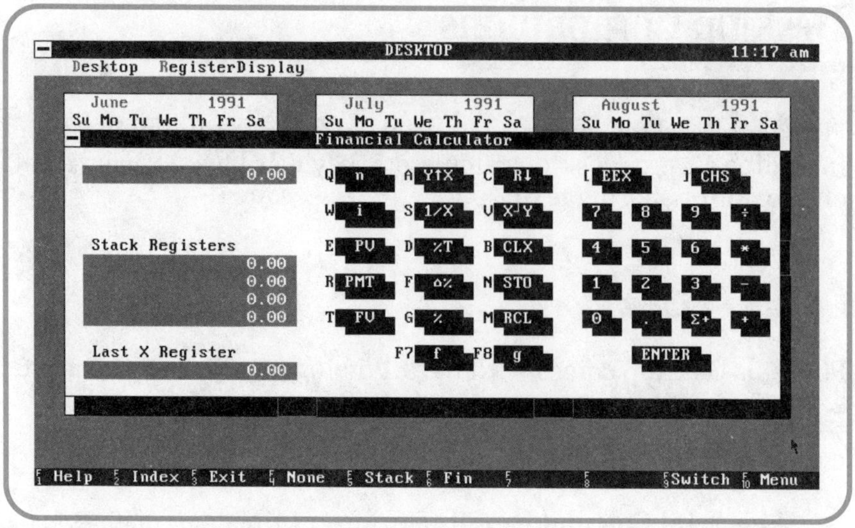

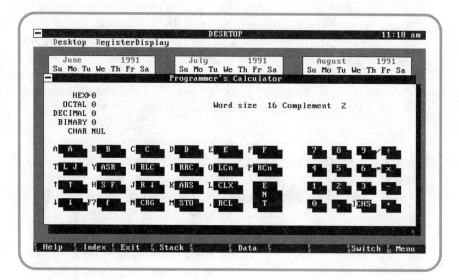

Figure 12.29   *The Financial Calculator.*

354

Figure 12.30   *The Programmer's Calculator.*

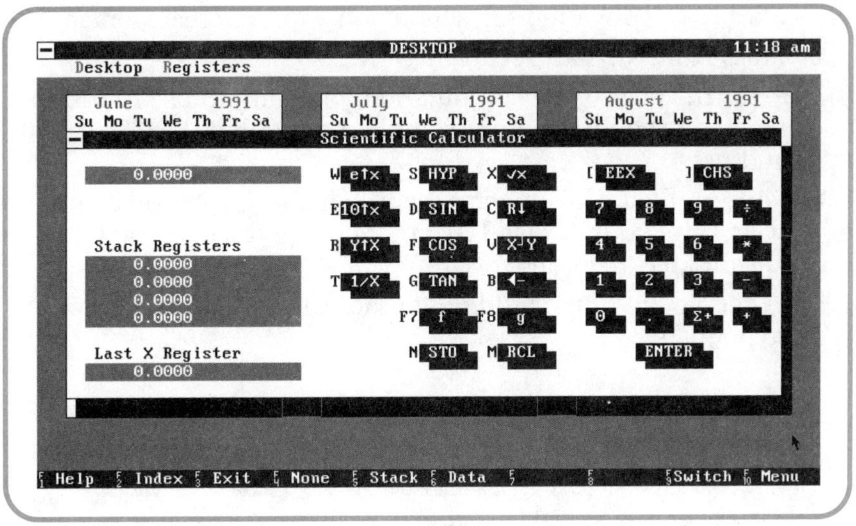

Figure 12.31   The Scientific Calculator.

The Algebraic Calculator includes *paper tape* that scrolls like a regular PC Tools window. As you complete your computations, the results print out on the tape. You can easily go back and view a previous result by scrolling the tape window in the usual manner.

Keyboard Macros

Keyboard macros are preprogrammed shortcuts. A *macro* is akin to a tape recording. What you record on the tape can be instantly played back. With PC Tools macros, you enter a series of keystrokes into the PC Tools Desktop Macro Editor. To play back the keystrokes you recorded, press the one or two special hot-keys you assigned to the macro.

The Macro Editor, shown in Figure 12.32, operates like the Notepads Desktop accessory. You can create macros by entering the keystrokes explicitly into the Macro Editor window, or by turning on the Learn mode and recording those keys you press on the keyboard. To turn on the Learn mode, pull down the Controls menu and select Learn Mode; a check mark next to the option indicates it's active. To record your keystrokes in Learn mode, you must be running Desktop in memory-resident mode. You can then create your macro:

1. Start the application for which you want to create a macro.
2. Press Alt-+ to start recording.
3. Press the macro key combination you want to use to run the macro in the future. For example, hold down the Ctrl key and press R.
4. Perform the task you want recorded, using your keyboard. (Don't use your mouse.) As you perform the task, each keystroke is recorded.
5. When you're done, hold down the Alt key and press the hyphen key (-).

356

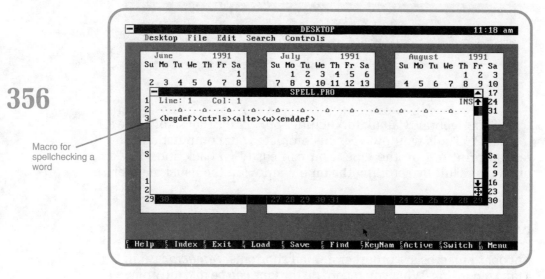

Macro for spellchecking a word

Figure 12.32   Sample Macro Editor document.

You can use the macros you create with the Macro Editor for a variety of functions. For example, you can use macros to embed special printing codes in your Notepads documents (to turn on bold print or to change the font size, for example).

You can use the macros you define with the Macro Editor within Desktop or another application (such as PC Tools Shell, WordPerfect, and Lotus 1-2-3). When used in another application, you must load Desktop in memory-resident mode.

Data Clipboard

The Clipboard is a PC Tools feature that lets you temporarily store snippets of text you've cut or copied from another application. As long as Desktop is loaded in memory-resident mode, you can use the Clipboard to transfer text between two different word processors—WordStar and Microsoft Word for example—even though these two applications aren't data file compatible.

To use the Clipboard:

1. Pull down the Desktop menu and select Clip**b**oard.
2. When the Clipboard window opens (shown in Figure 12.33), pull down the Copy/Paste menu and choose the **C**opy to Clipboard command.
3. Move the cursor to the beginning or end of the block of text you want to copy and press Enter.
4. Move the cursor to the opposite end of the block you want to copy and press Enter. The block appears on the Clipboard.
5. Move the cursor where you want to paste the text (or start another application). You can paste the text into a different document.
6. Pull down the Copy/Paste menu and select **P**aste from Clipboard. The text from the Clipboard is pasted into the document.

357

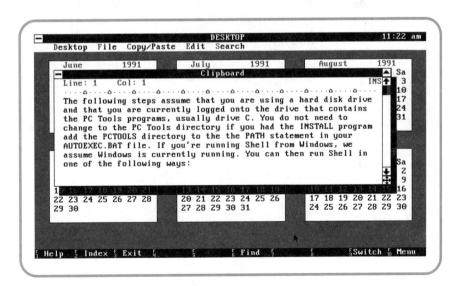

Figure 12.33   A clipping of text temporarily stored in the Desktop clipboard.

What You Have Learned

This chapter introduced you to the accessories included in the PC Tools Desktop program. You also learned:

► You can load Desktop as a stand-alone program at the DOS prompt or as a memory-resident program.

► Notepads, the Desktop word processor, can read and write documents in WordStar format.

► You can easily cut and copy text by selecting the text and using the Copy and Cut to Clipboard commands from the Edit menu.

► The built-in spell-checker checks for spelling and typographical errors.

► Outlines is a "thought organizer" that lets you easily create and format outlines using headlines and multiple levels.

► Creating a database with the Databases module of Desktop involves three steps: defining the structure of the new database, customizing a new form file, and entering record data.

► You can readily sort records and display records using selection criteria you enter.

► The Appointment Scheduler can help you keep track of meetings and things you must get done. It can also notify you of upcoming meetings.

► With the Keyboard Macro Editor, you can record your keystrokes to play them back later.

► Desktop offers a variety of calculators for use in your daily work.

Communicating with Other Computers

In This Chapter

▶ *Using PC Tools on a Network*
▶ *Transferring files between laptop and desktop computers*
▶ *Sending and receiving information via modem*
▶ *Sending and receiving FAX messages and E-Mail*
▶ *Remote computing*

In the past, personal computers (PCs) were fairly isolated. A computer user who wanted to share information had two choices: print the file and send the printout to another user, or copy the file to a floppy disk and send the disk. The process was about as efficient as trying to communicate through the mail—it was reliable, but slow. Conscious of this inefficiency, more and more users are connecting their PCs to other computers through the phone lines or by way of network cables. In this way, the user gains direct access to the information and power of other computers.

For computers to communicate, they require two items: *hardware* (a physical connection such as a phone line and modem, a network cable, or a null-modem cable) and *software* (a program that coordinates the communication). PC Tools provides support for the following communications tasks:

Networking. PC Tools can be installed on a Novell NetWare server (version 2.12 or higher) or on an IBM PC LAN server. You then can perform most of the tasks described in this book over the network.

Transferring Files. DeskConnect lets you transfer files between two computers connected by a null-modem cable.

Telecommunications. Desktop offers the Telecommunications program that lets you send and receive FAX messages and E-Mail lets you communicate with other computers via modem.

Remote Computing. The Commute program lets you take control of another computer from a remote location (provided you have security clearance). You'll have access to all the programs and information on the other computer.

Using PC Tools on a Network

Before you can use PC Tools on a network, your network manager (the person who manages your network) must install PC Tools on the network server, the network's central computer. (Network installation guidelines appear at the end of Chapter 4.) Once PC Tools is installed, you can use the PC Tools programs as you would on any PC. Figure 13.1 shows FileFind running on a network. As you can see, it looks the same as it does when it runs on a single PC.

Because the network server requires greater security than individual computers, you will not have access to many commands and programs that can affect the network server's disk. These commands include:

- ▶ Rename Volume
- ▶ Sort Files in Directory
- ▶ Disk Information
- ▶ Disk Map
- ▶ File Map
- ▶ Search Disk
- ▶ Verify Disk
- ▶ View/Edit Disk
- ▶ Format Disk

In addition, you won't be able to run DiskFix or Unformat, or change to any drive or directory you're not specifically given access to.

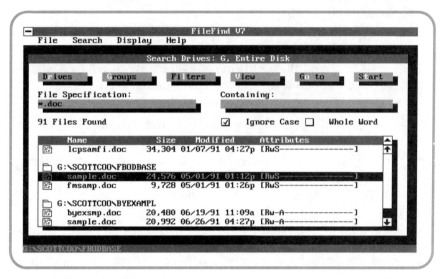

Figure 13.1   You can use PC Tools on a network in the same way you use it on a single PC; FileFind is shown here.

Viewing Network Information

The System Information utility, described in Chapter 11, includes an option that lets you view information about the various users connected to the network and the amount of space available on the network server. To view Network Information, start the System Information program by entering `si` at the DOS prompt or by selecting **S**ystem Info from the Shell's Special menu. Select **N**etwork from the Computer panel or from the System pull-down menu. The Network Information screen appears, as shown in Figure 13.2.

This screen displays information about the network server(s) installed on the network. This information is helpful if you need to know whether a program you want to use is compatible with a specific network server. This screen also informs you of how many users are currently logged in to each server. At the bottom of the screen are the following buttons that let you access additional network information:

► **U**ser List displays a list of users currently logged in to the network server, as shown in Figure 13.3. Below the User List are additional buttons:

> The **S**elect User button lets you select one or more users from the list.

> You can send a brief message to selected user(s) by pressing the **M**essage button.

> The **D**isk Space button indicates how much disk space each selected user is currently using.

> The **P**rev button lets you view the previous screen.

> The **O**K button lets you return to the main System Information screen.

► **V**ol Info displays a Volume Information dialog box for the selected server. This information can tell you if there's adequate space on a server to hold any files you want to transfer to the server.

► **G**roup List displays the names of work groups on the server. Additional options let you view a list of all members in a group or only those members who are currently logged in.

► **F**ile Info provides information about file usage on the selected server.

► **D**etails displays additional details about the network server.

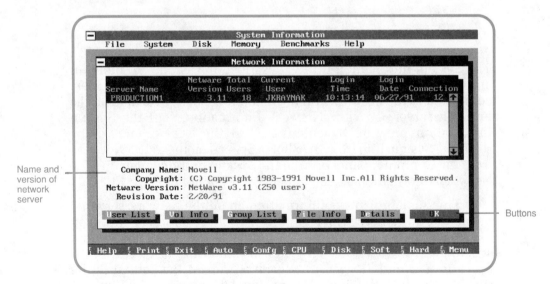

Figure 13.2   The Network Information screen.

Coordinating Work Schedules with Desktop's Appointment Scheduler

In Chapter 12, you learned how to use the Appointment Scheduler to keep track of your daily appointments on an individual computer. On a network, the Appointment Scheduler offers an additional feature that lets you make appointments for an entire group of users. For example, a department manager can schedule meetings for everyone in the department. Each member can then view the schedule to keep informed of upcoming meetings.

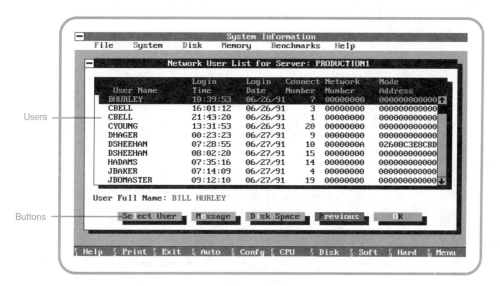

Users ——————

Buttons ——————

Figure 13.3   You can view a list of users currently logged in to the network server.

Before you can use the Appointment Scheduler in this way, your network manager must create a directory (on the network server) that all users in the group can access. The network manager should also assign the proper read/write privileges to each user. For example, the department manager should have read/write access in order to schedule appointments. Other members of the group should be given read privileges only, so they can read the schedule without changing it.

Once the proper directory is set up, the group must decide on a name for itself, and the department manager must create an appointment file (explained in Chapter 12). The users can then add themselves to the group. Each user must perform the following steps:

1. Start Desktop and choose **A**ppointment Scheduler from the Desktop pull-down menu.

2. Load an appointment schedule from the File list. You can load the appointment schedule you created in Chapter 12.

3. Pull down the File menu and select **G**roups. The Subscribe to a Group dialog box appears.

4. Press the **N**ew button. The Group Membership dialog box appears, as in Figure 13.4, prompting you to type the name of the group you want to join.

5. Type the name that your group decided on in the Group Name box.

6. Type the complete path and file name of the group appointment schedule in the Path and Filename text box. For example, type `g:\market\market`. Desktop will automatically add the extension .TM to the file name.

7. Press the **O**K button.

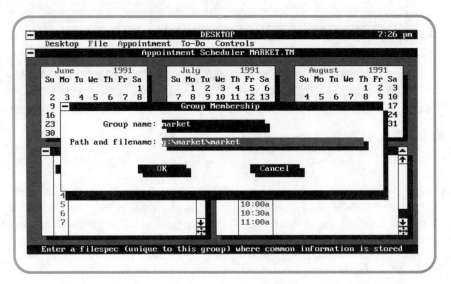

Figure 13.4   The Group Membership dialog box lets you join a group.

To find out about upcoming meetings, log in to the network, start the Appointment Scheduler, and load the group appointment file. The Appointment Scheduler appears, showing all meetings scheduled for today. You can view meetings scheduled for another day by selecting the day in question from the calendars at the top of the screen.

Assuming that you have read/write privileges for the directory created earlier, that you're logged in to the network, and that the Appointment Scheduler is running, you can make appointments for the members of the group. The following Quick Steps lead you through the process:

 Making Group Appointments

1. Move to the desired Monthly Calendar and highlight the day on which you want to set an appointment.	Selects a date for the appointment.
2. Move to the Daily Schedule.	
3. Highlight the time of the appointment and press Enter.	The Make Appointment screen appears as in Figure 13.5.
4. Type a brief entry and press Enter.	This entry will appear on the group's Daily Schedule.
5. To define a time block of more than one day, enter a start date and end date in the corresponding boxes.	
6. Set the duration of the meeting in days, hours, and minutes.	This will help prevent you and others from scheduling conflicting meetings.
7. Select **S**ettings to enter special appointment settings. Select **OK** when you're done.	Use this screen to schedule the meeting on a regular basis and to notify group members in advance of the meeting.
8. Select **G**roup to enter the appointment.	A list of groups appears.
9. Select the group for which you want to enter the appointment and then press the **M**ake button.	The appointment appears in the Daily Schedule, as shown in Figure 13.6.

365

> **Caution:** If you want Desktop to notify group members of upcoming meetings, each member must be running Desktop in memory-resident mode. Otherwise, each member will have to load the group appointment schedule individually and check for appointments on a regular basis.

366

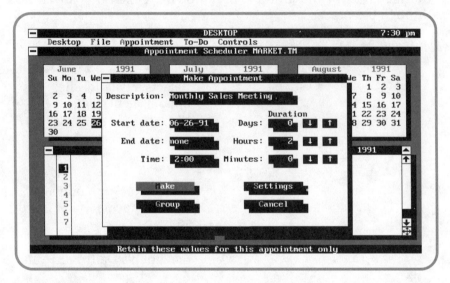

Figure 13.5   Use the Make Appointment dialog box to schedule meetings.

Using DeskConnect to Transfer Files between Two Computers

If you have two computers—a laptop to take home and a desktop at work for instance—and you transfer files between the two, you can save time by using DeskConnect. Once the two computers are connected and running DeskConnect, you simply copy files from one to the other, just as you would copy files from one disk or directory to another. To use DeskConnect, PC Tools must be installed on both computers.

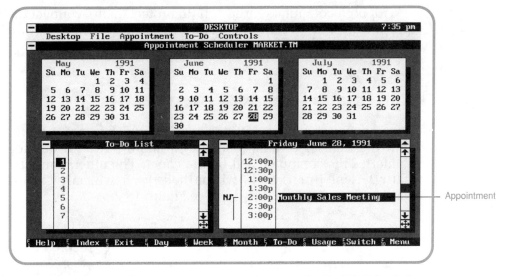

Appointment

Figure 13.6   The appointment appears on the Daily Schedule.

367

Connecting the Two Computers

The first step in establishing a connection is to purchase the proper serial null-modem cable (RS-232) for each computer. Make sure the cable is a null-modem cable—not just a standard serial cable (it should be marked). You can convert a serial cable to a null-modem cable by connecting a null-modem adapter to the cable. You need a cable to connect a COM port on one computer to a COM port on the other computer. Check the back of your computer to see if the ports are marked. If they are, you're in luck; if not, refer to the documentation that came with your computer or call your dealer. Write down how many pins each COM port has (9 or 25) and whether the port is male (has pins) or female (has receptacles for pins). The serial ports are usually male, but don't bet on it. When you've figured out what you need, obtain the required cable and any necessary adapters from your local computer store.

> ▶ **Note:** Your printer is probably connected to the parallel port at the back of your computer. If you have a mouse or modem, it's probably connected to your serial port. If you have only one COM port on your computer, you'll have to disconnect any device that's connected to it before you can proceed.

With both computers turned off (to protect them), connect the COM ports on the two computers using the cable. Then, boot (turn on) each computer.

Setting Up the Client and Server

Before you perform the next step, decide which computer will control the transfer of data (usually the more powerful desktop computer). This computer will be the *client*. The other computer (usually the laptop or portable) will be the *server*; it will only do what the client computer tells it to do. (See Figure 13.7.)

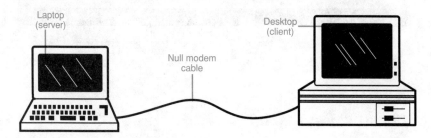

Figure 13.7   Connection of a laptop (server) and desktop (client) computer using a null-modem cable.

DeskConnect requires you to run a different program on each computer; you'll run DESKSRV.EXE on the server and DESKCON.EXE on the desktop, as explained in the following steps. If you run these programs without additional parameters, DeskConnect will run DESKSRV as a stand-alone program, using the COM 1 port at a *baud rate* (transmission speed) of 115200. You can add the parameters shown in Table 13.1 to change these default settings.

1. On the server (laptop or portable computer), type `desksrv /parameters` at the DOS prompt and press Enter.
2. On the client (desktop computer), type `deskcon /parameters` at the DOS prompt and press Enter.

Table 13.1   DeskConnect parameters

Parameter	Function
/B:nn	Sets the baud rate. Substitute a number from 300 to 115200 for *nn*. The settings must be the same on both computers.

Parameter	Function
/C:n	Specifies which COM port to use.
/I:n	For use with the /C:3 or /C:4 parameter. Specifies the IRQ. Substitute a number from 2-15 for the correct interrupt number.
/P:nnn	For use with the /C:3 or /C:4 parameter. Specifies the port address of the COM port.
/U	Unloads DESKCON from memory, keeping all other PC Tools memory-resident programs in memory.
/?	Provides help for using the DeskConnect parameters.

▶ **Tip:** If you transfer files often, you can have DeskConnect loaded automatically on the client computer by adding the DESKCON command to the AUTOEXEC.BAT file. To add the command, start the INSTALL program, choose PC **S**hell, and then select Load DeskConnect. Do not, however, select this option for the server. Doing so will prevent DeskConnect from running.

369

Establishing the Connection

Once both computers are set up for the connection, you can establish the connection through PC Shell:

1. Run PC Shell on the client computer.
2. Pull down the Special menu and select DeskConnect. A dialog box appears, as in Figure 13.8, telling you that the drives on the server will be appended to the drives on the client. For example, if the client computer has drives A, B, C, and D and the server has drives A and C, the server's drives A and C will be renamed E and F, giving the client computer six drives: A, B, C, D, E, and F.
3. Select **O**K. The new drives appear on the drive line of the client computer, just under the pull-down menu bar.

You can now transfer files from one drive to another as you normally would using PC Shell.

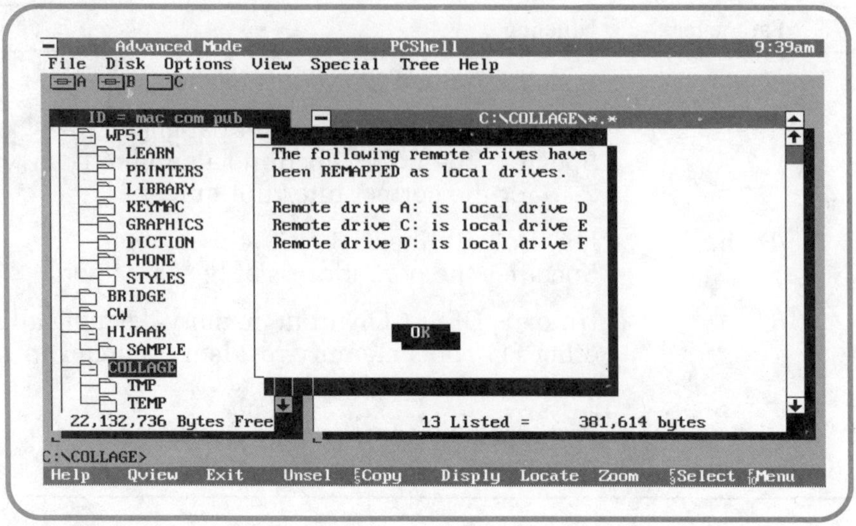

Figure 13.8 *When you connect the client and server computers, the server's drives are appended to the client's drives.*

370

Quitting DeskConnect

When you're done transferring files, you can exit DeskConnect and return to the DOS prompt or to PC Shell.

> **To Exit to DOS using the client computer**, press Esc and select OK.
>
> **To Exit to DOS using the server computer**, press Esc and select Yes.
>
> **To Exit to PC Shell using the client computer**, pull down the Special menu and select DeskConnect. Select Disconnect.
>
> **To Exit to PC Shell using the server computer**, press Esc and select Yes.

After you exit DeskConnect, the program remains in the client computer's memory. To remove it from memory, change to the drive and directory that contains PC Tools (C:\PCTOOLS), type `deskcon /u`, and press Enter. You can use the KILL command to remove DeskConnect from memory, but that will remove all PC Tools memory-resident programs as well.

Using Desktop's Telecommunications Program

If you have a modem connected to your computer, you can use it and PC Tools Desktop to converse with another computer anywhere on the globe. All you need to complete the link is a phone line connecting the modem on one computer to the modem on the other.

The communications program built into Desktop, called Telecommunications, is a *smart terminal*: Not only can you use it to dial a remote computer automatically, but you can also use it to send and receive files, even when you're busy working in another application. And you can transfer files to and from another computer that has a different telecommunications program installed. Telecommunications offers the following three options for communicating via modem:

371

> **Modem Telecommunications**—lets you send and receive files from any other computer similarly connected to a modem. The other computer does not need to have PC Tools, but it must have a telecommunications program. You can also connect to on-line computer services, including MCI Mail, EasyLink, CompuServe, and Central Point BBS.
>
> **Electronic Mail**—lets you exchange messages with other subscribers of MCI Mail, EasyLink, and CompuServe.
>
> **FAX Telecommunications**—lets you send FAX messages through a Novell NetWare network (assuming your computer is networked and a FAX board is installed in the network), or to other computers or FAX machines (assuming your computer has a FAX board).

Ø **Caution:** Keep in mind that using a modem means calling on a phone, and phone service isn't free. As long as your computer is using the phone you're being billed.

Using Modem Telecommunications

To start Telecommunications, pull down the Desktop menu and choose **T**elecommunications. Select **M**odem Telecommunications.

The PHONE.TEL window appears as in Figure 13.9. The entries in the window are preprogrammed communications settings. PC Tools comes with a collection of settings files, including MCI Mail, EasyLink, CompuServe, and Central Point BBS. You can edit these settings files or create your own. The settings files allow you to quickly select the number you want to dial and initiate the call automatically. There's no need to reset communications parameters manually for each call you make.

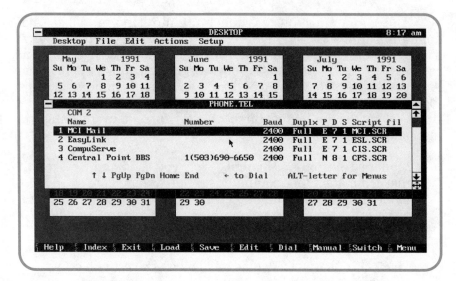

Figure 13.9   The Telecommunications PHONE.TEL window.

Editing and Entering Settings

Before you can use Telecommunications, you need to enter a phone number and other settings in the PHONE.TEL window. If you already subscribe to one of the services listed (Central Point BBS is free to all registered PC users), highlight the entry, pull down the Edit menu, and select **E**dit Entry. To add a new entry (for example, to exchange files with another user who has a modem), pull down the Edit menu and select **C**reate New Entry. You'll see an Edit Phone Directory dialog box like the one in Figure 13.10. This screen includes the following fields:

> **Name.** Type the name of the person or mail service you want to call (up to 50 characters).

Database. Lets you specify a database to use for sending E-mail and FAX messages automatically. This database contains information required to contact a particular individual or mail service.

Field 1 and Field 2. These commands let you use a database (assuming you created one) in conjunction with the Script feature to send messages automatically. For example, the Field 1 entry may contain the name of the person you want to contact, and Field 2 may contain that person's FAX number.

Phone. Type the phone number and any other commands your modem must execute to establish a connection with the other computer or with the mail service. If you need to dial a specific number to get an outside line, include that number.

Script. This option is used to automate the modem communication. You can create a separate script program with the .SCR extension, and then tell your computer to perform the operations listed in the script.

User ID. On-line computer services require that you identify yourself before logging in. Type the user ID provided to you when you subscribed to the service.

373

Password. Type the password required to access the other computer or on-line service.

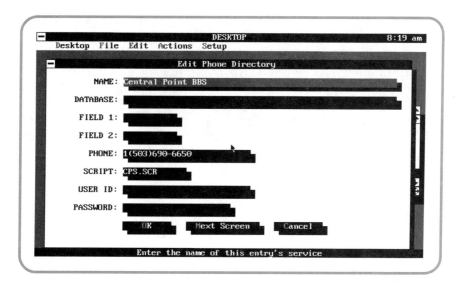

Figure 13.10   The Edit Phone Directory dialog box lets you enter information for one of your contacts.

At the bottom of the dialog box is a button labeled **Next** screen. Press this button to view the screen shown in Figure 13.11. You can use this screen to change the communications settings for your modem to match the settings used by the other computer or on-line service. The following is a list of the most common communications settings:

374

Baud Rate: 1200 or 2400 (depending on the capabilities of your modem and the modem you're connecting to). The higher the baud rate, the faster the two computers will transfer files. With slower baud rates, file transfer can be slow and cumbersome.

Parity: None. Parity tests the integrity of the data you send and receive.

Terminal—TTY. Sets the terminal emulation.

Flow Control—XON/XOFF. Tells the two computers to pause between exchanges.

EOL (End-of-Line) Receive—None. Tells the computer that's receiving information where a line of transmission ends.

EOL Send—None. Marks the end of an ASCII line when you press Enter.

Data Bits—Eight. Indicates the number of bits in each transmitted character.

Stop Bits—One. Indicates the number of bits used to signal the end of a character.

Duplex—Full. Tells the computer to send and receive data simultaneously. Half tells the computer to send data or receive data, but not to do both at any one time.

When you're finished entering or changing the settings, select **O**K. To store your settings permanently in the PHONE.TEL settings file, pull down the File menu and select **S**ave.

Placing a Call

After you've determined the number to call and the parameters to use, you can establish the modem link. Keep in mind that the computer you're calling must be set up to receive your call. The computer may use a different telecommunications program than the one offered by PC Tools, but a telecommunications program must be in operation in order to recieve your call.

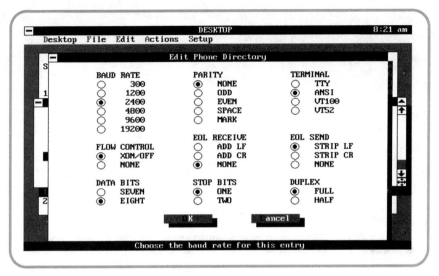

Figure 13.11   Page two of the Edit Phone Directory dialog box lets you change the settings for your modem.

To place your call, select the setting file you created and press Enter, or double-click on the setting file with your mouse. PC Tools Desktop establishes the connection and then displays the Telecommunications screen shown in Figure 13.12. You will use this screen to communicate with the other user and to transfer files. To display the pull-down menu bar at the top of the screen, select F10 Menu. You'll use the menus listed in this bar to send and receive files. If Telecommunications fails to establish a connection with the other computer, for whatever reason, a dialog box will appear, asking if you want to redial the number or cancel the operation.

> ▶ **Tip:** You don't absolutely need to dial a phone number by selecting it from the list of preset phone numbers. If the modem and computer you're talking to accepts 1200 Baud Generic or 2400 Baud Generic settings, you can use one of these to place the call. To dial the phone manually, display the screen that contains the list of phone numbers, pull down the Actions menu, and select **M**anual. The Telecommunications screen appears as in Figure 13.12. Type the dialing sequence specified in your modem manual followed by the phone number you want to dial. For example, type `atdt5743567` and press Enter. The Telecommunications program will dial the number and establish the connection.

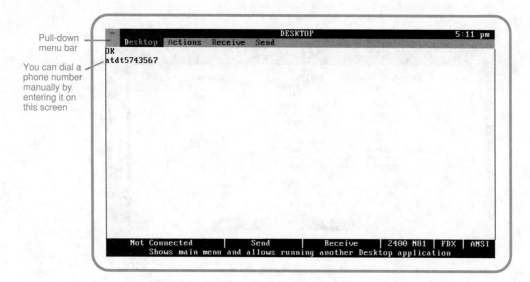

Pull-down menu bar

You can dial a phone number manually by entering it on this screen

Figure 13.12 *The Telecommunications screen lets you transfer files.*

Waiting for a Call

If you plan on receiving a call rather than placing one, you should set up the Telecommunications program to answer the phone. With the Telecommunications screen displayed, type `ate1` and press Enter. This tells the program to display whatever you type on your screen instead of on the other user's screen. Type `ats0=1` (that's a zero, not an O), and press Enter. This tells the program to automatically answer the phone on the first ring.

> ▶ **Tip:** If you want to continue working while waiting for a call, run Desktop in memory-resident mode. Set up Tele-communications to answer the phone. You can then work with another application in Desktop or quit desktop and work with your other DOS programs. When the call comes in, Telecom-munications will answer the phone. When you go back into Telecommunications, the Telecommunications screen will appear, allowing you to proceed with the file transfer.

Communicating with the Other User

Once a communications link is established, the message bar at the bottom of the screen displays the message Connected. You can now transfer files between the two computers and communicate with the other user. Communicating with the other user will take some getting used to. Whatever you type appears on the other user's screen—not on yours, so make sure you have your fingers on the right keys. Figure 13.13 shows a sample message.

Message from other user —

Figure 13.13   Whatever you type on the Telecommunications screen appears on the other user's screen, not on your screen.

377

Sending and Receiving Files

The PC Tools Telecommunications terminal can send and receive files using ASCII or XMODEM protocol allowing you to *upload* (send) files or *download* (receive) files from another user or on-line computer service. Both computers must be using the same protocol. For example, you cannot receive a file in XMODEM protocol that's been sent using ASCII protocol.

▶   ASCII protocol sends or receives plain text, one character at a time. ASCII protocol is susceptible to errors caused by noise on the phone line.

▶ XMODEM protocol sends data in discrete blocks. XMODEM includes a built-in error detection/correction scheme to ensure that transfers are error-free, even on relatively noisy phone lines.

ASCII protocol is appropriate for ASCII-only text documents. You need to use XMODEM when transferring binary text or binary-only files (program files). Although the XMODEM protocol is the most common error correction/detection file transfer method, it's not always supported. Both you and the remote computer must use the XMODEM protocol. To send or receive files, perform the following Quick Steps:

Q Sending a File Via Modem

1. Initiate the connection with the remote modem as explained earlier.

    Keep in mind that a telecommunications program must be running on both computers.

2. Press F10 to display the menu bar.

3. For an ASCII transfer, pull down the Send menu and choose ASCII. For an XMODEM transfer, pull down the Send menu and choose XMODEM.

    A dialog box appears, as in Figure 13.14, prompting you to select the file you want to send.

4. Select the file you want to send from the list that appears and press the Load button.

    If you selected XMODEM transfer, a dialog box appears telling you that the program is waiting for an OK from the other computer. Once the other user selects to receive the file, the dialog box will change to display the progress of the operation. If you selected ASCII transfer, a message appears at the bottom of your screen showing the progress of the transfer. □

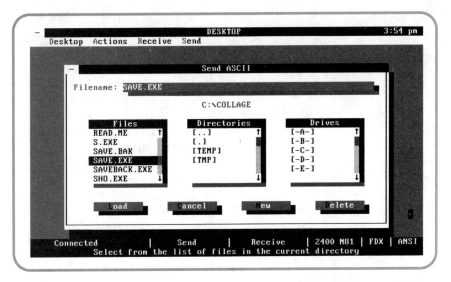

*Figure 13.14   To send a file, select it from the file list and then
press the Load button.*

 Receiving a File

1. Initiate the connection with
   the remote modem as
   explained earlier.

2. Press F10 to display the menu
   bar.

3. For an ASCII transfer, pull
   down the Receive menu and
   choose ASCII. For an
   XMODEM transfer, pull down
   the Receive menu and select
   XMODEM.

   A dialog box appears,
   prompting you to type a
   name for the incoming file.

4. Type a name for the file you
   will be receiving.

   Include a complete path
   name, telling the program
   where you want to store the
   file. You'll be *capturing* the
   incoming information into
   this file.

5. Select **S**ave.

If you selected XMODEM transfer, a dialog box appears, telling you that the program is waiting for the other computer to send the file. Once the other user sends the file, the dialog box will change to display the progress of the operation. If you selected to receive a file in ASCII protocol, the characters included in the file appear on-screen as they are received. See Figure 13.15.

6. When receiving an ASCII file, wait until the transfer is complete, and then choose the **E**nd Transfer command from the **A**ctions menu.

380

The ASCII text file is displayed as it is received

Figure 13.15   When receiving an ASCII file, the ASCII characters appear on-screen as they are received.

Terminating the Transfer

Once you've completed the file transfer you can terminate the transfer in either of two ways. If you want to continue transferring files between the two computers, press F10 to display the pull-down menu bar, pull down the Actions menu, and select **End Transfer**. The transfer is terminated, but the two computers remain connected.

To disconnect the two computers, pull down the Actions menu and select **Hangup**. The message bar will display the message Disconnecting, and communication between the two computers will stop.

⊘ **Caution:** Be sure to choose the **Hangup** command when you're done transferring files between the two computers. As long as you're connected to the other computer, whether you're transferring files or not, you're running up the phone bill!

381

Advanced Topics

The PC Tools Desktop Telecommunications module includes an enhanced *script* feature that lets you automate many common communications procedures. For instance, you can place a call to Dow Jones News/Retrieval, and a script previously written by you automatically navigates through the Dow Jones service and obtains the latest stock quotes on the stocks in your portfolio.

Telecommunications also provides for background communications using the Backtalk memory-resident program included with PC Tools. With Backtalk installed, you can use your computer for another task while it is sending or receiving files with the communications terminal. To load Backtalk, enter the command backtalk /n at the DOS prompt, where n stands for the number of the COM port your modem is connected to.

For more information on these advanced topics, refer to the Desktop Manager manual included with the PC Tools package.

Sending and Receiving Electronic Mail

Electronic mail (E-mail for short) allows you to exchange mail with other computer users through a mail service. You send mail (via modem) to the mail service, where it is stored until the other user (to whom you sent the mail) retrieves it.

Before you can send or receive E-mail, your computer must be connected, via modem, to an electronic mail service (MCI Mail, CompuServe, or Easy Link), and you must have an account with the service. You must then configure the Electronic Mail program for use by specifying the mail service you subscribe to and the directories you want to use for storing incoming and outgoing mail.

First, start the Electronic Mail program: Pull down the Desktop menu and select **T**elecommunications. Select **E**lectronic Mail. The INBOX dialog box appears. Because you haven't established a link with the mail service, the box is empty.

To select a mail service, perform the following steps:

1. Pull down the Setup menu and select **M**ail Service. A dialog box appears listing the three available mail services.
2. Select a mail service from the list and press the Configure button. The Configure Mail dialog box appears for the service you selected.
3. Type the phone number, your user ID, and the password supplied to you by the mail service.
4. Select a baud rate. The baud rate must be less than or equal to the baud rate of your modem and must match the baud rate for the mail service.
5. Select the dialing mode for your phone: *Tone* (for Touch-Tone) or *Pulse* (for rotary).
6. Select the COM port that your modem is connected to.
7. Select **O**K.

After you select a mail service, you must specify the directories you want to use for your mail. You'll need three directories:

INBOX—stores any mail which the program reads from the mail service

OUTBOX—for mail that's waiting to be sent to the mail service

SENT—for any mail that's been sent to the mail service.

You may have created these directories during the PC Tools installation. If not, you can create them now by selecting Mail **D**irectories from the Setup menu. Type a complete path for each directory you want to use, as shown in Figure 13.16.

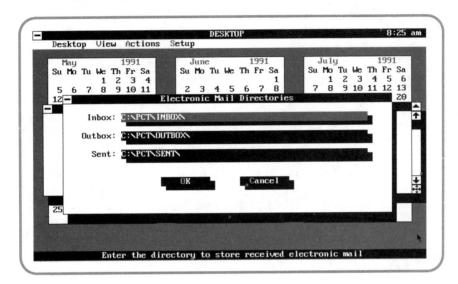

Figure 13.16   Create directories for incoming mail, outgoing mail, and mail that's been sent.

The Setup menu also contains two commands you can use to set a schedule for sending and reading E-mail. If you run Desktop in memory-resident mode, these commands tell the Electronic Mail program to automatically send mail or receive mail at specified times. Once Electronic Mail is set up, you can use the program to send and receive messages. To send a message, perform the following Quick Steps:

**Sending Mail**

1. Pull down the Actions menu and select **C**reate Mail Message.

   A Notepad screen appears, prompting you to create a message.

2. Type the requested information.

This includes the phone number of the person who is to receive the message, a brief summary of the message, and the complete message.

3. Pull down the File menu and select Send Electronic Mail.

A dialog box appears asking if you want to send the message now or at the scheduled time.

4. Select Send Immediately or Send at Scheduled Time, and then select OK.

The message will be sent to mail service when specified: either immediately or at the next scheduled time. □

Receiving messages from the mail service is a two-step process. You must first have Electronic Mail *read* the mail stored by the mail service and store the files in your INBOX directory. You can then *view* each message.

 Receiving Mail

1. Pull down the Actions menu and select Read Mail Now.

The program dials the mail service, reads any messages stored there, and puts them in your INBOX directory.

2. Pull down the View menu and select View Inbox.

A dialog box appears showing a list of all messages retrieved from the mail.

3. Highlight the message you want to read and press Enter, or double-click on the message with your mouse.

The message appears.

□

FAX Communications

PC Tools Desktop supports FAX communications. If you have a FAX board in your computer or on your network, the Desktop-Telecommunications submenu will include two FAX commands:

384

▶ Send a Fax lets you send FAX messages to FAX machines or to other computers equipped with FAX boards. You can use the Notepads word processor to create the FAX document and/or a cover sheet.

▶ Check the Fax Log lets you view a list of FAX messages that your computer received.

Desktop works with only a select number of PC FAX boards, specifically the Connection CoProcessor (Intel), the Satisfaxtion Board (Intel), and the SpectraFAX (SpectraFAX). The FAX board can be installed in a Novell network (but should not be installed in the network server PC).

The FAX Communications control panel allows you to enter the phone number of the recipient and, optionally, a time and date to place the call. That way you can use your computer to place FAX transmissions after hours, when the long distance rates are lowest. Conversely, you can keep your computer on and receive FAX messages at any time. It keeps a log of FAX messages sent and received.

385

Controlling Another Computer with Commute

Commute is a powerful program that lets you take control of another computer and access all its programs and information as if you were sitting at its keyboard. If you work at home, you can connect your home computer to your office computer, via modem, and use a program installed on your office computer to edit one of the documents stored on its hard disk. If your office is networked, you can access the network from a remote location to use its programs and information.

Commute is also useful if you work on team projects. You can connect two computers and then collaborate on a project with one of your colleagues, taking turns editing a document or spreadsheet. You can even *chat* with the other user, carrying on a dialog while you work.

> **Note:** Because the commands you enter must travel through phone lines or other cables, you'll notice that computer operations slow down quite a bit, depending on the program you're running. If you're running Windows via modem, for example, your computer will seem sluggish. Commute is also limited by the video driver installed on the two computers. Although Commute automatically translates between EGA, VGA, and CGA, the translations may be slow.

Connecting the Computers

Before you can use Commute's magic, the two computers must be connected by modem, by network, or by a null-modem cable. Commute must be installed on both computers. Once that's done, you must configure Commute on each computer to tell it how the computers are connected:

1. Change to the drive and directory that contains the PC Tools program files. If you installed PC Tools to run from any directory, this step is unnecessary.

2. Type `commute`, and press Enter. A dialog box appears, asking for your name.

3. Type your name and select **OK**. This name will identify you to other users. Another dialog box appears asking how the computers are connected.

4. Select Connect by **M**odem (phone line), Connect by **LAN** (network), or **D**irect Connection (null-modem cable).

   If you selected the LAN option, the configuration process is complete.

   If you selected the Modem option, select the type of modem you're using and select **OK**. Select the COM port to which the modem is connected and select **OK**.

   If you selected Direct Connection, select the COM port to which the null-modem cable is connected, and select **OK**.

5. Repeat the configuration process for the other computer.

Once Commute is configured you'll see the Call Manager window shown in Figure 13.17. You must now establish which computer will take control (the master) and which one will yield control (the slave).

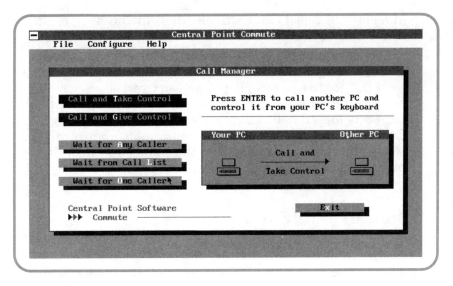

*Figure 13.17   The Call Manager window lets you start a
Commute session.*

First, you must set up the slave computer to wait for a call. On
this computer, Commute will run in the background until the master
computer calls on it to perform a task. To wait for a call, select Wait
for **A**ny Caller from the Call Manager window. A dialog box appears,
asking you to confirm the type of connection. Choose **O**K. Commute
loads and then returns to DOS so you can continue using the computer.

You can now take control of this computer using the master
computer. On the master computer, select Call and **T**ake Control
from the Call Manager window. The Private Call list appears. What
you do next depends on how the computers are connected:

Connected by Direct Connection, select MANUAL CALL
and then choose **O**K. In the dialog box that appears, select
Direct and then select **O**K. The master computer takes
control of the slave and displays the screen shown on the
slave computer. Both users can operate their computers, but
the user of the slave computer cannot access information or
programs on the master computer.

Connected by Modem, the Private Call list appears. Select
MANUAL CALL and then choose **O**K. Another dialog box
appears, asking for a phone number. Type the phone number
for the slave computer's modem in the Dial box, select

Modem, and select **OK**. Commute dials the number, establishes the connection, and gives you control over the slave computer.

Connected by Network, the Private Call list appears. Select LAN USER LIST to see a list of network servers. Select the network server you want to access and select **OK**. A list of currently logged in Commute-users appears. Select the Commute-user whose computer you want to control, and select **OK**. Commute establishes the connection with the other computer and puts you in control of it.

Performing Operations with the Session Manager

Now that the master and slave computers are linked, you can use the master computer to operate the slave. Is that all? Not quite. Hold down the Alt key and press the right Shift key. This displays the Commute Session Manager, shown in Figure 13.18. The Session Manager offers the following options:

▶ **E**nd the Session disconnects the two computers. The slave computer continues to wait for calls, so you can take control of it again at any time.

▶ **L**ook at Your PC lets you use the programs and files on the master computer. When you're done working with the master, type `exit` and press Enter to regain control of the slave.

▶ **C**hat with Other PC opens the dialog box shown in Figure 13.19. This is literally more like a dialog box than most of the dialog boxes described in this book; it lets you carry on a dialog with the other user. Whatever you type appears on your monitor and the other user's monitor; whatever the other user types appears on his or her monitor and on your monitor. To get the other user's attention, press F10; a tone will sound on the slave computer.

▶ **S**end Files to Other PC and **G**et Files from Other PC lets you transfer files between the two computers.

▶ **A**dvanced Options displays a dialog box that lets you reboot the slave computer, lock the keyboard on the slave, modify your display, and more.

▶ **H**elp provides help for using Commute.

Ending a Commute Session

When you're done using Commute, press Alt-Right Shift to display the Session Manager on the master computer. Select **E**nd the Session. This disconnects the two computers, but Commute is still running in memory-resident mode on the slave. To remove Commute from the memory of the slave computer, press Alt-Right Shift on the slave keyboard to view the Call Manager window. Pull down the File menu and select **U**nload From Memory. Commute is unloaded; the computer will no longer give control to the master computer.

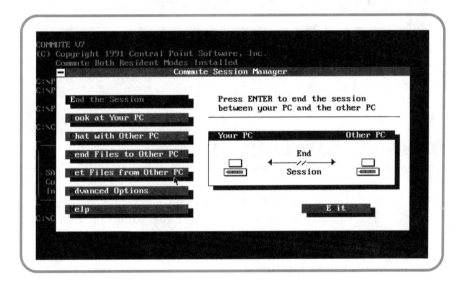

Figure 13.18   The Session Manager gives you more control over the Commute session.

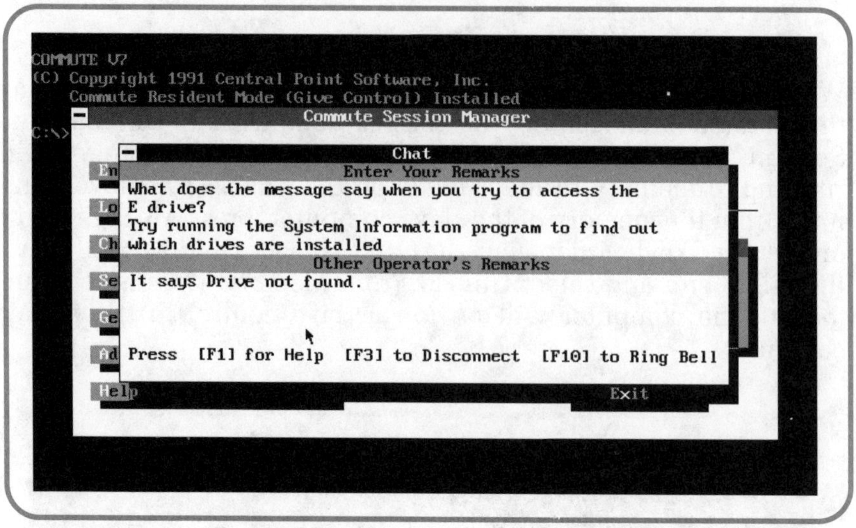

Figure 13.19   *The Chat box lets you carry on a conversation with the other user.*

What You Have Learned

▶ Once PC Tools is installed on your network server, it operates in much the same way as it operates on an individual computer.

▶ You can view information about your network by using the System Information program.

▶ You can use Desktop's Appointment Scheduler on a network to schedule meetings for groups of users.

▶ DeskConnect lets you transfer files quickly between two computers.

▶ Desktop's Telecommunications program lets you communicate to other computers via modem, send and receive E-mail, and send and receive FAX transmissions.

▶ Commute lets you take control of another computer from a remote location.

▶ Commute's Chat command lets you carry on a conversation with another user.

Appendix

PC Tools Program Files

Although the PC Tools programs are designed to work together, you may encounter problems running two or more programs simultaneously. For example, your computer may not have the memory required to run CP Backup from PC Shell. This rarely happens, but when it does, you can often get around the problem by running the program you want to use alone, from the DOS prompt. (This requires you to remove PC Shell and other memory-resident programs from memory.)

To run a program from the DOS prompt, you have to enter a command that initiates the program. The command consists of the base name of the program's *executable* file. For example, PC Shell's executable file is named PCSHELL.EXE. To run Shell, you enter `pcshell` at the DOS prompt. All the individual programs included in PC Tools have a corresponding executable file, ending in the extension .EXE or .COM. Some of these files can be executed from the DOS prompt; others require that you run them from within another PC Tools program.

The following sections describe some of the program files you're likely to use on a regular basis.

Setup and Configuration Files

These files are used for installing and configuring PC Tools. The INSTALL.EXE program is needed only when installing PC Tools on a hard disk. The KILL.EXE program is used only when PC Tools programs are loaded in memory-resident mode.

INSTALL.EXE	Installation program. You can run the program at any time to change the options you selected during the initial installation.
PCCONFIG.EXE	Configuration program. Lets you change screen colors, display options, mouse setup, and keyboard key repeat speed.
KILL.EXE	Removes all PC Tools memory-resident programs from memory.

Shell Files

These files manage the Shell program. All files are required when using the Shell application.

PCSHELL.EXE	Runs PC Shell.
PCTOOLS.EXE	Runs PC Shell and displays a list of PC Tools programs you can run from Shell.
PCRUN.COM	Shell run-time program; runs other applications when Shell is in TSR mode. You cannot run this as a stand-alone program; you must run it from within PC Shell.
FF.EXE	FileFind program. Helps you find files on a disk. Can be run from Shell or from DOS prompt.
DM.EXE	Directory Maintenance. Lets you add, move, and rename directories. Can be run from Shell or from DOS prompt.

VIEW.EXE — Lets you view a selected file's contents. Can be run from Shell or from DOS prompt, and from several other PC Tools programs.

Data Protection

The following files run the various data-protection programs:

MIRROR.COM — Runs Mirror which creates a copy of a disk's boot sector and FAT.

DATAMON.EXE — Runs the Data Monitor which lets you configure Delete Sentry and Delete Tracker.

WIPE.EXE — Erases a file or disk so that it cannot be undeleted.

PCSECURE.EXE — Protects files by encrypting them.

VDEFEND.EXE — Runs a virus-defense program in the background, providing early warning of virus infection.

PCFORMAT.EXE — Formats a disk safely to prevent you from formatting a disk that contains data.

393

Data Recovery Files

PC Tools includes several data recovery programs.

UNDELETE.EXE — Lets you undelete recently deleted files.

DISKFIX.EXE — Scans selected disk to reveal any problems, and helps you correct disk problems.

FILEFIX.EXE	Helps you undelete large database files including dBASE, Lotus, and Symphony files.
UNFORMAT.EXE	Unformats a disk that's been accidently formatted.
REBUILD.COM	Rebuilds the FAT, boot sector, or CMOS.

Desktop Files

The following program files operate Desktop:

DESKTOP.EXE	Runs the main Desktop program.
BACKTALK.EXE	Lets the Telecommunications program communicate in the background while you perform other tasks.

Utility Files

The PC Tools stand-alone utilities comprise the following files. The files are needed only when running the associated utility.

COMPRESS.EXE	Unfragments files on a selected disk to increase efficiency of disk.
PC-CACHE.EXE	Sets aside part of your computer's memory for disk-caching.

System Information Files

The following files are required for the System Information and Memory Information programs:

SI.EXE	System Information program.
MI.COM	Memory Information program.

Backup Files

The following files are required for the CP Backup utility.

CPBACKUP.EXE	Runs the CP Backup program.
CPBDIR.EXE	Identifies the number of the backup disk in the specified drive.
CPSCHED.EXE	Used for scheduling automatic backups.

395

Commute

You can run Commute by executing the following program file:

COMMUTE.EXE	Starts Commute on one of the computers you want to connect. You must run Commute on both computers.

DeskConnect

DeskConnect requires the following two program files:

DESKCON.EXE	Must be run on the client computer (desktop).
DESKSRV.EXE	Must be run on the server computer (laptop or portable).

Index

399

401

402

403

404

405

407

408

409

411

Reader Feedback Card

Thank you for purchasing this book from SAMS FIRST BOOK series. Our intent with this series is to bring you timely, authoritative information that you can reference quickly and easily. You can help us by taking a minute to complete and return this card. We appreciate your comments and will use the information to better serve your needs.

1. Where did you purchase this book?

☐ Chain bookstore (Walden, B. Dalton)   ☐ Direct mail
☐ Independent bookstore   ☐ Book club
☐ Computer/Software store   ☐ School bookstore
☐ Other _____

2. Why did you choose this book? (Check as many as apply.)

☐ Price   ☐ Appearance of book
☐ Author's reputation   ☐ SAMS' reputation
☐ Quick and easy treatment of subject   ☐ Only book available on subject

3. How do you use this book? (Check as many as apply.)

☐ As a supplement to the product manual   ☐ As a reference
☐ In place of the product manual   ☐ At home
☐ For self-instruction   ☐ At work

4. Please rate this book in the categories below. G = Good; N = Needs improvement; U = Category is unimportant.

☐ Price   ☐ Appearance
☐ Amount of information   ☐ Accuracy
☐ Examples   ☐ Quick Steps
☐ Inside cover reference   ☐ Second color
☐ Table of contents   ☐ Index
☐ Tips and cautions   ☐ Illustrations
☐ Length of book
☐ How can we improve this book?_____
☐ _____

5. How many computer books do you normally buy in a year?

☐ 1–5   ☐ 5–10   ☐ More than 10
☐ I rarely purchase more than one book on a subject.
☐ I may purchase a beginning and an advanced book on the same subject.
☐ I may purchase several books on particular subjects.
☐ (such as _____)

6. Have your purchased other SAMS or Hayden books in the past year? _____
If yes, how many _____

7. Would you purchase another book in the FIRST BOOK series? _____

8. What are your primary areas of interest in business software? _____

☐ Word processing (particularly _____)
☐ Spreadsheet (particularly _____)
☐ Database (particularly _____)
☐ Graphics (particularly _____)
☐ Personal finance/accounting (particularly _____)
☐ Other (please specify _____)

Other comments on this book or the SAMS' book line: _____
_____

Name _____
Company _____
Address _____
City _____ State _____ Zip _____
Daytime telephone number _____
Title of this book _____

Fold here

- -

NO POSTAGE
NECESSARY
IF MAILED
IN THE
UNITED STATES

BUSINESS REPLY MAIL
FIRST CLASS   PERMIT NO. 336   CARMEL, IN

POSTAGE WILL BE PAID BY ADDRESSEE

SAMS

11711 N. College Ave.
Suite 141
Carmel, IN 46032–9839